John Dobson

Chronological annals of the war from its beginning to the present time

In two parts

John Dobson

Chronological annals of the war from its beginning to the present time
In two parts

ISBN/EAN: 9783742836557

Manufactured in Europe, USA, Canada, Australia, Japa

Cover: Foto ©Andreas Hilbeck / pixelio.de

Manufactured and distributed by brebook publishing software (www.brebook.com)

John Dobson

Chronological annals of the war from its beginning to the present time

Chronological Annals

OF THE

WAR;

FROM ITS BEGINNING

TO THE

PRESENT TIME.

IN TWO PARTS.

PART I. Containing from *April* 2, 1755, to the End of 1760.

PART II. ——— from the Beginning of 1761. to the signing of the PRELIMINARIES of the PEACE.

WITH AN

INTRODUCTORY PREFACE to each Part, a CONCLUSION, and a GENERAL INDEX to the Whole.

BY MR. DOBSON.

OXFORD,

AT THE CLARENDON PRESS. MDCCLXIII.
Sold by DANIEL PRINCE: By JOHN RIVINGTON in St. *Paul*'s Church-Yard. R. and *J. Dodsley* in *Pall-Mall*, and *J. Walters* at *Charing-Cross, London*.

ERRATA.

Page iv. *(Introduction) line* 25 *read* happens, — p. 6, l. 23, r. mutually. — p. 8. l. 7. p. 32. l. 18. p. 46. l. 29. p. 133. l. 29. p. 185. l. 15. r. Ammunition. — p. 9. l. 2. *after* Philip *add* in Minorca. — p. 9. l. 29. r. Battalions. — p. 10. l. 2. r. Cannon. — p. 12. l. 26. r. Swivels. — p. 16. l. 17. *after* had r. also. — p. 18. l. 5. p. 33. l. 5. p. 38. l. 9. p. 71. l. 13. p. 121. l. 15. p. 125. l. 26. p. 149. l. 4. p. 186. l. 1. *and* 32. r. driven. — p. 38. l. 5. r. Unicorn. — p. 38. l. 6. r. Captain. — p. 39. l. 6. *and* 7. r. Compte *and* Privateer. — p. 43. l. 16. *after* her *add* from. — p. 44. l. 13. r. Indigo. — p. 47. l. 33. r. come. — p. 53. l. 15. p. 62. l. 19. r. Pounds. — p. 62. l. 11. *after* Fermor *add* at Zorndorf. — p. 63. l. 5. r. livres. — p. 64. l. 11. r. flute. — p. 69. l. 31. p. 112. l. 31. *read* Millions. — p. 71. l. 17. r. William. — p. 73. l. 2. *read* le. — p. 79. l. 27. r. Captain. — p. 85. l. 9. *after* without *add* its. — p. 98. l. 34. *after* Squadron *add* was falsly reported to have, and w. wounds. — p. 105. l. 25. *and* p. 163. l. 23. r. broken. — p. 131. l. 25. *after* Flora *add* or Flores one of the Azores. — p. 162. l. 2. *after* withdrawing *add of* l. 25. *after* Michelon *add* or even that of St. Pierre only. l. 24. r. them. l. 25. r. their. p. 162. l. 29. p. 165. l. 19. r. Sr. — p. 163. l. 3. r. Companies. — p. 177. l. 31. r. shaken. — p. 181. l. 10. r. Sovereign. — p. 19 . l. 22. *after* Lummria *add* on Belleisle. — p. 209. l. 29. r. Prussian. — p. 211 l. 8. *after* certain *add* than — p. 242 l. 12. r. diminished. — p. 252. l. 13. r. honour. — p. 275. l. 14. r. Entrance. — p. 318. l. 2. *from the bottom*, r. Possession of

N. B. *The Reader is desired to correct any literal Mistake, which occurs to him, in the proper Names of Persons and Places.*

TO THE
RIGHT HONOURABLE
WILLIAM EARL TALBOT,
LORD TALBOT BARON OF HENSOL IN THE COUNTY OF GLAMORGAN, LORD STEWARD OF HIS MAJESTY'S HOUSHOLD, AND ONE OF THE LORDS OF HIS MAJESTY's MOST HONOURABLE PRIVY COUNCIL.

My LORD;

A STEADY, regular, and uniform Oeconomy can alone give the Nation any Relief under that Oppreſſion of Debt, which it feels from the Length and Extent of the late memorable War; or teach it to ſet a juſt Value upon the Bleſſings of Peace. The firſt Step to this Oeconomy is the Baniſhment of Fraud and Corruption from the ſeveral Offices of
Govern-

Government. Your Lordship has taken the Lead, with Success, in the Reformation of some scandalous and inveterate Abuses in the King's Houshold: But the Houshold is only his Majesty's private Family; His public one is the whole Kingdom; and I flatter myself that the latter will, at a proper Time, reap the Benefit of your Lordship's Example and Perseverance. I am, with the greatest Respect,

My LORD,

Your most humble,

And most obedient Servant,

John Dobson.

INTRODUCTION.

THE War between *Great Britain* and *Spain*, which commenced in the Year 1739, on the Refusal of the latter to fulfil the Terms of the well-known CONVENTION; and *that* which afterwards became so general in *Europe*, upon the Death of the Emperor *Charles* the sixth, the last Heir Male of the House of *Austria*; were both terminated by the Treaty of *Aix-la-Chapelle*. All the Parties, fatigued rather than satisfied, suffered themselves to be comprehended in this Peace. *France* had the Glory to dictate the Terms of it, and the Moderation to give up all her Conquests in the *Netherlands*. *Great Britain* was obliged to restore *Cape-Breton*, and to pass over in Silence the favourite Claim of No SEARCH. *Spain* obtain'd the Dutchies of *Parma*, *Placentia*, and *Guastalla*, for the Infant Don *Philip*, after having spent more Treasure than the Fee-simple of them was worth. The Empress Queen relinquish'd her Rights to those three Dutchies; confirm'd the Cession of *Silesia* and the County of *Glatz* to the King of *Prussia*; that of the *Vigevanasque*, of a Part of the *Pavesan*, and of the County of *Anghiera*, to the King of *Sardinia*; and retain'd the Rest of the *Austrian* Dominions, which had been guarantied to her by the Pragmatic Sanction. Of all the great Potentates engaged in this War, the King of *Prussia* seem'd to be the only one who had acquir'd a clear Advantage, almost without Expence. Victory had been render'd familiar to his Troops; Rich Provinces had been added to his paternal Possessions; His own military Conduct and political Genius had made him the Object of personal Admiration; His Strength was dreaded by his Enemies, and respected by his Friends. But this very Situation, assisted by some unforeseen and critical Events, plung'd him into a new War, more extensive in its Operation, and checquer'd with a much greater Variety of Fortune. *Silesia* was too fertile and opulent a Province, to be surrender'd without Regret; and perhaps the Empress Queen gave it up to her Antagonist, and form'd the Plan for its Recovery, in the same Moment. Few Princes think themselves accountable for Success. If the Course of publick Affairs happen to fall in with their private Views, they seldom neglect the favourable Opportunity, and every Victory becomes an Apology for their Conduct. I do not think it at all necessary to labour the Defence of the King of *Prussia*, and to justify his first Invasion of *Silesia*. FACTS generally speak best for themselves; these I shall endeavour to state with Brevity, and

INTRODUCTION. v

and then leave it to the Reader to deduce his own Inferences from them.

The House of *Brandenburg* had ancient Pretensions upon four Dutchies in *Silesia*, those of *Iægerndorf*, *Lignitz*, *Brieg*, and *Wohlau*. The Margrave *George*, Cousin and Governor of *Lewis* King of *Bohemia*, sold his Estates in *Hungary*, and purchas'd the Dutchy of *Iægerndorf* of the Lords of *Schellenberg*, in the Year 1524; King *Lewis* gave him the Investiture of that Country, as of an hereditary and alienable Fief; and this whole Transaction was confirm'd by King *Ferdinand* the first, in 1527; the Son of this Margrave, having no Issue, bequeath'd the Dutchy of *Iægerndorf*, by his last Will and Testament, to the Electoral House of *Brandenburg*. *Joachim Frederic*, who was then Elector, and from whom the present King of *Prussia* is descended, entered upon the peaceable Possession of it; and gave it, in 1607, to the Margrave *John George*, his younger Son. The Margrave, having unfortunately attach'd himself to the Interests of *Frederic* the fifth Elector Palatine, (who had assum'd the Title of King of *Bohemia* in Opposition to the Emperor *Ferdinand* the second) was dispossess'd of his States, and put to the Ban of the Empire, under which he died in 1624. *Ernest*, his innocent Son, and a Minor, in vain made Application for the Restitution of his Father's Patrimony; and dying in 1642, without Issue, the elder Branch of the electoral Family put in an immediate, tho' unsuccessful, Claim to the Dutchy of *Iægerndorf* with its Dependencies.

In Regard to the Dutchies of *Lignitz*, *Brieg*, and *Wohlau*, the Rights of the House of *Brandenberg* were more complicated and involv'd. The ancient Dukes of *Lignitz* &c, were, at first, independent Sovereigns; but Duke *Bogislaus* submitted in 1329, of his own voluntary Concession, to become a Vassal of the Kingdom of *Bohemia*, on the Condition of holding his Dutchies, as a true hereditary Fief, to himself, his Heirs, and Descendants. King *Uladislaus*, in his Letters Patent of 1511, gave the Dukes of *Lignitz* a Power of alienating their Estates by Will; and the same Power was twice renewed by King *Lewis* in the Years 1522 and 1524; the Words of whose Letters Patent are to this Effect — "That as the Dukes of *Lignitz* had always "enjoy'd the Power of alienating their Es- "tates, and disposing of them between living "Persons *(inter Vivos)*, so they might also "do it for the future, by Way of Testament, "and Declaration of their last Will." A general and full Confirmation of all Privileges, bestow'd at any Time on the Dukes of *Lignitz*, was granted by King *Ferdinand* the first to the then reigning Duke, in 1529.

Under

INTRODUCTION. vii

Under these Circumstances, *Frederic* Duke of *Lignitz* and his two Sons on the one Part, and *Joachim* Elector of *Brandenburg* on the other Part, enter'd into a Treaty of hereditary Co-fraternity in 1537. The youngest Son of the Duke of *Lignitz* was to marry the Elector's Daughter, and the eldest Son of the Elector was engag'd to the Daughter of the Duke. In Consequence of this Treaty and double Marriage, the Possessions of the House of *Lignitz* were settled, on Failure of the male Line of Duke *Frederic*, upon every male Branch of the House of *Brandenburg*, to whom the Marches of *Brandenburg* and the Electoral Dignity should successively descend; and in Case of Failure of such Issue Male in the House of *Brandenburg*, the Fiefs, belonging to the Elector in *Bohemia*, were to be entail'd, in like Manner, upon the Male Heirs of the House of *Lignitz*. This Treaty was made with the Consent of the Clergy and States of the Country, confirm'd by the Oath of the contracting Parties, and an eventual Homage was paid to the Elector of *Brandenburg*. In 1546, *Ferdinand* the first, in Quality of Prince and supreme Judge of the States of *Silesia*, annull'd and cancell'd the whole Treaty, by a formal Decree pass'd at *Breslau*; against which the Councellors of *Brandenburg* protested, in the Presence of that King, who did not oppose their Proceeding. The Dukes of *Lignitz* were afterwards

wards compell'd to declare, that their Dominions, upon the Death of the last Male of their Family, ought, of right, to revert immediately to the King of *Bohemia*; but they wrote to the Elector of *Brandenburg* in these memorable Terms; " Tho' a superiour Force " pretends to deprive you of your Rights, " their Foundation is unshaken; the Inhe- " ritance is not yet fallen; Time changes all " Things; what appears now impossible, your " Posterity will find Means to effect."

The Male Line of the Dukes of *Lignitz* became, at last, extinct in 1675; and the Elector *Frederic William*, firnam'd the Great, insisted upon his Pretensions to the Succession. The Emperor tempted the Elector with a considerable Sum of Money, which was constantly refused. After reiterated Solicitations, the House of *Austria* apparently resolv'd, in 1686, to satisfy the Elector by a Treaty, which ceded to him the Circle of *Schwibus*, together with smaller Advantages, in Compensation of all his Demands. But what was formally given with one Hand, was virtually taken away with the other: For whilst the Emperor was amusing the old Elector with this Cession, he employ'd Intrigues and Menaces at *Berlin*, to seduce the Electoral Prince (afterwards the first King of *Prussia*) into a secret Promise of re-delivering the Circle of *Schwibus*, as soon as he should succeed to his paternal Dominions;
the

the Design took Place, and the Prince gave an Act of Security in Writing, according to the Desire of the Court of *Vienna*. Upon the Elector's Death, the *Austrian* Ministry demanded the Circle of *Schwibus*. The young Elector summon'd his Council, who declar'd on mature Deliberation, that he was not bound by such an illegal and extorted Obligation. After negotiating till the Year 1695, to little Purpose, the Elector yielded the Country in Dispute, for a small pecuniary Consideration; but at the same Time he charg'd his Posterity with the Assertion of his Pretensions. "I have given my Word "(says he) and I will keep it. I leave it to "my Descendants to make good my Claims "upon *Silesia*, since, in my present Circum-"stances, I cannot do it myself. When it "pleases Providence to change the Face of "Affairs, my Descendants will well know "how to act the Part that shall be found "most convenient for them."

The present King of *Prussia* is that Descendant, who avail'd himself of the critical Moment, and march'd a numerous and disciplin'd Army into *Silesia*, to vindicate the Pretensions of his Progenitors. Unhappily for the Queen of *Hungary*, a zealous Vote of the House of Commons, and the spirited Warmth of the *British* Nation, strengthen'd the natural Constancy of her Temper, and engag'd her to reject the Terms offer'd her

by

by her Adverfary. Conceffions made with a tolerable Grace in that delicate Conjuncture, might have eafily turn'd a young Enemy into a warm Friend. A different Syftem of Policy was embrac'd; the final Refult of which was, the abfolute Ceffion of the nobleft Part of *Silefia*, with the County of *Glatz*, to the King of *Pruffia*, by the feveral Treaties of *Breflau*, *Drefden*, and *Aix la Chapelle*.

Europe continued arm'd after the Conclufion of the General Peace. It was reafonable to expect that this very Circumftance fhould affure its Tranquillity for a Length of Time. No State would probably venture upon Hoftilities, when its Rival was prepar'd for a vigorous Refiftance. Yet this Expectation was blafted. Mutual Sufpicion and Jealoufy dictated defenfive Meafures, which mutual Animofity and Revenge were ready to turn into offenfive Ones, upon the fmalleft Alteration of the political Balance. Diffenfions arofe between *Ruffia* and *Sweden*, which threatened the Repofe of the North; the King of *Pruffia* interfered, with a Spirit and Refolution, which the Emprefs of *Ruffia* never forgave. Commiffaries met at *Paris*, on the Part of *Great Britain* and *France*, to regulate the difputed Limits of *Nova Scotia*, and wafted much Time in fruitlefs Conferences. The Affairs in *Germany* were, in the mean while, ripening into Confufion. The Minifters of *Vienna* and *Drefden* had not been idle; and,

whilft

whilst they projected the Ruin of the King of *Prussia*'s Greatness, they push'd the Empress of *Russia*'s Resentment against that Monarch into an implacable Aversion. The two Empresses had concluded at St. *Petersburg* what they call'd a defensive Alliance, so early as *May* 1746: By a secret Article, it was resolv'd, that any War made by *Prussia*, upon *Austria*, *Russia*, or *Poland*, should be consider'd as an Infraction of the Treaty of *Dresden*; tho' the two latter Powers were not at all concern'd in that Treaty. Thus the Empress Queen put in three Claims at once, for the Recovery of *Silesia*. The Court of *Dresden* declar'd their Readiness, both in 1747 and 1751, to accede to the Alliance of St. *Petersburg*; if they might only previously obtain a sufficient Provision for the Safety of their hereditary Dominions, and be admitted to a Share of the Spoils, in Proportion to the Extent of the Conquests.—Towards the Close of 1749, the *Austrian* Ministers at *Petersburg* and *Berlin* endeavour'd, in an artful Manner, to convey remote Hints to the *Russian* Minister at *Berlin*, that a Plot was forming in *Sweden* against the Life of the Empress of *Russia*, in which the *Prussian* Court had a large Share. — The Grand Council of *Russia* was held in *October* 1755; and it was determin'd in that Assembly, to embrace the first Opportunity of attacking the King of *Prussia*, without discussing the Point of Aggression, and to erect Magazines, for that Purpose,

pose, at *Riga, Mittau, Liebau,* and *Windau,* capable of supporting 100,000 Men. — In *April* 1756, the Secretary of the *Saxon* Embassy at St. *Petersburg* recommended it to Count *Brühl,* to take Care that Intelligence might be communicated, through different Channels, to the *Russian* Ministry, of the King of *Prussia*'s reconnoitring the *Ukraine,* and stirring up a Rebellion in that Country: The Secretary clos'd his Advice with these remarkable Words; "That the King of *Prussia* "had given *Saxony* a Blow, which it would "feel for 50 Years; but he should receive "one himself, which he should feel for an "100." Count *Brühl,* in his Answer to the Secretary's Letter, promis'd to execute this Commission. — Thus Fuel was prepar'd in Abundance, on every Side; a little Spark only was wanting, to light it up into a general Flame. The Troubles which arose in *America,* united *Austria* with *France,* and *Prussia* with *Great Britain.* Nothing more was necessary, to involve the principal Powers of *Europe* in the Calamities of War.

In the Course of the Year 1754, the great Designs of the *French* in *America* began to appear. These were, to open a Communication between *Canada* and *Louisiana,* by Means of Forts erected on the River *Ohio,* which falls into the *Mississippi*; and to secure the fertile Countries, wash'd by that River, to themselves, by the Establishment of numerous Settlements.

tlements. Thus, in Progress of Time, the *British* Colonies would be hemm'd in between those Settlements and the Sea, and the allied *Indians* would be easily tempted to forsake their Interest, and to form Connections with the *French*.—To accomplish these Designs, the *French* attack'd and took one of the small Forts belonging to the *English*, on the Straight of the River *Monongahela*, obliging Mr. *Ward* and his little Garrison of 44 Men to capitulate, and retire. They afterwards made themselves Masters of the Fort of *Logs-town* on the River *Ohio*, in the Territory of *Virginia*. On the first of *June*, a Party of 35 Soldiers, detach'd to intercept an *English* Convoy, was routed by 45 Men under Mr. *Washington*; seven of the *French* were kill'd, and the rest made Prisoners, together with their commanding Officer M. *la Force*; three unhappy Persons fell into the Hands of the *Indians*, and were massacred. On the third of *July*, M. *de Villiers* obliged Mr. *Washington* to surrender *Fort-Necessity* in the *Great Meadows*, upon Articles of Capitulation.

The Situation of *Great Britain*, at this critical Period, with Respect to *America*, was beautifully describ'd by a General Officer of distinguish'd Abilities, in Part of two Speeches in the House of Commons. "We seem, says he, to be driving upon the Edge of an high Mountain; on every Side, a dreadful and

and tremendous Precipice; too much Expence makes us Bankrupts, too little makes us Slaves. Some Years ago, the *French* were by no Means a Match for the five Nations; now, they have a Communication, by a Range of Forts, from the River St. *Laurence* in *Canada*, to the *Ohio* near the *Miſſiſippi*. Hence it is, that they hold our Colonies between the two Ends of a Net, which if they tighten by Degrees, they may get all of them into the Body of it, and then drown them in the Sea. When the Ship is sinking, the Man at the Helm in vain lays the Blame upon the Labourer at the Oar, or the Labourer at the Oar recriminates upon the Man at the Helm; we are all in one Veſſel; it is our Intereſt, as well as our Duty, to unite heartily in the common Cauſe; and, laying aſide private Ambition and Animoſity, to act with Alacrity and Confidence; and to perform every Thing in our Power, for the Preſervation, Honour, and Happineſs of our Country."

This was the fatal Spark, which kindled the Flame of War in every Quarter of the World; and which afterwards raged (particularly in *Europe*) with a deſtructive and unrelenting Fury, beyond the Example of former Times. *France* and *Auſtria*, to whom *Francis* the firſt and *Charles* the fifth had left a Kind of hereditary Antipathy, mutually ran into each other's Arms. *Great Britain* was put under the diſagreeable Neceſſity of expending

INTRODUCTION. xv

pending more Treasure against the Empress Queen, than had been employed, in the preceding War, for her Support. *France, Austria, Russia, Sweden,* and the Empire, combin'd their Strength to crush one Monarch, the King of *Prussia*; That Monarch, assisted by *Great Britain,* maintain'd his Ground with a Resolution and Activity, which deserved Success. *France* weaken'd her Credit and tarnish'd her Glory, as a Friend to the House of *Austria*; to which, for upwards of two Centuries, she had been a constant and victorious Enemy. *Great Britain* felt the unhappy Effects of Party Division at home, in some early Misfortunes; united within herself, and favour'd by Providence, she became irresistible.

The principal Events of this astonishing War, reduced to a short chronological Series, make the Subject of the following Pages. They are only design'd to assist the Memory in the easiest Manner, and to serve as a copious Index to any larger Work; which, by reasoning upon Matters of Fact, and explaining the Motives of political Actions, may throw a full Light upon the Conduct of the Powers engag'd in the War, and enable the Reader to form his Judgement upon the Nature, Solidity, and Duration of a Peace. — A Work, of this Character, belongs, not to the ANNALIST, but the STATESMAN.

CHRONOLOGICAL ANNALS

Of the WAR.

1755.

April 2. Commodore James, Commander in chief of the East India Company's marine force, in the Protector of 44 guns, with the Swallow of 16, together with the Viper and Triumph bomb vessels, attack'd and made himself Master of the fort of Severndroog of 54 guns, Fort Goa of 40 guns, and two smaller forts of 20 guns each; these belong'd to Angria; and were deliver'd up to the Marattas, according to treaty.

April 9. Bancote, the most northern port of consequence in Angria's dominions, surrender'd to Commodore James upon summons, and was kept by the East India Company with the full consent of the Marattas. It is now called Fort Victoria. The Harbour is good; and the country about it abounds in cattle, which are much wanted for the use of the garrison and squadron at Bombay.

June 8. The Alcide of 64 guns and 480 men, M. Hocquart Commander; and the Lys pierced for 64 guns, but mounting only 22, with 8 companies of land forces on board, M. de Largeril Commander; having been separated from their squadron commanded by M. du Bois de la Mothe, were

were attack'd and taken, at the distance of 25 leagues from Newfoundland north-north-east of capeRace, by the Dunkirk and Defiance, part of the squadron under the orders of Vice-Admiral Boscawen.

June 16. The French fort of Beau-Sejour, on the Isthmus of Chignecto, surrender'd to Lieutenant Colonel Monckton.

June 17. Gaspereau, a small fort near Bay Vert, surrender'd to the same Officer: and soon afterwards, the French abandon'd Fort St John, near the mouth of the river of that name; after having ruin'd it to the utmost of their power. This compleated the reduction of Nova Scotia.

July 9. General Braddock receiv'd a total defeat from an ambuscade of French and Indians, within 10 miles of Fort Duquesne, which he was marching to besiege: the conduct of this unhappy General has been greatly censur'd, but his personal courage was indisputable; he had five horses kill'd under him, and died of his wounds. The English lost near 1000 men, kill'd and wounded, in this action; among the former, were Sir Peter Halket Baronet, Colonel of the 44th regiment of Foot, and General Shirley's eldest son, Secretary to Mr. Braddock; among the latter, were the Lieutenant-Colonels, Gage and Burton, and Mr. Orme, and Captain Morris Aid-de-Camps. The French became masters of all the artillery, provisions, baggage, and the military chest; the usual fruits of a decisive victory. General Braddock's papers fell into their hands, of which they afterwards avail'd themselves, in a large memorial which they publish'd against the British Ministry: by their own account, they had in this battle only 250 French Soldiers, and 650 Savages, commanded by the Sr. Beaujieu (kill'd in the engagement) and under him by the Srs. Dumas and Ligneris.

July 17. The Doddington Indiaman struck upon a barren uninhabited rock, in the latitude of 33 degr. 44 min. south, and distance about 250 leagues east of the Cape of Good Hope: out of 270 persons, 23 only gain'd the rock: upon which, they providentially subsisted themselves with the provisions collected from the wreck, till the 18th of February, being seven months complete; on that day they set sail from the rock (to which, at parting, they gave the name of Bird Island from the quantity of water-fowl, call'd Gannet, found upon it) in a sloop, built by the carpenter out of the fragments of the ship. After a difficult and distressful voyage, they reach'd St. Lucia river on the coast of Africa the 6th of April; and from thence, anchor'd in de la Goa Road at 4 o' clock in the afternoon, on Wednesday the 21st. This sloop was afterwards sold to Captain Chandler of the Rose galley, for 2500 rupees, or about 500 l. sterling, and sail'd in company with him to Madagascar. — It were to be wish'd, that all ships which happen to sail near any desart island or coast, would give themselves the charitable trouble of sowing a few seeds, and putting on shore a few animals, male and female, for the benefit of those unfortunate people; who, in any future time, might be expos'd to greater calamities, than those which befel the Doddington Indiaman.

Sept. 8. Colonel *Johnson*, who commanded the Provincial regiments design'd for the attack of Fort Frederick or Crown-Point, obtain'd a victory over the

the French Regulars, Canadians, and Indians, under the command of the Baron de Dieſkau. The French march'd up to Colonel Johnſon's intrenchments in good order, and behaved with courage and ſpirit; but the ſteadineſs of the Provincials, and the fire of a ſuperior artillery directed by Captain Eyre, obliged them to fly with precipitation. The Baron de Dieſkau was wounded and taken priſoner; the loſs of the French amounted to ſeven hundred men; that of the Provincials (in this action, and in the defeat of their detachment under Col. Williams, which immediately preceded it) fell ſhort of 300 men kill'd and wounded: among the former, were the Colonels Williams and Titcomb, one Major, ſix Captains, and old Hendrick the famous Indian Sachem. Col. Johnſon himſelf was wounded. Some time afterwards the King created him a Baronet, and the Parliament made him an handſome preſent in money, for this acceptable ſervice. The battle was fought on the banks of lake George.

November 11. L'Eſperance of 74 guns, but mounting only 24, M. le Vicomte de Bouville Commander, was taken by the Orford of 70 guns, Capt. Steevens. This ſhip was afterwards obliged to be ſunk.

Supplies granted by Parliament for the ſervice of the year 1755.

Four millions, ſeventy three thouſand, ſeven hundred, and twenty nine pounds.

1756.

1756.

Jan. 16. A Treaty was sign'd between the Kings of Great-Britain and Pruſſia, for keeping all foreign troops out of the Empire.

February 13. Colonel Yorke, the King's Miniſter Plenipotentiary at the Hague, demanded the 6000 men, which the Dutch were bound to furniſh by treaty, when Great-Britain was in danger of an Invaſion.

Feb. 13. Rear-Admiral Watſon, with the Kent, Cumberland, Tiger, Saliſbury, Bridgewater, and King's Fiſher ſloop; and the following ſhips belonging to the Company, viz. the Protector of 40 guns, the Revenge, Bombay, Grab, and Guardian frigates, the Drake, Warren, Triumph, and Viper bomb-ketches, attack'd and reduc'd the ſtrong fort of Geriah, belonging to Angria, and the capital of his dominions. There were found in the fort, 200 pieces of cannon, 6 braſs mortars, a great quantity of ammunition of every kind, and money or effects to the value of 120 or 130,000 pounds ſterling. The whole fleet of Angria was ſet on fire and deſtroy'd, by a ſhell from one of the ſhips. It conſiſted of eight galliots, one ſhip, two others building (one of which was to have carried 40 guns) together with a conſiderable number of ſmall veſſels call'd gallivats. Colonel Clive landed his troops, to blockade the fort, and prevent the Marattas from getting poſſeſſion of it clandeſtinely, to whom the Governor intended to ſurrender it. The walls were of ſuch an extraordinary height and thickneſs, that no weight of metal could have effected a breach; the garriſon was subdued by the terror alone of so brisk and unusual a fire.

Mar. 11. The Chev. d'Aubigny in the Prudent of 74 guns, together with the frigates Atalanta M. de Chaffault, and Zephyr M. le Touche de Treville, took the Warwick of 60 Guns Captain Shouldham, near Martinico.

March 27. The Sr. de Lery, Lieutenant of the troops of the Colony, at the head of 500 Regulars, Canadians and Indians; attack'd, and took Fort Bull (at a considerable distance from Oswego) by assault, putting the garrison of 100 men to the sword; the fort, after it was taken, blew up by accident, with its magazine of Powder, (of 40,000 pound weight) bombs, bullets, grenades, other utensils of war, and a considerable quantity of provision.

May 1. A treaty was sign'd at Versailles, between the French King and the Empress-Queen, by which the contracting Parties reciprocally obliged themselves to the guaranty of all their European dominions; and, in case of an attack from any Power whatsoever, they mutuallw engag'd to furnish each other with 18000 foot and 6000 horse; or with a proportionable sum of money, after the rate of 8000 German florins for 1000 infantry, and 24000 German florins for 1000 cavalry.

May 17. Great-Britain declar'd War against France.

May 17. There was a very warm engagement off Rochfort, between the Aquilon of 48 guns M.
de

de Maurville, and the Fidelle of 36 guns M. de Litardais, on the one fide; and the Colchester of 50 guns Captain Obrian, with the Lyme of 20 guns Captain Vernon, on the other. The combat began about fix in the evening, and lasted till half an hour past eleven between the Lyme and Fidelle, and till half an hour past twelve between the Colchester and Aquilon. This action did great honour to the marine of both Nations.

May 20. The unfortunate engagement happen'd in the Mediterranean, between the British squadron of 13 men of war exclusive of frigates, commanded by admiral Byng; and the French squadron of 12 men of war exclusive of frigates, under the orders of the Marquis de la Galassionere. Rear-Admiral West engaged briskly with his division; the Intrepide, Chesterfield, Captain, and Defiance, suffer'd considerably. The English had between 40 and 50 kill'd, among whom were the Captains Andrews and Noel, and 168 wounded. The French acknowleged the loss of 38 kill'd, and 184 wounded. Admiral Byng, return'd to Gibraltar; and the Marquis de la Galassionere, to his station before Port-Mahon.

May 25. The States General came to a resolution, to observe an exact neutrality in respect to the war in America, between Great-Britain and France.

June 4. The Suba, or Vice-Roy, of Bengal, obliged the factory of Cossimbuzar to surrender, having previously made Mr. Watts, the chief of it, prisoner; whom he had inveigled out of the fort, under the pretence of an accommodation.

June 9. France declar'd War against Great-Britain.

June 12. The Litchfield and Norwich, part of Commodore Spry's squadron, took off Louisburg the Arc-en-Ciel, a French man of war of 50 guns, 578 men, of whom 190 were soldiers, with a great quantity of provisions and amunition for the use of the garrison of Louisburg.

June 20. The Suba of Bengal made himself master of Fort-William or Calcutta, the principal settlement of the English down the bay. It is situated on the eastern banks of the westermost branch of the Ganges, 25 miles below Hughly, and about 21 below Chandernagore. One reason which induced the Nabob to make this attack, was the imprisonment of Omychund, a Gentoo, and a very considerable merchant of the country, confin'd at that time in Calcutta. After the surrender of the fort; Mr. Holwell the Commander, together with the officers and private persons belonging to the factory, to the number, in the whole, of one hundred and forty six, were thrust into a close room, a cube of eighteen feet, commonly call'd the Black-Hole Prison. The night was sultry, and this miserable place was open only towards the west by two windows strongly barr'd with iron, which hardly admitted the least circulation of fresh air. Mr. Holwell has given an account of the miseries they endur'd, in a very elegant letter; and indeed they are not to be describ'd, but by one who felt them. Twenty three Persons, came out of the Black-Hole alive; after having been confin'd from eight in the evening, till a quarter after six the next morning.

June

June 29. General Blakeney furrender'd Fort St. Philip to the Marſhal Duke de Richelieu, after a fiege of more than feven weeks from the opening of the French batteries againſt the place. The loſs of the Engliſh amounted to 3 officers kill'd and 5 wounded, 71 private men kill'd, 326 wounded (25 of whom died of their wounds) 10 deſtroy'd by difeafe, and 17 miſſing. The French acknowleg'd the loſs of 13 officers and 419 private men kill'd; and 92 officers and 996 private men wounded.

July — The Sr. de Villiers, Captain in the troops of the Colony, under the orders of the Marquis de Vaudreuil, deſtroy'd an Engliſh convoy on the river Choeguen, compos'd of near 200 loaded veſſels, and kill'd or made prifoners 500 men.

July 27. Le Heros M. Beauſſier, L' Illuſtre M. de Montalais, with the frigates La Lycorne and and La Syrene, failed out of Louiſburg to engage Captain Holmes, who was cruifing off the harbour with two ſhips of the line and a frigate. By the French account the Heros fought the two great ſhips alone, for 6 hours; the Illuſtre being prevented by a calm from giving her any affiſtance. The Heros was a fine new ſhip, but ſo feverely handled in the engagement, that ſhe return'd into the harbour in a ſhatter'd condition.

Auguſt 14. The Marquis de Montcalm Marechâl de Camp, with near 3000 men, compos'd of the batalions of Sarre, Guyenne, and Bearn, (amounting to 1300) the troops of the colony, Canadians, and Savages, attack'd and took Fort-Oſwego on the lake Ontario. Colonel Mercer, the Engliſh Commandant, was kill'd. The capture made upon

this

this occasion consisted of seven brass, and 48 Iron, canon; fourteen brass mortars; forty-seven swivel guns; twenty-three thousand pound weight of powder; eight thousand pound weight of lead and ball; two thousand nine hundred and fifty bullets of different sizes; one hundred and fifty bombs of nine inches, and three hundred of six inches; one thousand four hundred and seventy six grenades; seven hundred and thirty fuzees for grenadiers, three hundred and forty common fuzees; seven hundred and four hogsheads of biscuit; a very great quantity of pork, beef, and meal; thirty-two oxen; fifteen hogs; together with a small sum of money in the military chest. The French burnt a skiff upon the stocks; and took a vessel pierc'd for 18 guns; a brigantine of 16; a vessel of 10; one batteau of 10, and another of 8 guns, with a skiff of 18 swivels. A full detail of this important conquest was publish'd in Italian, under the direction of the French Ambassador at the court of Naples; to sink the credit of the English, and to impress a favourable idea of his master's power, in that part of the world. The English garrison in Fort-Oswego of 1600 men, among whom were eighty officers, were obliged to surrender themselves prisoners of war. — About the same time, the French took Fort-Granville on the frontiers of Pensilvania.

October 1. The battle of Lowoschitz was fought between the King of Prussia and Marshal Brown. Both parties claim'd the victory. The King order'd Te Deum to be sung, and a sermon to be preach'd on Psalm 20. v. 6. "Now know I, that "the Lord saveth his Anointed: he will hear him "from his holy heaven, with the saving strength "of his right hand." The Saxon army, on the
con-

contrary, celebrated the victory of the Austrians in a sermon upon Psalm 10. v. 12, 13, 14, 17, 18. " Arise, O Lord; O God, lift up thine hand: " forget not the humble. Wherefore doth the " wicked contemn God? he hath said in his heart, " thou wilt not require it. Thou hast seen it; for " thou beholdest mischief and spite to requite it " with thy hand: the poor committeth himself " unto thee; thou art the help of the fatherless. " Lord, thou hast heard the desire of the humble: " thou wilt prepare their heart, thou wilt cause " their ear to hear; to judge the fatherless and " the oppress'd, that the man of the earth may no " more oppress." — The action lasted seven hours. The Prussians computed their loss at 523 kill'd, among whom were the Generals Luderitz, D'Oertzen, and Quadt, 600 wounded, and 250 taken prisoners; in all, 1373. The Austrians own'd 19 officers kill'd, among whom was General Radicati, and 105 wounded; 420 private men kill'd, and 1729 wounded; and 711 missing; in all, 2984. General Lascy, on their side, distinguish'd himself by his conduct and intrepidity.

October 16. The Saxon troops, inclos'd on every side, were obliged to surrender themselves prisoners of war. They amounted to near 16000 men, according to an article in the Berlin Gazette.

November 22. The Concord of 30 guns, one of the best frigates in the French navy, founder'd upon some rocks in her passage from Morbihan to Bourdeaux, and was irrecoverably lost; the men and guns were sav'd.

December 30. Colonel Clive, with the assistance of the squadron under Admiral Watson, made self master of the fort of Busbudgia, which, though a place of strength, and capable of a good defence, was taken with little loss.

Supplies granted by Parliament for the service of the year 1756.

Seven millions two hundred twenty nine thousand one hundred seventeen pounds, four shillings, six pence three farthings.

December — The Juno, a French frigate cruising off Minorca, struck upon a rock at the entrance into Mahon harbour, and sunk; but the crew and guns were saved.

A list of some considerable privateers and armed merchantmen, taken by his Majesty's ships of war, from the first of December 1755. *to the first of January* 1757.

1755.	guns	men	captors
A vessel of Prince d'Angola privateer	20		Savage sloop
	18	40	Essex
1756.			
A vessel of	14	57 sailors 183 soldiers for Cape Breton	Orford
Le Grand Cerf of	22	225	Tartar C. Lockhart
The Rose of	10	90	Tartar C. Lockhart
A privateer of Dunkirk after a smart engagement	8 carriage 8 suivels	86	Hazard sloop
Grand Judeon	24	190	Tartar C. Lockhart
A Merchant Man	22		Bristol Bigot

1756.	guns	men	captors
Bigot privateer of Dunkirk	6 carriage 10 swivels	50	Dispatch sloop
Cigalle privateer of St. Maloe	14	102	Unicorn C. Edwards

1757.

Jan. 1 and 2. Part of the fleet under Admiral Watson cannonaded the batteries, which had been constructed by the Nabob for the defence of Calcutta, with such success, that upon the debarkation of the troops, they were abandon'd; the English re-possess'd themselves of their demolish'd settlement, and found a numerous artillery on the batteries and in the fort.

Jan. 5. Captain Smith in the Bridgewater, with a sloop of war and all the arm'd boats of the fleet, sail'd up the river to Hughley, a populous town full of warehouses and magazines, which was reduced after a short but warm fire: in obedience to orders, given with much reluctance, the houses were burnt, and all the magazines on both sides of the river were effectually destroy'd.

Jan. —— The Captains Rogers and Speakman, with 70 Provincials under their command, were attack'd on their return to Fort Edward near Lake George or St. Sacrament, by a party of 200 French, whom they obliged to retreat after a very obstinate engagement: the latter lost, at least, 50 men; Captain Speakman, Lieutenant Kennedy, with 16 private men, were kill'd on the side of the English; and Captain Rogers was wounded in several places.

Jan.

Jan. — The Vengeance Privateer of St. Maloe fought the Terrible Privateer Captain Death, for 7 hours; the prize belonging to the Terrible was first taken by the Vengeance, and then Captain Death was attack'd by the joint force of those ships; at last the Terrible struck, having only 26 men left out of 144: the brave Captain lost his life in this bloody engagement. The Vengeance suffer'd extremely, two thirds of her crew having been destroy'd; almost all the officers on both sides were kill'd. The contributions which were generously raised for the relief of the survivors, and the widows of the slain, amounted to upwards of 500 pounds.

Jan. — The Pondicherry, of 1000 tons, an East-India ship, bound from China to Port L'Orient, and valued at 160,000 pounds sterling, was taken by the Dover of 40 guns Captain Hill.

Jan. — The gallant Captain Fortunatus Wright of the King George privateer, fought the Hirondelle, a French polacco of a much superior force, mounting 26 guns with 283 men; and, after two vigorous engagements, obliged her to put back into Malta to refit.

Jan. — The Greenwich of 50 guns, was taken by a French squadron, consisting of 5 sail of the line and a frigate.

Jan. — The Duke Packet, of 8 carriage guns 6 swivels and 26 men, was taken by the American Privateer, of 10 carriage guns 16 swivels and 110 men; Captain Owen Phillips commanded the packet, and engaged the privateer, about 6 leagues to windward of Cape-Tiberoon, for near eleven glasses. The crew of the packet were cruelly used after the capture.

February 5. A detachment of seamen under Captain Warwick, having join'd the land forces commanded by Colonel Clive; the Colonel attack'd the army of the Nabob, compos'd of horse and foot to the number of 40,000 men and upwards; the English artillery, consisting of six field pieces and one haubitzer, play'd so successfully on the right and left, that the Nabob was dislodged from his camp, and even obliged to abandon some of the posts that he took after his retreat. The small army of the English obtain'd this victory with inconsiderable loss, having only 41 kill'd and 65 wounded. This success brought on a treaty with the Nabob, by which the possessions, immunities, and privileges of the East-India Company were confirm'd, satisfaction was to be made for past injuries, permission was given to fortify Calcutta, and the Company were allow'd to coin their own imports of bullion and gold into siccas.

March 8. The Suffolk captain William Wilson, Houghton C. Richard Walpole, and Godolphin C. William Hutchinson, all in the service of the East-India Company, engag'd a French man of war of 60 and a frigate of 26 guns, which they obliged to sheer off; and afterwards pursued their voyage without interruption.

March 22. Fifteen hundred men, under the orders of the Governour of Canada, sent upon an expedition to Fort-William-Henry on Lake George or St. Sacrament, set fire to, and destroy'd, 4 brigantines from 10 to 14 guns, two gallies with 50 oars,

50 oars, upwards of 350 battoes, a large quantity of ship-timber, a great number of field carriages, and some small magazines. The fort was preserv'd by the want of wind.

March 23. Chandenagore, the chief of the French settlements in Bengal, situated on a branch of the Ganges, at a small distance below Hughley, was reduced by Admiral Watson and Colonel Clive. This place was fortified with various outworks and batteries, and contain'd a garrison of 500 Europeans and 700 Blacks, with some mortars, and near 200 pieces of cannon mounted. The French had sent away some of their merchandize and the best part of their effects. Besides ten ships, sunk above and below the Fort, the French lost four sloops and a snow, which fell into the hands of the English; they had 40 men killed and 70 wounded. On the part of the English, Mr. Samuel Perreau first Lieutenant, Mr. Rawlins Hey third Lieutenant of the Kent, the Master of the Tyger, and the son of Captain Henry Speke were kill'd, together with 32 private men; Admiral Pocock, Mr. Stanton, and Captain Henry Speke (the latter by the same cannon ball which kill'd his son) were wounded, together with 100 private men.

April 21. The Duke of Bevern, with about 20,000 men, defeated General Count Konigsegg at the head of 28,000 men, who was advantageously posted at Reichenberg in Bohemia; the Austrians lost 1000 men in kill'd, wounded, and prisoners; the Prussians 300.

May 6. The King of Prussia gain'd an important victory near Prague, over the Austrian army com-

commanded by Prince Charles of Lorrain and Marſhal Browne. 4000 priſoners, (exclufive of the wounded and thoſe taken in the purſuit) 60 pieces of battering cannon beſides field pieces, 10 ſtandards, and the military cheſt, fell into the hands of the conquerors. Marſhal Browne died of a wound he receiv'd in this battle, which was rendred mortal by the chagrin that attended his defeat. The Pruſſians loſt 2500 kill'd and 3000 wounded; Marſhal Schwerin was in the number of the former; an aged General of conſummate merit, and the King of Pruſſia's maſter in the art of war. The following compliment is the beſt encomium upon Marſhal Schwerin's abilities; his Pruſſian Majeſty told him in the winter, that he intended to give him the command of 40,000 men; upon looking over the liſt of the regiments, the Marſhal obſerved to the King, that he could find but 30,000; I do'nt know, Marſhal, replied his Majeſty; but including you, I am ſure there are full 40,000. ⎯⎯ In conſequence of the victories at Reichenberg and Prague, the King of Pruſſia made himſelf maſter of many conſiderable magazines in the kingdom of Bohemia.

May 23 and 24. The Auſtrian army beſieg'd in Prague, made a ſally in the night, but were repuls'd with the loſs of above 1000 men kill'd and wounded.

May ⎯ The America of 600 tons from St. Domingo, valued at 30,000 pounds, was taken and brought into Yarmouth by the Squirrel.

⎯⎯ The Superb of 750 tons, 24 guns, 50 ſeamen and 250 ſoldiers; and the Renown of 350 tons, 12 guns, 86 ſeamen and ſoldiers; both from

B   Bour-

Bourdeaux to Quebec, and rich prizes, were taken by the Somerset Captain Geary, in company with the Rochester.

—— The Aquilon man of war, of 48 guns, 450 men, was drove on shore, and destroy'd, by the Antelope of 50 guns, near la Hogue Bay.

—— The Merlin sloop of war was taken by the Machault privateer, and carried into Brest.

June 14. The French attack'd Bielfeld, in Westphalia, (50 miles east of Munster) and carried it after a vigorous resistance; the Count de Chabot charg'd the rear of the Hanoverians in their retreat, without success.

June 18. The King of Prussia with 32,000 men, attack'd Marshal Daun at the head of near 60,000 near Kollin; the latter was posted on a rising ground, defended by intrenchments, and by a numerous and well serv'd artillery. The action began at half an hour after two in the afternoon, and lasted till eight at night; after seven different unsuccesful attacks with his infantry, the King brought up his houshold troops and some dragoons to the charge, but with the same bad fortune. His loss was prodigious in the battle, and its necessary consequences. The Austrian Grenadiers behav'd with remarkable intrepidity, and the Prince de Lichtenstein directed the Artillery with judgment. The kill'd and wounded, on the side of the conquerors, amounted to near 5000 men.

June 19. The town and fort of Cutwa, near the island of Cassimbuzar, was attack'd and taken by Colonel Clive.

June

June 23. Colonel Clive, at the head of 1000 Europeans, 2000 Seapoys, 50 seamen under the command of a lieutenant, with 7 midshipmen, and 8 pieces of cannon, engag'd the army of the Suba or Nabob of Bengal, in the plain of Plaissy, which consisted of near 15,000 horse and between 20 and 30,000 foot, with upwards of 40 pieces of heavy cannon directed by Frenchmen, in whom the Suba placed great confidence. A grove, cover'd on every side by mud banks, in the midst of the plain, shelter'd the English from the enemy's cannonade; who withdrew their formidable artillery within their camp, upon the falling of a smart shower of rain: Colonel Clive avail'd himself of this capital error; and, by a well-plac'd detachment, prevented them from bringing out their artillery any more. He then storm'd the eminences near their camp; which, together with the loss of some persons of distinction kill'd about this time, dispirited the Nabob's forces, and the right wing and center fled, abandoning their camp and artillery: their loss in this decisive action, was computed at about 500 men; but their precipitate flight, and the number of cannon taken, answer'd all the purposes of the most bloody victory. On the side of the English, there were 20 kill'd and 50 wounded, the greatest part of which were Seapoys. Meer Jaffier, who commanded the Nabob's left wing, was in treaty with the English, and kept hovering at a distance with a great body of horse, till the fate of the day was determin'd. —— In consequence of this success, Colonel Clive was invited to Muxadavad, where he made his publick entry, and saw Meer Jaffier seated in form upon the musnud or carpet of state, and unanimously saluted Suba of Bengal, Bahar, and Orixa: the unfortunate Nabob Suraja Dowlat was privately put to death in the 25th year

year of his age; the treaty made with Meer Jaffier, before his acceffion, was executed, as far as the circumftances of the time would admit; and one moiety of the fum of two millions two hundred and twelve thoufand five hundred pounds, was paid in a fhort fpace; and funds were afterwards affign'd for the payment of the other; the French were for ever prohibited from fettling in the three provinces; the territory of the Company was enlarg'd; the Nabob engag'd to erect no new fortification near the Ganges, below Hughley; and he gave the Company a leafe of the falt-petre of Patna, which had formerly occafion'd continual difputes between them and the Dutch. He alfo diftributed 625,000 pounds fterling between the fea fquadron and the troops. The importance of thefe events, juftifies the minute detail that has been given of them.

June 26. Vizagapatam furrender'd to M. de Buffy; the Chief, the Council, and all the Officers, civil and military, were made prifoners of war on their parole; the Europeans in the garrifon, to the number of 140, were to remain prifoners during the continuance of the war, unlefs fooner exchang'd; the country troops had leave to retire where they pleas'd. The French fat down before this place with 850 Europeans, 6000 Seapoys, and a fmall body of horfe.

June 27. Lieutenant John Peighin, commander of the James and John tender; having receiv'd two broadfides from a large fnow with a tier of guns fore and aft, and finding he could not board her according to his firft defign, order'd his men to fire into her, which they did for an hour and an half; the floop at laft ftood from the tender, and

Lieute-

Lieutenant Peighin made for the Downs in a shatter'd condition. In *January* 1758, he had the command of the Alderney sloop given him for his gallant behaviour in this action.

June 28. Count Colloredo, Minister Plenipotentiary from the Empress Queen, acquainted Lord Holderness by letter, that he had receiv'd orders from his Mistress to leave the Kingdom, and desir'd the necessary Passports.

June —— The Borrine of 14 guns and 60 men, with stores for Canada, was taken, and brought into Portsmouth, by the Harwich Capt. Rowley.

—— The Duc d' Aquitaine East-Indiaman, of 50 guns 18 pounders, and 493 men, was taken by the Eagle and Medway, after an engagement of three quarters of an hour.

—— The Nymph of 32 guns, a French frigate, M. de Caillan Commander, was destroy'd by the Hampton-Court, Captain Hervey, off Majorca.

July 1. The Britannia privateer of Bristol, of 32 guns, nine and six pounders, and 220 men, Captain Fowler Commander, engag'd the Granville Privateer very close, for three hours; she mounted 36 guns, *viz.* 22 nine, and 4 twelve pounders on the main deck, 2 twelve pounders between decks, and 8 four pounders on the quarter deck, besides 5 swivel guns; she carried 278 men; her rigging being very considerably damaged, the first and second Captains kill'd, and about 50 or 60 private men kill'd and wounded, she was obliged to sheer off; three quarters of an hour afterwards, she blew up; all the crew perished, except 4 persons ions who were saved by the Britannia's boat. The Britannia's rigging was cut to pieces; but she had only 3 kill'd and nine wounded in this memorable action.

July 1. The Prince of Conti Indiaman, outward bound for Pondicherry, M. le Mott Commander, of 800 tons, 50 guns eighteen, twelve and nine pounders, and 195 men, was taken by five privateers; she was laden with stores, and had a considerable sum of money on board.

July 3. Embden surrender'd to the Marquis d' Auvet, Commander of the French troops in East Frizeland: part of 400 Prussians, who compos'd the garrison, went on board the Squirrel Captain Hyde Parker; the rest were made prisoners of war.

July 5. The city of Memel surrender'd to the Russians.

July 13. The French took possession of Cassel.

July 16. Gottingen surrender'd to the Marquis d' Armentieres.

July 19 and 20. Ostend and Newport admitted French garrisons, under the command of Lieutenant General de la Motte.

July 22. Colonel John Parker of the New-Jersey Regiment, with 350 men, making an excursion by water on Lake George or St. Sacrament, fell into an ambuscade; the French kill'd about 90 of this party, took upwards of 100 prisoners, the rest made their escape.

July —

July — Gabel was taken by the Auſtrians.

July 23. Zittau, in upper Luſatia, was taken by the Auſtrians, after a cannonade from eleven in the morning till five in the evening: 547 houſes, including brewhouſes, two cathedrals, all the ſteeples except that of Bautzen, the orphan houſe, eight parſonage houſes and eight ſchools, the town-houſe, public weigh-houſe, and the priſon, were laid in aſhes; the archives, plate, and other things of value, were conſum'd.

July 25. The Southampton Captain Gilchriſt, fell in with two French frigates, and three ſmall privateers, off the High-land of St. Albans; he engag'd one of them upwards of an hour and a half, when ſhe made ſignals for the other to bear down to her aſſiſtance; Captain Gilchriſt was put for ſome time between two fires; the firſt ſhip continued the engagement upwards of an hour longer, till ſhe receiv'd a whole broadſide, which ſilenc'd her entirely: the other ſhip then came up, fought ſmartly for about a quarter of an hour, after which ſhe dropt a-ſtern. The Southampton was left a perfect wreck, and unable to purſue; ſhe receiv'd eight very dangerous ſhot between wind and water, had 10 men kill'd and 38 wounded, half of them mortally: the frigate's weight of metal was the ſame with that of the Southampton.

July 26. After ſome ſkirmiſhes on the 24th and 25th, the French army, under the marſhal D'Etrées, attack'd that of the Allies commanded by the Duke of Cumberland, near Haſtenbeck: the diſpute was long and vigorous; but, in the end, his Royal Highneſs found himſelf obliged to retreat

to

to Hamelen. The hereditary prince of Brunſwick, and the Colonels Bredenbach and Dachenhauſen, diſtinguiſh'd themſelves in this engagement. The loſs of the Allies, in the three days, amounted to 327 kill'd and 1127 wounded and miſſing; by a liſt publiſh'd in France, the kill'd and wounded of the enemy exceeded 2000 men.

July 28. Hamelen ſurrender'd to the French: Hanover being no longer cover'd, the Regency ſent deputies to the French army, to treat about the contributions.

July 31. The French took poſſeſſion of Minden.

Auguſt 1. The Sea-Horſe Captain Thomas Taylor, and the Raven and Bonetta ſloops, engag'd two ſhips from Breſt, each of which carried 40 guns, ſomething more than 12 pounders: the action began at half an hour paſt 12, off Oſtend; and the two French ſhips bore away to the leeward. at three quarters paſt three. Captain Taylor, and Captain Bover of the Raven, were wounded: the Sea-Horſe had two men kill'd; eight very dangerouſly, and nine ſlightly wounded. The names of the French frigates were, Le Chauvelin, and Le Marechal de Belliſle; the Sea-Horſe mounted 20 guns.

Auguſt 9. The Marquis de Montcalm, with near 10,000 regular troops, Canadians, and Indians, made himſelf maſter of Fort-William-Henry, after a ſhort ſiege; the garriſon, conſiſting of more than 2000 men, were diſabled from ſerving againſt the French or their allies, for the ſpace of 18 months; the Marquis found magazines of proviſions and ſtores

stores in the fort, the former of which were of of great service to him; before he departed, he raz'd the fort, and the buildings round it, to the ground.

August — The French took Possession of Brunswick and Wolfenbuttle.

August 23. The French enter'd the Hanoverian camp at Verden.

August 23. Gueldres capitulated to the French upon honourable conditions.

Aug. 24 and 25. The Prince Edward of 36 guns, Captain William Fortescue: engag'd, about 30 leagues from Scilly, a French ship of 48 or 50 guns, from six in the evening till seven; they renewed the combat at eleven the same night, which lasted till one in the morning; they fought a third time, from five till past eleven in the morning, when the French ship was oblig'd to sheer off. The Prince Edward had 10 men kill'd and 30 wounded.

August 30. Marshal Lehwald, with less than 30,000 men, attack'd 80,000 Russians under Marshal Apraxin, near Grofs Jægersdorf, or Norkitten in Prussia; the battle was obstinate and bloody, and both sides had some pretensions to victory: three thousand Prussians were kill'd and wounded, and the Russians left 8000 men on the field of battle: the latter occupied a very advantageous Camp, fortified with a great number of cannon.

August — The Merlin sloop of war was retaken, and brought into Plymouth by the Rochester and Chichester. *Sep.*

September 1. At 7 o' clock in the evening, about 19 leagues to windward of Barbadoes, the Fawkner packet captain John Humphry, was attack'd by a Schooner privateer of 14 guns and near 140 men; a close engagement began, which continued for four glasses, when the privateer sheer'd off; at 10 o' clock the next morning she attack'd the packet again for four glasses more, and was forced to sheer off a second time; at one she made a third attack, hoisting her bloody flag, and order'd the packet to strike: but after fighting for two glasses, her men abandon'd their quarters, and the packet got safe into Barbadoes the next day. Captain Humphry had eight carriage guns and twenty six men.

September — The Swedes invaded Prussian Pomerania.

September — The city of Bremen was taken possession of, by the French.

September 6. Bautzen was taken by General Haddick.

September 7. The Generals Nadasti and D'Aremberg, attack'd and forced an eminence near Hennersdorf, planted with cannon, and defended by three Prussian battalions; General Winterfeld was kill'd by a cannon ball, as he march'd out of his camp to support the eminence; upon which, his troops retir'd to the Neiss. This affair cost the Prussians 1000 men, 6 pieces of cannon, and as many colours. The loss of the Austrians was considerable.

September — The Auftrians enter'd Gorlitz, upon the retreat of the prince of Bevern.

September 8. A convention was fign'd at the camp at Clofter-Seven, by which the troops of Heffe, Brunfwick, Saxe-Gotha, and Lippe-Buckebourg, were to be fent back to their refpective countries; fifteen Hanoverian battalions, and fix fquadrons, were to pafs the Elbe; the remaining ten battalions, and twenty eight fquadrons, with the whole body of Hunters, were to be placed in the town of Stade, or canton'd within the line, drawn between the mouth of the Luhe in the Elbe, and the mouth of Elmerbeck in the Ofte, and not to be recruited on any pretext whatfoever; and the French were to keep all the pofts and countries, of which they were then in poffeffion.

September 8. The Efcarboucle, a French frigate of 16 guns and 110 men, was carried into Guernfey by the Ifis.

September 13. The Ruffian army retreated out of Pruffia, with great precipitation.

September 23. The Magnanime Captain How, and the Barfleur, C. Greaves, part of Sir Edward Hawke's fquadron, obliged the garrifon in the fort of Aix, to ftrike their colours, and furrender; eight mortars and thirty pieces of cannon were found in the fort, the works of which were blown up and demolifh'd.

Sept. 24 and 25. The fleet under the command of Vice-Admiral Holbourne fuffer'd great Damage in a ftorm; towards the evening of the 24th, they
were

were about ten leagues south of Louisburg, when it began to blow very hard at east; but veering round to the southward, it blew a perfect hurricane till near eleven the next day. Ten ships of the line were dismasted, eighty guns thrown over-board, and ten men drown'd: the Tilbury of 60 guns captain Barnsley, drove on the rocks off Cape Foucett, and was lost: out of all the Officers, three Lieutenants, one Lieutenant of Grenadiers, two Master's Mates, and nine Midshipmen were saved; part of the private seamen were also providentially preserv'd.

September 26. The Prince of Bevern abandon'd Lignitz in Silesia, to the Austrians.

September 29. Sir John Mordaunt and the land Officers agreed, in a council of war, to return to England. Sir John was afterwards tried, by a general court martial, for the failure of the expedition to Rochfort, and was unanimously and honourably acquitted of the charge exhibited against him.

October — The Lutine a French frigate, founder'd in a storm at sea, and every Person perish'd.

Octob. 16. General Haddick enter'd the suburbs of Berlin, and levied a contribution of 200,000 crowns upon that city.

October 21. The Augusta of 60 guns 390 men, Captain Arthur Forest, with the Dreadnought Captain Suckling of 60 guns 375 men, and the Edingburgh Captain Langdon of 64 guns 467 men, had the confidence to engage a French squadron, off Cape François, composed of the following line of battle ships and frigates — The Intrepide of 74 guns 900 men M. de Kerfin, the Sceptre of 74 guns 750 men M. Clavau, the Opiniatre of 64 guns 640 men M. de Molean, the Greenwich of 50 guns 400 men M. de Faucault, the Outarde of 44 guns 350 men, the Sauvage of 30 guns 200 men, and the Unicorn of 30 guns 200 men. The action began about 20 minutes after three in the afternoon, with great briskness on both sides, and continued for two hours and an half, when the French Commodore made a signal, and one of the frigates immediately came to tow him out of the line, and the rest of the French ships followed him. The English ships had suffer'd so much in their masts, sails, and rigging, that they were unable to pursue them. The loss of the French amounted to near 500 kill'd and wounded; that of the English only to 23 kill'd and 89 wounded.

November 5. The King of Prussia with less than 20,000 men, attack'd the combin'd army of French and Imperialists, near Rosbach, amounting to 50,000 fighting men, and gave them an entire defeat; three thousand of the enemy were left on the field of battle; and, in the course of the action and pursuit, eight French Generals, 250 Officers of different ranks, and 6000 common men were made prisoners; sixty three pieces of cannon, 15 standards, two pair of kettle drums, and seven pair of colours were taken. The Count de Revel, brother to the Duke de Broglio died, at Merseburg, of his wounds. The vanquish'd army was commanded by the Princes Soubise and Saxe-Hildberghausen. The loss of the Prussians in kill'd and wounded did not amount to 300 men.

November 12. The Austrians took Schweidnitz, the garrison of 4000 effective men surrendering themselves prisoners of war.

November — The garrison of Schweidnitz, on hearing the News of the King of Prussia's victory at Rosbach, fell upon their escourt, and defeated it; and afterwards join'd the King upon his march.

November 22. The Hermione frigate of 26 thirteen pounders and 2 nine pounders, was taken, after a five hours engagement, by the Unicorn of 28 guns Captain Moore.

November 22. Prince Charles of Lorrain, and Marshal Daun, attack'd and forced the intrenchments of the Prince of Bevern, near Breslau. The heat of the action lasted near five hours; and the Austrians purchas'd victory with the blood of their best troops; General Wurben on their side, and General Kleist on that of the Prussians, were kill'd in this desperate engagement. The Prince of Bevern was taken prisoner in the morning of the 24th, as he was reconnoitring the position of the Austrian army.

November 23. The Hussar of 28 guns Captain Elliot, together with the Dolphin of 24 guns, sunk a two-deck'd French ship, with one tier of guns mounted; not a single man was saved.

November 25. The City of Breslau capitulated; and the garrison had leave to depart, on condition of their not serving against the Empress Queen, during the whole course of the war.

December 5. The King of Pruffia left Leipfick on the 12th of November; and after having pafs'd he Elbe at Torgau, he purfued his march with all diligence, by Groffenhayn, Koningfbruck, Canentz, Bautzen, Gorlitz, Naumburg on the Queifs, Deutmanfdorf, Lobedau, and arrived at Parchnitz near the Oder on the 28th, where he was join'd by the Prince of Bevern's army on the 2d of December, which had crofs'd the Oder at Glogau. On the 4th the King proceeded to Newmarck, and on the 5th gave battle to Prince Charles and Marfhal Daun near the village of Leuthen, obtain'd a moft amazing victory, and purfued the Auftrians as far as Liffa. The Pruffian Officers and common foldiers behav'd to admiration in the action. In this, and the following days of purfuit, the Auftrians loft 307 Officers and 21500 foldiers made prifoners, befides 116 pieces of cannon, 51 colours and ftandards, and 4000 waggons of ammunition and baggage taken. Their kill'd amounted to 6000 men. The Pruffians eftimated their lofs at no more than 500 kill'd and 2300 wounded. This famous action began at one o' clock in the afternoon, and ended at four. The Auftrian army was at leaft, one third more numerous, than that of the King of Pruffia.

December 6. The Bien Acquis, or Abenakife, a French frigate of 38 guns and 300 men Captain M'Cartney, was brought up to Portfmouth by the Chichefter Capt. Willet.

December 20. The city of Breflau furrender'd to the King of Pruffia, and the garrifon of near 14,000 men fick and wounded included, were made prifoners of war. 144,000 florins were found in the mili-

military cheſt; 37 pieces of Pruſſian cannon loſt in the action of the 22d, were retaken, with 4 pieces of Auſtrian cannon, and all the artillery of the place.

December 29. Lignitz ſurrender'd to the King of Pruſſia.

December 29. The caſtle of Harburg capitulated, and the garriſon obliged themſelves not to ſerve againſt the King of Great Britain during the War. The Kings of Great Britain and France mutually accuſed each other of infringing the capitulation of Cloſter Seven.

December 29. The Swedes in Demmin capitulated.

December 30. The Swedes abandon'd Anclam, which Marſhal Lehwald took poſſeſſion of, and found in it 150 priſoners with a conſiderable magazine of proviſions and amunition, ſeveral pieces of iron cannon, and a large quantity of regimental cloathing.

Before the end of the year, the Pruſſian General Werner, with a corps of cavalry, took poſſeſſion of Jagerndorf, Troppau, and Teſſchen in Upper Sileſia.

Supplies granted by Parliament for the ſervice of the year 1757.

Eight millions, three hundred fifty thouſand, three hundred twenty five pounds, nine ſhillings and three pence.

A list of many considerable privateers and armed merchantmen, taken by his Majesty's ships of war from the 31st of December 1756. to the 31st of December 1757.

January.	guns.	men.	captors.
A French privateer drove ashore on the coast of France	10		by the Hunter sloop.
La Gloire privateer			Prince Edward.
A cutter privateer burnt	6		Mermaid and Eagle.
A ship of war	12		Otter sloop Captain Harrison.
A privateer			Ditto. — made a Post-Captain for his gallant behaviour.
A small privateer			Scorpion and Ranger sloops.
The Victory, a merchantman	11		blown up by the Trial sloop Captain Falkingham.
February.			
The Swan of Calais	6	50	Diligence sloop.

	guns.	men.	captors.
Prince of Soubise privateer	14 carriage 10 swivels	100	by the Dunkirk.
A privateer	10 carriage	150	Porcupine sloop.
St. Thomas of Dieppe	6	45	Hazard sloop.
Post-Boy of Morlaix	10		Fire-Drake sloop.
Duke de Penthievre	12		Aldborough.
A Dogger privateer	6		Badger sloop Captain Taylor, afterwards promoted to the Seahorse.
A privateer Ketch	8 swivels	60	Bonetta sloop.
The Revenge Privateer.	10 carriage	70	Lyme Captain Vernon.
Glaneur Privateer	16		Gibraltar.
A Privateer	18	180	Tartar Captain Lockhart.
A Privateer	16 eight pounders	150	Badger sloop Captain Taylor.

The Badger mounted only 12 guns six pounders; the engagement lasted two hours; the Privateer had 53 men kill'd; the Badger 7 kill'd; the Captain and others wounded; the Badger was much shatter'd in the action.

	guns.	men.	captors.
The Mount Ofier Privateer	20 nine pounders		by the Tartar Captain Lockhart.

She boarded the Tartar, after she had struck her colours, but was repulsed with great loss.

March.

	guns.	men.	captors.
Entreprenant privateer	16	130	Lyme Capt. Vernon.
Le Procureur privateer	6 carriage 6 swivels	36	Grampus sloop Cap. Knackstone.
Infernal privateer of Havre de Grace	6 six pounders 8 four pounders 6 swivels	73	Happy Sloop Capt. Burnet: who was made a Post-Captain in May for his bravery.
Victory of Havre a new privateer	26 nine pounders besides swivels	230	Tartar.

The engagement lasted an hour and an half; Captain Baillie commanded during the indisposition of Captain Lockhart; this ship was afterwards put into commission under the name of the Tartar's Prize, and the command given to the gallant Captain Baillie.

La Victoire privateer schooner	10 carriage 20 swivels	109	Blandford Captain Middleton.
A Privateer sloop	10 carriage 20 swivels		Ditto.

April.	guns.	men.	captors.
The Ruby from St. Maloe to Louisburg with stores provisions and soldiers	22 nine pounders		by the York Capt. Pigott; he took two other store ships at the same time.
The general Sally privateer	14 carriage 4 Swivels	110	Flamborough.
Duc d'Aiguillion	24 nine pounders 2 four pounders	264	Tartar Captain Lockhart.

The privateer was a ship of 500 tons, and each large gun weigh'd 300 pounds heavier than the Tartar's; she was taken off the isle of Wight after an engagement of one hour and twelve minutes; she had 50 men kill'd and wounded; the Tartar fired 42 broadsides, and had four kill'd and one wounded.

La Victoire of Bayonne	26 nine pounders 4 swivels	340	Somerset, Devonshire and Rochester.
Ruby of St. Maloe	14 carriage	110	Lowestoffe Captain Gambier.
A ship from Marseilles to Martinico	26	150	Fortune sloop of 14 guns 100 men Captain Hotham; and carried into Alicant.

	guns.	men.	captors.
La Fortune privateer	10		by the St. Anne and Princefs of Wales arm'd fhips.
The Chevalier Baft of Dunkirk.	10 carriage 8 fwivels	78	Solebay Capt. Craig; with 3 Ranfomers on board.
May Le Faucon privateer	10		Swallow and Cruizer floops.
L'Automne privateer	4 carriage 6 fwivels	48	Falmouth.
Ardencour privateer	14 carriage 6 fwivels	86	Trident, Hind and Loweftoffe.
La Difficulte privateer	6 carriage 6 fwivels	57	Loweftoffe.
Lantore privateer	8 carriage	45	Stafford, Sheernefs and Seaford.
Invincible of St. Maloe	24 nine pounders	286	Unicorn of 20 guns Cap. Rawlins, who being kill'd in the action, Lieu. Clements fucceeded to the command, and carried the Privateer into Crookhaven.

	guns.	men.	captors.
Le Poſtillion privateer	12	70	burnt by the Rocheſter.
La Philippine privateer	6 carriage 6 ſwivels	31	Grampus ſloop.
Counteſs of Noialles priv.	14 ſix pounders	119	Unicorn Lieutenant Clements.
La Penelope of Morlaix	18	180	Tartar Captain Lockhart.
La Marquiſe du Barail	12 carriage 6 ſwivels		Dolphin.
A Dogger privateer	6 carriage 8 ſwivels	60	drove on ſhore near Oſtend by two Cutters under the command of Mr. Barkley one of Admiral Smith's Midſhipmen.
L'Heuruſe Union Privat.	6	50	Antelope.
A Privateer			Hound ſloop and St. Anne.
Le Nouveau Saxon Privateer	16	150	Lancaſter and Dunkirk.
A Privateer	8	38	carried into Port Royal by the Lively.
A Schooner privateer	10	85	carried into Port Royal by the Lynn.

June.	guns.	men.	captors.
Duc d'Aumont of Dunkirk	12 six pounders 4 four pounders 6 swivels	100	by the Grampus sloop Captain Allen.
Prince de Conti with sugar, coffee and indigo.	14 carriage	40	St. Albans.
Le Conte de Gramont, drivateer	36	370	Lancaster and Dunkirk.
Jean Baptist of St. Malo	8	41	Rochester Captain Duff.
Privateer of Dieppe	8	80	Aldborough.
A Privateer	16		Hind.
Mars of Bayonne	16	180	York.
A Schooner privateer	4		Ditto.
Telemachus privateer of Marseilles, with 30 musquetoons and 250 stands of small arms.	22	400	boarded and taken by the Experiment of 24 guns 135 men, Captain Strahan.
July. Ursula privateer	8 carriage 12 swivels	56	Dolphin Captain Marlow.

	guns.	men.	captors.
Port-Mahon of St. Maloe	14 carriage	114	Sheerness.
A Privateer	4	22	Brighthelmstone Cutter.
A Dogger Privateer of St. Maloe	14	94	
A large Cutter privateer			Rochester.
A Snow privateer			Medway arm'd Buss.
Prince of Turenne privateer	10	84	
Comte de Harville of Bourdeaux	16	180	All three by the Isis Captain Wheeler.
Preceaux of St. Maloe	26	240	
L'Hiver of Brest	6	50	Lizard Captain Vincent Pierce.
Vainqueur privateer	24 nine & twelve pounders	350	Ambuscade Captain Gwynn.

August.

Comte de Florentine	16		Essex.
A privateer	16	100	Litchfield and Centaur.
A snow privateer of Brest	14	133	Lowestaffe captain Haldane.

September.

October.	guns.	men.	captors.
A Privateer	2 carriage 6 swivels	24	by the Wolf sloop and Flamborough's Prize.
A Schooner privateer.	6 carriage	54	Isis.
Prince de la Borde	10		Rochester and Unicorn.
A large privateer		115	carried into Antigua by the Cambridge Commodore Moore.
A privateer	16		carried into Antigua by the Amazon.
Two stout privateers cruising to the windward of Barbadoes			Blandford of 20 guns Captain Cummin.
Countess of Grammont	18	155	Tartar Captain Lockhart.
A store ship from Martinico to Hispaniola	26	85	sent into Jamaica by an English man of war.

November.	guns.	men.	captors.
The Melampe privateer of Bayonne of 700 tons	36	320	Tartar Captain Lockhart of 28 guns 200 men. The Melampe was afterwards purchas'd by the Government, and the command given to Captain Hotham.
St. Louis of Dunkirk pierced for	10	33	Southampton Captain Gilchrift.
Hazard privateer	4		Pallas Juno and Shannon.
A small privateer			Pallas.
A schooner privateer of Cape Breton			Gosport.
A privateer	10		Lynn.
A privateer	16	120	blown up by Ditto.
Moras privateer of Bayonne	22 carriage 12 swivels	245	taken by the Antelope Captain Saumarez.
A privateer	12 carriage		Nottingham.
A privateer sent into Lisbon			Greyhound.

Two snows and a privateer schooner, destroy'd in Tiberon Bay by the Assistance Captain Weller. One of the snows was the Duke packet, taken last January, and mounted 18 guns. These vessels were defended by a battery of 5 guns.

December.	guns.	men.	captors.
Le Frere of Dunkirk	10	55	Dispatch Captain Hodges.
A privateer	14	120	A man of war, off the Lands End.
The Diamond, richly laden with a cargo of the finest furs	14	70	blew up in firing her stern chase at the Brilliant; only 27 men were saved.
Dragon, a new privateer of Bayonne	24 nine pounders many swivels	284	taken by the Coventry.
Intrepid of Bayonne	14	130	sunk by the Brilliant; the crew was saved in the Brilliant's boats.
A lugsail boat of Dieppe	6		taken by the Shannon
A large ship mounting	16		burnt by the French in Tiberon Bay to prevent her falling into the hands of the Augusta.

	guns.	men.	captors.
A privateer	8 carriage 10 swivels		taken by the boats of the Marlborough, Augusta, and Princess Mary.
A privateer	4 carriage 8 swivels		Ditto.
A snow of	12 carriage		by the Hornet sloop off Cape Rosa.
A small privateer schooner	—		Ditto.
Eight merchantmen and a brigantine, the richest ships that ever sail'd from Port au Prince			taken by the Augusta Captain Arthur Forest, under the orders of Vice-Admiral Cotes.
A large letter of marque ship, with 400 hogsheads of sugar, some indigo	12	64	taken in sight of the Havannah by the Wager Captain Shur-

1758.

January 2. A Merchant-man of 300 tons, 8 guns, 23 seamen, and 19 soldiers, was taken by the Sterling-Castle and Essex, and another merchant-man of 350 tons, 20 carriage guns, 10 swivels, 61 seamen and 20 soldiers, by the Loweftoffe; both bound to Louifburg, with provisions.

Jan. 17 and 18. Captain Richard Tyrrell of the Buckingham, in company with the Cambridge, deftroy'd a fort in Grand Ance Bay which mounted seven guns 18 and 24 pounders, and made himself master of four privateers; near 90 Frenchmen were kill'd in this action: he afterwards took a schooner, and oblig'd the inhabitants to sink another privateer, to prevent her from falling into his hands. — The sailors, flush'd with victory, earneftly desir'd permission to destroy a village that lay close to the fort, to whom their generous Commander made this remarkable answer, " Gentle-
" men, its beneath us to render a number of poor
" people miserable, by destroying their habitations,
" and little conveniencies of life; brave English-
" men scorn to distress even their enemies, when
" not in arms against them." This prevail'd; his people answer'd him with three cheers, weigh'd anchor, and sailed.

Jan. 22. The Ruffians took possession of Koningfberg, the capital of Pruffia.

Jan. — The Opiniatre of 64 guns, and th[e] Greenwich of 50, were loft in a fudden fquall [of] wind, as they were going into the harbour [of] Breft; their cargoes were valuable, out of whic[h] little was faved, except indigo in a bad conditio[n].

February 18. The Marquis de Ville, diflodg'[d] the Pruffians from Troppau, in upper Silefia.

Feb. 19. The Invincible of 74 guns Capt. Bent[-]ley, ran afhore on a fhoal of land call'd the Dean about four miles to the fouthward of South Se[a] Caftle, and was loft; the men, ftores, and mof[t] of the guns were faved.

Feb. 20. The caftle of Rottenbourg furrender'd to the Hanoverians, after a refiftance of fix hours, and the garrifon of about 150 men were made Pri[-]foners of war.

Feb. 23. The French evacuated the city of Bre[-]men.

Feb. 23. The Hereditary Prince of Brunfwick with two battalions of Hanoverians, two of Brunf[-]wickers, and fome hundred Chaffeurs, Huffar[s] and light troops, attack'd and made himfelf mafte[r] of the town of Hoya upon the Wefer; the actio[n] was fharp and memorable; many of the Frenc[h] were kill'd, and 670 made prifoners: the Cou[nt] de Chabot retreated with two battalions into th[e] caftle; to whom the hereditary Prince granted [a] honourable capitulation, on the condition of h[is] leaving all the cannon, amunition, and provifio[n] behind. The lofs of the Allies, in kill'd and woun[d]ed, did not amount to 100 men.

Feb. 26. The Marquis d'Armentiers, and the Marquis de Rochepine, withdrew the French garrison from Zell.

Feb. 28. The Prince de Clermont, and the Duke de Randan, evacuated Hanover.

Feb. 28 and 29. The Revenge of 64 guns Captain Storr, supported by the Berwick of 64 guns Captain Hughes, and the Preston of 50 guns Captain Evans, took the Orpheé of 64 guns 502 men, commanded by M. de Herville; and the Monmouth of 64 guns Captain Gardiner, supported by the Swiftsure of 70 guns Captain Stanhope, and the Hampton Court of 64 guns Captain Harvey, took the Foudroyant of 80 guns 800 men, on board of which was the Marquis du Quesne, Chef-d'Escadre: the Mountagu of 60 guns Captain Rowley, and the Monarch of 74 guns Captain Mountagu, ran the Oriflamme of 50 guns on shore under the castle of Aiglos, but spared her out of respect to the neutrality of the coast of Spain: the Pleiade of 24 guns, outsailed the English ships, and escaped. — Captain Storr lost the calf of one of his legs, and Captain Gardiner was kill'd; Lieutenant Carket succeeded to the command of the Monmouth, and continued the engagement with distinguish'd bravery. During the action, Admiral Osborne, with the body of his squadron, stood off the Bay of Carthagena, to watch the French fleet, in that harbour, under the command of M. de la Clue. The Foudroyant and Orpheé suffer'd so severely in the battle, that they probably would have surrender'd to the Monmouth and Revenge, if no other ships had came up.

March

March 3. Six hundred Pruffian Dragoons an Huffars, attack'd and defeated, near Lauenau, party of 600 French horfe and 300 foot, of whic 300 were kill'd and 176 made prifoners.

Mar. — Minden furrender'd to the Hanove rians, and the garrifon of 3516 men were mad prifoners of war.

Mar. 13. Major Rogers, the famous Ranger having march'd with about 180 men from For Edwards towards Ticonderoga, was attack'd by th French and Indians to the number of 300, at the diftance of about 5 miles weft from that place of thefe he kill'd 40, the greateft part Indians; but the French being reinforc'd from their fort, renew'd the engagement, when Major Rogers af- ter an obftinate difpute was obliged to make a pre- cipitate retreat, with the lofs of 137 men kill'c and prifoners; the French were reported to be 700 men; they fuffer'd confiderably in the Ac tion.

Mar. 13. The Swedifh garrifon in the Fort o Pennamunde on the Ifle of Ufedom, confifting o 8 officers and 180 foldiers furrender'd prifoners o war.

Mar. 19 and 20. The French and Auftrians, t the number of 3720, evacuated Embden, on th arrival of Commodore Holmes with the fhips Sea Horfe and Strombolo.

Mar. 20. The French evacuated the town c Munden, without committing the leaft diforder.

Mar 21. The French evacuated Caſſel.

March — The Pacifique of Nantz, from Mauritius to Port L'Orient, with a rich cargo, was taken by the Windſor Captain Faulkner, and brought into Plymouth.

March — The French abandon'd the town of Munſter, on the march of Prince Ferdinand to Saſſenberg; they alſo evacuated Paderborn and Lipſtadt about the ſame time.

March — A Corps of Huſſars of the allied army, attack'd the rear guard of the French near Soeſt in the county of Mark, made a conſiderable number of priſoners, and took ten 24 pounders, five 6 pounders, together with a large magazine.

April — The caſtle of Vechte, in which there was a garriſon of ſeven companies, ſurrender'd, by capitulation, to an Hanoverian Captain with a detachment of 150 men from Bremen; upwards of 100 pieces of cannon and mortars were found in the place.

April — The Mount-Martin Eaſt-Indiaman, of 16 guns 75 men, homeward bound, laden with coffee and bale goods, was taken by the Dublin Captain Rodney.

April 4. Sir Edward Hawke, with 7 ſhips of the line and 3 frigates, oblig'd a French ſquadron, lying off the iſle of Aix, and conſiſting of 5 ſhips of the line and ſix or ſeven frigates, with 40 merchant ſhips, to cut, and ſlip their cables, and run in great confuſion; they threw over board their guns,

guns, stores, and ballast; some of the men of war got as far up as the mouth of the Charante; the merchant ships were aground towards Isle Madame; the boats of the English frigates cut away about 80 buoys, which were laid on their anchors, and on what they had thrown over board. The shallowness of the water prevented Sir Edward from doing a more essential service to his country.

April 7. The Galatheé frigate of 22 guns 200 men, was taken by the Essex Captain Campbell.

The Prince George of 80 guns Captain Payton, in which Admiral Broderick hoisted his flag, took fire, and was consum'd; the people on board of her were about 780, but the number lost far exceeded the number saved.

April 16. Schweidnitz surrender'd to the King of Prussia, after 15 days open trenches, one of the works of the place having been taken the night before by storm. The garrison of 173 officers, 3439 soldiers, 1300 sick, in all 4912, were made prisoners of war. 150 pieces of cannon with the Prussian arms, 40 with those of the Empress Queen, 19 mortars, and near 18000 muskets, were found in this fortress. During the long blockade, the Austrians lost between three and four thousand men by diseases.

April — A French frigate of 32 guns, was reported to be taken by Sir Charles Hardy.

April 28. The Bridgewater of 24 guns, and the Triton of 20, being surrounded in St. David' Roa

Road by the French fleet, were obliged to be run ashore, and burnt.

April 29. Admiral Pocock engag'd M. D'Aché, about seven leagues west by north of Alamparvey, from three o' clock in the afternoon till past half an hour after four, when M. D'Aché broke the line, put before the wind, and was follow'd by the fleet under his command. The French, according to the reports of the Dutch, and of several of their own officers, had 600 men kill'd and many wounded in the action; the English lost no more than 29 kill'd and 30 wounded, which disparity can only be accounted for, by the enemy's endeavouring to dismast the English ships, while those, on the contrary, fired at the French hulls. Admiral Pocock, in his letter to the Admiralty, commended the gallant behaviour of Commodore Steevens, the Captains Kempenfelt, Latham, Somerset, and Harrison, and of all the Officers and Men belonging to the Yarmouth. The French, if they did not lay claim to victory, resolv'd, at least, not to confess any defeat: they acknowledged that the action continued till night, with great vivacity on both sides; that a second engagement was expected the next Day; but that the English retired to Madrass to repair the damage they had received.

A state of the two fleets, from the journal of Count D'Ache's squadron.

ships.	guns.	ships.	guns.
Le Zodiaque	74	Yarmouth	70
Le Comte de Provence	58	Elizabeth	70
not in the action.		Cumberland	70
Le Bien Aimé	58	Newcastle	70
Le Vengeur	54	Weymouth	60

ships.	guns.	ships	guns.
Le Duc d'Orleans	50	Tyger	60
Le Duc de Bourgogne	50	Salisbury	60
Le St. Louis	50	Protector	44
Le Condé	50	Queenborough	20
Le Moras	50		
La Sylphide	30		
La Diligente	26		

not in the action.

A state of the two fleets, from Admiral Pocock's letter.

ships.	guns,	ships.	guns.
Le Zodiaque	74	Cumberland	66
Le Bien Aimé	74	Yarmouth	64
Le Comte de Provence	74	Elizabeth	64
to leeward of the French line.		Weymouth	60
		Tyger	60
Le Vengeur	74	Newcastle	50
Le St. Louis	64	Salisbury	50
Le Duc d'Orleans	60	Queenborough frigate.	
Le Duc de Bourgogne	60		
Le Condé	50	Protector storeship.	
Le Moras	50		
La Sylphide	36		
La Diligente	24		

to leeward of the French line.

The Bien-Aimé, of 74 guns, receiv'd so much damage in the action, that the French were oblig'd to run her on shore a little to the southward of A-lemparvey, where their squadron was at anchor.

April 29. The Dorsetshire of 70 guns, 520 men, Captain Dennis, engaged the Raisonable of 64 guns.

guns, 630 men, the Prince de Mombazon Chevalier de Rohan Commander; the latter ſtruck, after a fight of near two hours, having had 61 men kill'd, and 100 wounded: ſhe was a new ſhip, not five months off the ſtocks; on board the Dorſetſhire, 15 men only were kill'd, and 21 wounded. The lower-deck guns of the Raiſonable were 36 pounders; thoſe of the upper-deck, 24. The lower-deckers of the Dorſetſhire were 24 pounders; the upper, 12.

May 1. Fort Lewis, upon the river Senegal, capitulated to Captain Marſh and Major Maſon; 232 French officers and ſoldiers, 92 pieces of cannon, with treaſure, ſlaves, and merchandize to a conſiderable value (ſome ſaid 200,000 pound) were taken in this fort. By the articles of capitulation, every thing belonging to the French company on the river Senegal, was to be put into the hands of the Engliſh.

May 3. Cuddalore (commonly called Gondelour) ſurrender'd to Lieutenant General Lally, on condition that the garriſon ſhould have liberty to retreat to Fort St. David the next morning.

May — The Bolton Tender from Falmouth to Milford, was taken off Mounts-Bay, by a ſnow privateer of 16 guns, after an engagement of three hours.

May 26. The ſhips of war employ'd in the reduction of Senegal, made an attack upon the French ſettlement at Goree, but after an engagement of an hour and an half, were obliged to deſiſt.

May 29 and 30. M. Scheither, with his corps, pafs'd the Rhine at Duyſbourg, defeated three French battalions that oppos'd him, and took five pieces of cannon with all the new cloathing of the regiment of Navarre, and afterwards repaſs'd the Rhine without moleſtation.

May 30 and 31. The allied army attack'd Kaiſerſworth in the night, and carried it.

June 2. The allied army, under the command of Prince Ferdinand, paſs'd the Rhine without any loſs, and made themſelves maſters of Cleves.

June 2. The garriſon of Fort St. David, conſiſting of 720 Engliſh, and 1700 Blacks, were made priſoners of war; the French army, which form'd this ſiege, was compos'd of 3500 Europeans. The fortifications were afterwards reduced to an heap of ruins; the villas, and many beautiful ſtructures in the neighbouring country, were deſtroy'd: reaſons of war juſtified the former; but the latter was the effect of wanton and inexcuſable ſeverity. —— Davecotah, a fort about eleven leagues from St. Davids, was evacuated by orders from Madraſs, and the garriſon retired through the Tanjore country to Trichinopoly. 180 pieces of cannon or mortars, were found in Fort St. David, and 80 pieces in Davecotah.

June 9. The Duke of Marlborough burnt and deſtroy'd at St. Maloe, one ſhip of 56 guns, one of 36, one of 30, another of 30 (in part deſtroy'd) one of 22, four veſſels of 20, one of 18, two of 16, one floop of 12, ſixty ſeven merchant ſhips, ſix ſloops, together with great quantities of pitch,

pitch, train-oil, rosin, and deals, in the storehouses.

June 23. Prince Ferdinand of Brunswick gain'd a victory over the Prince de Clermont, near **Crevelt**. The right wing of the allied army was commanded by the Hereditary Prince and Major General Wangenheim; the left wing by Lieutenant General Sporcken. After a violent and well supported cannonade, the Hereditary Prince put himself at the head of the first line, and attack'd the left wing of the French with a continued fire of small arms, for two hours and an half; but this not producing the desir'd effect; he, in conjunction with the Generals Kilmansegge and Wangenheim, order'd the grenadiers to attack two ditches in the wood, that were lin'd with infantry; these were forced one after the other, and the enemy quitted the wood in the utmost disorder, owing their safety to the spirited behaviour of their cavalry, which protected their flight, and prevented the allies from a farther prosecution of their success. The right wing and center of the French army, never engaged; but retir'd, on the defeat of their left, in the greatest order, toward Nuys. The loss of the allied army consisted in 296 kill'd, 754 dangerously, and 429 slightly wounded, in all 1512. This smart action cost the French between 7 and 8000 men in kill'd, wounded, and prisoners. No more than 2 kettle-drums, 5 standards, 2 pair of colours, and eight pieces of cannon, were taken. The Count de Gisors only son of the Marshal Duke de Belleisle, a gallant young Nobleman, who headed the Royal Carabineers, died in the 26th year of his age, of the wounds he receiv'd in this battle, after having given distinguish'd proofs of a courage worthy of his high birth.

June

June 25. The French abandon'd Nuys, having first given away or destroy'd their great magazine.

June —. The Loire frigate of 36 guns (pierc'd for 44) and 300 men, Captain Gautier commander, bound from Toulon to Quebec, with upwards of 1000 tons of provisions, was taken by the St. Albans man of war.

July 1. The Generals Laudohn and Ziskowitz having, in two attacks on the 28th and 29th of *June*, defeated and destroy'd the greatest part of a large convoy coming from Troppau, and made General Putkhammer with several hundred men prisoners, in the defiles of Domstadt; the King of Prussia found himself obliged, after near five weeks open trenches, to raise the siege of Oltmutz in Moravia; which he effected with little other loss.

July 1. The Rose, a French frigate of 36 guns (which had taken several prizes) was burnt near the island of Malta, by the Monmouth and Lyme men of war.

July 6. The army under General Abercrombie, marching through a thick wood to invest Ticonderoga, Lord Howe fell in with a French party suppos'd to consist of about 400 regulars; of these, many were kill'd and 148 taken prisoners: but this advantage was more than balanc'd by the loss of Lord Howe, who was kill'd in the beginning of the skirmish; a nobleman greatly and deservedly regretted.

July 7. The town of Dusseldorff capitulated, and the garrison engaged not to serve against the Allies

lies for a year; a large quantity of ammunition and provisions, and a fine train of French artillery, were found in the place.

July 8. General Abercrombie, with 6367 regulars, and 9024 provincials, attack'd the Marquis de Montcalm; by whom he was unfortunately defeated. The French were formidably entrench'd near Ticonderoga, and General Abercrombie engaged without his Artillery. The British army, including provincials, had 551 kill'd 1356 wounded and 37 missing, in all 1944. The Chevalier de Levis commanded the right wing of the French army, and M. de Bourlamaque the left; the Marquis de Montcalm reserv'd the center to himself. According to the French accounts, their force did not exceed 3650 men; they acknowledged the loss of 104 kill'd and 273 wounded.

July 23. The Duke de Broglio, with a superior force, attack'd and defeated the Prince of Isenbourg, near Sanderhausen or Sangershausen: the battle was obstinate, and lasted six hours. The French had, by their own confession, 785 kill'd and 1392 wounded. The Prince of Isenbourg lost above 1000 men kill'd, and the number of the wounded was confiderable. Seven pieces of cannon were taken in the field, and eight more in the town of Munden.

July 26. Louisburg surrender'd to Admiral Boscawen and General Amherst. Brigadier General Wolfe, who commanded the left division of the army, made good his landing on the 8th of June, notwithstanding the fire of the enemy, and the violence of the surff; then the center and right divisions follow'd in proper order, and landed in the same

same place; three 24 pounders, seven 9 pounders, seven 6 pounders, two mortars, and 14 swivels, were taken on this occasion. On the 12th, B. G. Wolfe took possession of the Light-House Point, which the French had abandon'd; and having erected batteries on this Point, he silenc'd the Island battery on the 25th in the evening. On the 9th of July, six or seven hundred of the garrison made a sally, and surpriz'd a company of Forbes's grenadiers, but were easily repulsed. In the night between the 25th and 26th, the Captains Laforey and Balfour, with the boats of the squadron, burnt the Prudent of 74 guns, and took the Bienfaisant of 64. The articles of capitulation were sign'd on the 26th, by which 3031 soldiers, and 2606 seamen and marines, were made prisoners of war. Eleven colours were taken; 221 pieces of cannon, 18 mortars, with a considerable quantity of ammunition and stores, were found in the place. The French marine suffer'd a severe loss, in the destruction or capture of the following ships:

	guns			guns	
Prudent	74	burnt	Apollon	50	sunk
Entreprenant	74	burnt	Diana	36	taken
Capricieux	64	burnt	Fidelle	36	sunk
Celebre	64	burnt	Echo	26	taken
Bienfaisant	64	taken	Chevre	16	sunk
			Biche	16	sunk.

In consequence of the reduction of Louisburg, the French settlements at Gaspey, Meremichi, and other places situated on the gulph of St. Lawrence, and on St. John's river in the bay of Fundy, were afterwards entirely demolish'd.

July 26. Admiral Pocock took a fnow off Alamparvey, loaded with fire wood for Pondicherry, and burnt feven empty chelingas.

July 27. The Swedes made themfelves mafters of the fort of Pennamunde, the Pruffian garrifon of 350 men furrendering prifoners of war. About the fame time, 2060 Swedifh infantry took poffeffion of the ifle of Ufedom.

July 28. Admiral Pocock drove on fhore, and burnt, the Reftitution, bound to Pondicherry from Carical, where fhe had been fent with ordinance ftores, and other materials, for M. Lally's army.

July — The French took poffeffion of Gottingen, and demanded a contribution of near 150,000 Florins.

July 31. Eight hundred of Fifcher's corps occupied Nordheim.

Auguft 3. About one o' clock in the afternoon, Admiral Pocock made the fignal for battle, and engaged the French fleet under M. d' Aché, with his whole fquadron. The Comte de Provence fupplied the place of the Bien-Aimé, and the Diligente frigate that of the Sylphide, which had been difarm'd. The Englifh fquadron was exactly the fame, one circumftance only excepted, viz. that fome of the fhips were put under the command of different Captains: Captain Martin, who had before been left ill at Madrafs, was appointed to the Cumberland; Captain John Stukely Somerfet was advanc'd from the Salifbury to the Weymouth; Captain Colville had the Newcaftle, and Captain Brereton

ton the Salisbury. The French made a running fight till near three o' clock, when they set all the sail they could, and got out of the reach of the English squadron, which was obliged to leave off the chace, and anchored at 8 o' clock, off Carical, a French settlement. The French lost upwards of 500 men kill'd and wounded; M. d'Aché and his Captain were in the number of the latter. 31 English were kill'd and 116 wounded; among the latter were, Commodore Steevens, who receiv'd a musquet ball in his shoulder, and Captain Martin, who was wounded in his leg by a splinter. All the officers and men, in this engagement, behav'd to the Admiral's entire satisfaction.

August 2. M. de Besenwald, a French Lieutenant General, at the head of a corps of Austrians, took possession of Ruremonde, which had been abandon'd by the Hanoverians.

August 3. The Hereditary Prince forc'd the post of Wachtendonck, a little island surrounded by the Niers, having forded the river with some companies of grenadiers, and attack'd the French with bayonets fix'd. By this gallant action, the allies were enabled to repass the Niers without difficulty.

August 5. M. de Chevert, with a force vastly superiour, was defeated by General Imhoff, at Meer near Rees. The action did not last more than half an hour. The French were driven under the cannon of Wesel, with the loss of many kill'd, 354 men (eleven officers included) made prisoners, eleven pieces of cannon, several waggons and ammunition carriages taken. The whole of General Im-

Imhoff's loss amounted only to 200 kill'd and wounded.

August 8. Major Rogers, with 65 regulars and two officers, 80 light-arm'd infantry, 80 rangers, a body of Provincials, making in the whole 700 men, fell in with a party of 450 French, Indians, Canadians, and Colonists, near Fort Anne at a little distance from Wood-Creek: the engagement lasted above two hours; upwards of 100 of the enemy were kill'd; the rest were pursued two miles, but without success. The loss on the side of Major Rogers was considerable.

August 8. Cherburg surrender'd at discretion to Lieutenant General Bligh and Commodore Howe. There were about 27 ships in the harbour; 22 pieces of fine brass cannon and two brass mortars were taken, and 173 iron cannon with three iron mortars were destroy'd. The bason and the two piers at the entrance of the harbour were afterwards demolish'd; all the batteries and forts, at that place, and along the coast, were effectually ruin'd.

August 9. The Hanoverians evacuated Duffeldorp.

August 9. The Tanjorean sepoys (Indian soldiers, disciplined by Europeans) and Collaries (inhabitants of the woods, under the government of the Polygars, who are Lords of small districts) sallied out upon the strong army of Europeans and sepoys, commanded by Lieutenant General Lally, attack'd at once the French camp and batteries, kill'd 100 Europeans, took one gun, one tumbril of ammunition, two elephants, and some horses,

blew

blew up four tumbrils of ammunition, and then return'd into the town. Upon this succeſs, M. Lally abandon'd the ſiege of Tanjore, left his guns ſpik'd upon the batteries, and retreated towards Carical.

Auguſt 9 and 10. The allied army repaſs'd the Rhine without any loſs.

Auguſt 23. The Ruſſians raiſed the ſiege of Cuſtrin.

Auguſt 25. The King of Pruſſia defeated the Ruſſian General Count Fermor. The action began at nine in the morning, and laſted till ſeven at night. The Pruſſians took, in and after the battle, 103 pieces of cannon, 27 colours, and made upwards of 2000 priſoners, among whom were five Generals, and 80 Officers: more than 20,000 Ruſſians were kill'd on the ſpot, and the wounded they carried off, amounted to 9000; their military cheſt of 900,000 rubles (upwards of 200,000 pound ſterling) fell into the king's hands. In this great day, the Pruſſians loſt near 1000 kill'd, and 1100 wounded; four officers, and 300 private men, were made priſoners, and 13 cannon taken. On the other hand, the Ruſſians laid claim to victory in this deſtructive battle; according to a liſt, ſpecious if not exact, which was ſent by the Sieur d'Arnfeld to the Swediſh General Count Hamilton, their total loſs in kill'd, wounded, and priſoners, did not exceed 21529 men. Their ſecond line, as it advanc'd, fir'd upon the firſt, and did very great execution; the ſoldiers plunder'd their own baggage, got drunk with brandy, mutinied againſt their officers, and made no diſtinction between friends and foes.

Auguſt

August 27. Lieutenant Colonel Bradstreet took Fort Frontenac; in which he found 60 pieces of cannon, (half of them mounted) 16 small mortars, with an immense quantity of provisions and goods, valued by the French at 800,000 livers; he also took nine vessels, from 8 to 18 guns, one of which was richly laden: seven of these vessels, together with the fort, provisions, artillery, and stores, were effectually destroy'd. The garrison of 110 men, surrender'd prisoners of war, until exchang'd for equal numbers and rank.

August — The Stork sloop of war was taken in the Windward Passage, by a French man of war of 74 guns.

August — The Garland, a French frigate of 22 guns from Brest, was taken by the Renown Captain Mackenzie, in company with the Maidstone and Rochester.

September 6. The fortress of Sonnenstein capitulated to the Prince de Deux-Ponts, and the Prussian garrison of 1442 men were made prisoners of war. 10 standards, 29 pieces of brass and nine of iron cannon, with seven iron mortars, were taken. The Prussians evacuated Pirna the same day.

September — General Retzow dislodg'd the Austrian General Laudohn from Fishbach, made 300 prisoners, and possess'd himself of the Austrian camp.

September 11. At the Re-imbarkation of the English troops from the Bay of St. Cas, the French fell upon the rear guard and broke it, and kill'd, wounded,

wounded, or made prisoners 822 men, officers included.

September 14. Major Grant, having march'd with 838 men from Loyal Hannon, and advanc'd close to Fort du Quesne, was attack'd, and defeated by the garrison, who sallied out upon him with such success, that he lost about 300 of his party, and was himself taken prisoner.

September —— The Russians evacuated Stolpe and Butow, and retired into Poland.

September 15. The Robuste, a Flate of 24 guns, was taken by the Alcide and Acteon; she was laden with six 24 pounders, twelve 18, six iron mortars, 3000 shells of 13 inches diameter, cordage, canvas, flour, and stores, for the French fleet at Hispaniola.

September 21. The Russians evacuated Landsberg.

September 28. Major General Wedel attack'd the Swedes in Fehrbellin, and drove them out of that town, with the loss of upwards of 500 men, and two small pieces of cannon.

October 2. The Duc d'Hanover, a French frigate of 14 guns and several swivels, was taken, off Brest, by the Lizard Captain Hartwell: the Captain engaged the Heroine frigate at the same time, for more than an hour, when she made off for the rocks, near the opening of the passage of Fontenoy.

October 10 The Prince of Soubise, with an army of 30,000 men, attack'd and defeated General Oberg,

berg, at Luttenberg or Lanwerenhagen, near Munden. The latter retreated to Gunterſheim in tolerable order, through the defile of Munden, under favour of the night; having loſt 1168 men kill'd, wounded, and miſſing, eleven pieces of cannon, two colours, one ſtandard, and a conſiderable quantity of artillery and ammunition.

Octob. 12. Eleven hundred French and Indians, commanded by M. de Vetri, attack'd the Engliſh poſt at Loyal Hannon or Hanning, during the ſpace of three hours, when they were happily repuls'd. The loſs, on the ſide of the Engliſh, was only 12 kill'd, 18 wounded, and 31 miſſing; 29 of the latter were upon graſs guards, when the French made this attack.

October — The Winchelſea man of war of 24 guns, was taken, in her paſſage from South Carolina, by a French man of war of 64 guns, and a frigate of 36.

October 14. Marſhal Daun, having march'd through thick woods, by very difficult roads, with the greateſt ſecrecy and conduct, came upon the King of Pruſſia about 4 o' clock in the morning, and artfully ſurpriz'd him in his camp. At five, all the columns deſtin'd for the firſt attack, charg'd at once; before day light, the advanc'd guards of thoſe columns, and the corps under M. de Laudohn, made themſelves maſters of Hoch-Kirchen, and the eminences behind the camp; at day-break, the Auſtrian infantry form'd in order of battle in the Pruſſian camp. Notwithſtanding theſe conſiderable advantages, the Pruſſians fought in every part with an obſtinate bravery; they once oblig'd the Auſtrian van guard, and grenadiers, to retire;

they

they forc'd the cavalry of their left to give way; and retook part of the village of Hoch-Kirchen, after returning three times to the charge: but the fortune of the day depending upon that post, the Austrians made so vigorous a resistance, that the King depriv'd of all hope of success, retreated about nine o' clock under the fire of a numerous artillery. Marshal Keith and Prince Francis of Brunswick, were kill'd on the Prussian side; the Prince of Anhalt Dessau was wounded and taken prisoner. The Austrians own'd the loss of 1020 kill'd, and 3972 wounded, exclusive of the missing: they reckon'd that of the Prussians at 10,000; which the latter, in their accounts of this battle, considerably reduced. 101 pieces of cannon, 44 cover'd and 17 open waggons, with nine chests of balls, were taken. The camp of the Prussians was given up to pillage.

October 26. The Prussians attack'd a body of Austrian cavalry near Gorlitz, broke it, and made 600 prisoners, besides officers.

October 29. Major Heydon, Governour of Colberg, oblig'd the Russian General Palmbach to raise the siege of that place, after two unsuccessful assaults on the 13th and 17th, which cost him 700 men, and two more in the night between the 26th and 27th, in which he was likewise repuls'd with very considerable loss. The corps of Russians consisted of 15,000 men. The garrison was weak, and the town defended only by a rampart, without any outwork whatsoever. The King of Prussia rais'd Major Heydon to the rank of Colonel, and conferr'd upon him the Order of Merit for this gallant defence.

October — The York Indiaman was loft in Maharee Bay in the County of Kerry.

October — The Rhinoceros of 36 guns, 700 tons, from Quebec, was taken by the Ifis Captain Wheeler, who took out her people and funk her.

November 1. The Belliqueux of 64 guns (pierc'd for 66) with 417 men, was taken in Lundy Road, by the Antelope Captain Saumarez, without any refiftance.

Nov. 3. The Buckingham of 65 guns mounted, and 472 men able to do duty, Captain Richard Tyrrel Commander, attack'd the Floriffant of 74 guns 700 men, a frigate of 38 guns 350 men, and another of 28 guns 250 men. Notwithftanding this difparity of force, the French fhips were oblig'd to fheer off, after an obftinate engagement. Captain Tyrrel was wounded, and compell'd to leave the deck. Mr. Marfhal, his firft Lieutenant, after he had brought the Buckingham clofe up to the Floriffant with great gallantry and fpirit, was unfortunately kill'd by the firft broadfide. The command then devolv'd on the fecond Lieutenant, who fought the fhip with equal bravery. Captain Troy, at the head of the marines, acquitted himfelf like an able officer, and did great execution. The lofs of the Buckingham in feamen and marines, amounted to 7 kill'd, 17 dangeroufly wounded (two of whom died foon afterwards) and 31 wounded flightly.

November 5 and 6. General Harfch rais'd the fiege of Neifs with precipitation on the approach of the King of Pruffia, abandoning a large quantity of ammunition.

E 2 *Nov.*

Nov. 8. Marſhal Daun appear'd before Dreſden.

Nov. 9 and 10. The Auſtrians retir'd from Coſel, which they had blockaded for 4 months.

Nov. 12. General Wedel oblig'd the Auſtrian General Haddick to abandon his deſign upon Torgau.

Nov. 14. General Haddick having encamp'd upon an eminence above Eulenburg; with the Mulda in his front, and a village, before that town, defended by Pandours; Major General Malachowſki and Colonel de Hordt attack'd and put the Auſtrians to flight, made 100 priſoners, took three pieces of cannon, two ammunition waggons, and ſome baggage. After this affair, the Auſtrians rais'd the blockade of Leipzick, at which the Prince de Deux-Ponts commanded, and retir'd towards Freyberg: the Pruſſians took poſſeſſion of Freyberg ſoon afterwards.

Nov. 16. Marſhal Daun, on the King of Pruſſia's arrival at Lauban, rais'd the ſiege of Dreſden.

Nov. 22 and 23. The French evacuated Munden and Caſſel.

Nov. 24. The French burnt and abandon'd Fort du Queſne, of which Brigadier General Forbes took poſſeſſion the ſame evening, and gave it the name of Pittſburg.

Nov. 29. The Litchfield of 50 guns Captain Barton, having been ſeparated from Commodore Keppel's ſquadron by a ſtorm off Cape Cantin, was ſtranded on the coaſt of Barbary. Out of 350 men, 130 were loſt; the reſt were afterwards carried into ſlavery.

December 1. The Marquis de Caſtries took St. Goar and Rhindfels; the garriſon of the latter, conſiſting of 700 men, ſurrender'd without oppoſition, and were made priſoners of war.

Dec. 7. The French army in Golconda, conſiſting of 500 Europeans, 8000 Sepoys, beſides black troops, with 36 pieces of cannon, and ſome mortars, under the orders of the Marquis de Conflans, was defeated by Colonel Forde; who took their camp with all the ordnance, (except 4 field pieces) ammunition, ſtores, tents, and camp equipage. The French loſt 156 Europeans kill'd and wounded; the Engliſh 44. Great numbers of Black forces fell on both ſides.

Dec. 8. Captain Knox took poſſeſſion of the fort of Rajamundry, which is the barrier and key to the Vizagapatam Country: it was given up to the Raja of Viſanapore according to agreement, but afterwards retaken by the French.

Dec. 19. The iſland of Goree, with its forts, ſurrender'd at diſcretion to his Majeſty's ſquadron under the command of Commodore Keppel. 94 pieces of cannon of different bores, ſome ſwivels and mortars, a conſiderable quantity of ammunition, with proviſions of every ſpecies for the ſubſiſtence of 400 men for four months, were found in the forts. The French garriſon amounted to 300 men.

Supplies granted by Parliament for the ſervice of the year 1758.
Ten million, four hundred eighty ſix thouſand, four hundred fifty ſeven pounds, and one penny.

A list of many considerable privateers, &c. and arm'd merchantmen, taken by his Majesty's ships of war, from the 31st of December 1757 to the 31st of December 1758.

January.	guns.	men.	captors.
The Machault privateer of Dunkirk	14 nine pounders	182	taken by the Adventure arm'd ship Captain Bray, who was made Captain of the Princess Amelia an 80 gun ship, for his services.
A privateer of Bayonne	22		by the Vanguard, Biddeford, and Dolphin.
The Actif privateer of Dunkirk	12	70	by the Chichester.
A privateer	6 carriage 4 swivels	56	by the Dispatch sloop Captain Hodges.
A privateer of Dunkirk	4 carriage 6 swivels	40	by the Ranger, Hound, and Peggy sloops.

	guns.	men.	captors.
The Vengeance Privateer of St. Maloe, pierced for 32 guns, mounting	24 twelve and nine pounders: and about 20 swivels.	319	taken after a smart engagement of an hour and three quarters, by the Huffar Captain Elliot. In the action, she had 5 guns dismounted, 52 men kill'd and 37 wounded. The Huffar had only 6 men kill'd and 15 wounded.
La Rayton of Boulogne	6 carriage 6 swivels	45	by the William and Anne arm'd ship.
A privateer			by the Dispatch sloop.
A small privateer	6 carriage	25	by the Savage sloop.
A privateer	14		drove ashore, near Port au Prince, by the Augusta Captain Forest.
A privateer	16	145	carried into Gibraltar by the Monmouth.
February.			
Count d'Argenson of Calais	10	80	by the Willian and Anne arm'd ship, the Richmond and Flamborough.

	guns.	men.	captors.
A privateer of Boulogne	4 carriage 4 swivels		by the Peregrine.
La Fidelle of Havre de Grace	8 carriage 8 swivels	48	by the Penguin Captain Man.
The Roston of Bourdeaux, fitted out to take the tartar	26 carriage, four of them 20 pounders, the rest 14	400	by the Torbay and Chichester.
A cutter privateer	6	50	by the Dispatch sloop.
A privateer			by the Badger sloop.
Le Vilmure of Dieppe	6	50	by the Flamborough and Richmond.
March.			
A new dogger privateer	6 carriage 6 swivels	50	by the Hound sloop.
The Marquis de St. Adge of Dunkirk	8 carriage	54	by the Grampus & Wolf sloops.
April.			
The Nymphe of Granville	20	160	by the Brilliant Captain Parker.

	guns.	men.	captors.
La Vengeur of Dunkirk	12	90	Ditto.
A Letter of marque	20		by the Pluto firefhip.
A veffel from Breft to Cape-Breton laden with ordnance ftores	16		by the Sutherland Captain Rous.
A brig	14		by the Boreas frigate.

May.

	guns.	men.	captors.
A privateer	18	100	by the Loweftoffe.
A fhip of 400 tons from Bourdeaux to Port au Prince	22		fent into Antigua by the Weazel floop Captain Boles.
A privateer	10		taken by the Antigua floop Captain Codrington.
A privateer	10		by a fhip of Commodore Moore's fquadron.

July.

A privateer of Bayonne
A privateer of Martinico
A store ship from Bourdeaux to Louisburg.
A store ship with a rich cargo from Bourdeaux to Quebec
} taken off Louisburg by the Boreas frigate the Hon. Capt. Boyle.

	guns.	men.	captors.
A privateer	10	100	by the Seaford.
A privateer			by the Dreadnought.

August.

A cutter privateer	6	30	by the Falmouth.
A privateer	22	200	by Commodore Howe's squadron.
L'Heureux Mallouin from Martinico to St. Maloe with white sugar, coffee, and cotton.	22	70	by the Hussar, America, and Achilles.

September.

The Lizard Captain Hartwell, engaged the Thetis and Calipſo frigates for two hours near Breſt, when the Calipſo ran on ſhore upon the rocks near Point de Leven, and Captain Hartwell concluded ſhe would break up, as ſhe ſtruck very hard upon the rocks, and her yards and ſails were ſhot all to pieces.

	guns.	men.	captors.
The Printemps privateer of Dunkirk.	6		taken by the Biddeford.
Duc d'Harcourt ſnow privateer of Dunkirk	8		by the Unicorn.
Caumartin privateer of Dunkirk, new from the ſtocks, of 280 tons	16 ſix pounders and full of ſwiv. and muſquetoons	147	by the Southampton Captain Gilchriſt.

October.

The Diamond privateer of Martinico			by the Barbadoes ſloop.
A privateer ſchooner			by the Dreadnought.

November.	guns.	men.	captors.
A large French ship bound to Cape François, call'd Le Mareschal de Broglio	full of warlike stores and provisions		by the Woolwich Captain Parker.
A privateer	5		by the Antigua sloop.
December.			
L'Entreprenant of Dunkirk, with two ransomers on board for small sums	6	50	by the Richmond Captain Hankerson.
The Gronyard a French ship from St. Domingo for Cadiz worth 40,000 pounds.	26 nine pounders	130	by the Favourite man of war, after a smart engagement.

1759.

January 1. GEneral Dohna took Damgarten, and obliged the Swedish garrison not to serve against the King of Prussia for the space of a year; in five days afterwards, he repossess'd himself of Swedish Pomerania, and forc'd a superiour army of the enemy to retire under the cannon of Stralsund.

January 2. The Prince de Soubise seiz'd upon Frankfort.

Jan. 4. The Grantham, a rich East-India man, with diamonds on board to the value of 30,000 pounds, was taken by two French men of war, off Cape Falso.

January 16. Commodore Moore's squadron destroy'd the batteries, and drove the French from their intrenchments at Point des Negres on the island of Martinico, and landed the troops without opposition the same night: but the following night the troops were reimbarked, on account of the difficulties which attended the transportation of heavy cannon, stores, and provisions, to Fort-Royal, which was design'd to have been attack'd. The loss at Martinico was 22 kill'd, and 47 wounded.

Jan. 17. The Swedish garrison of Demmin capitulated to Lieutenant General Manteuffel; 1275 men, officers included, were made prisoners of war:

war: 24 pieces of cannon, 6 pair of colours, and some warlike stores and provisions, were found in the place. The garrison of Anclam, consisting of 1421 men, capitulated on the same footing, but had liberty to return to Sweden, on promising not to serve against the King of Prussia, or his Allies, before they were exchang'd or ransom'd. 238 horses, 6 pair of colours, and 36 pieces of cannon, mortars, or haubitzers, were taken in Anclam, together with a considerable magazine.

Jan. 23 and 24. Commodore Moore, with the squadron under his command, silenc'd the Fort of Basseterre on the island of Guadalupe, and all the batteries; and put the land forces under Major General Hopson, in possession of that fort. The loss, in this attack, amounted to 17 kill'd, and 30 wounded.

Jan. 30. Two French merchant ships, of 300 tons each, bound for Martinico with provisions, some cloathing, and 500 stand of arms, were taken by the Brilliant, Captain Lendrick.

Febr. 17. On the 14th of December 1758. M. Lally, a Lieutenant General, at the head of 3500 Europeans, 2000 Sepoys, and 2000 horse, took possession of the Black Town near Madrass, or Fort St. George, which had been abandon'd by the English. The same day Colonel Draper with 500 men and two field pieces, made a spirited Sally upon the enemy in the Black Town; but his men not paying a just obedience to his orders, he was oblig'd to retreat, with the loss of nine officers, and upwards of 200 private men, kill'd, wounded, and prisoners: the French, by their own account, had 30 officers and 220 men kill'd and wounded:

the

aing, a Brigadier General, was
the beginning of the affair. On
nber, Lieutenant Airey, sent from
aptain Preston, destroy'd a consisting of tents sufficient for the
men, a large mortar, two guns,
ne ammunition and bullocks. On
ember, Captain Preston repuls'd
ny under Colonel Kenelly, who
him on the mount near Madrass,
ill'd 15 of the French on the spot,
Colonel, one Captain, and 25
d of January 1759, M. Soupire, a
nd second in command, attack'd
and Isouf Cawn near Trevambore,
division, took two guns and some
e broken troops being rallied by
n, the French were put to flight,
50 Europeans kill'd on the spot,
l prisoners were retaken. On the
three boats, with a Frenchman in
1 150 shot of 24 pounds, 1000
, 50 steel caps, 50 barrels of pow-
and-bags, were carried into Ma-
atman, who secur'd the soldiers
asleep. On the 27th of January,
nd Isouf Caun routed, at Pona-
detachment that was sent against
9th of February, M. Lally sent a
it of 600 Europeans, 1500 Sepoys,
an dragoons, 100 Hussars, and
rse, with ten pieces of cannon, to
aillaud and Captain Preston from
Madrass; the action lasted several
ous success; but, in the end, the
l with the loss of 170 Europeans
led, and near 300 Sepoys. On the
10th

10th of February, the English fleet arriv'd from Bombay, and landed 600 regulars; upon which the French raised the siege on the 17th, after the garrison had been shut up 67 days, and the enemies batteries had been open 46. During the siege, small parties of the garrison made successful sallies. Colonel Lawrence, and under him, Colonel Draper and Major Brereton, commanded the forces; Mr. Pigot was Governor of the town; Mr. Call, chief engineer. To the abilities of these Gentlemen, in their respective employments, the preservation of Madrass, is, under Providence, to be principally attributed. The retreat of M. Lally was so precipitate, that the Black Town escap'd destruction; at the Mount, he ungenerously order'd three barrels of gunpowder to be lodg'd in Colonel Lawrence's house, and blew it up.

Febr. — Captain Knox took Narsipore in Golconda, where the French had a factory, in which place he found two 24 pounders, three 12 pounders, and some small guns, with several vessels, boats, and marine stores.

Febr. 21. The Bellona frigate of 32 guns, the Count de Beauhonoir Commander, was taken by the Vestal of 32 guns Captain Samuel Hood, after an engagement of three hours and an half.

Febr. — The Russian magazines at Revel were burnt by accident; and the damage was computed at five millions of rubles. A ruble is four shillings and six pence sterling.

Feb. 26. Captain Maclean took the small fort of Concale in Golconda.

Febr.

Febr. 28. Erfurth capitulated to the Pruſſian General Knobloch.

Febr. — General Woperſnow took poſſeſſion of 'oſen, and deſtroy'd a Ruſſian magazine of flour ſtabliſh'd at that place, ſufficient for the ſubſiſtence of 50,000 men for three months.

Mar. 1 and 2. Hirſchfeld, Vacha, and all the Heſſian Bailiwicks, were abandon'd by the Auſtrians, on the approach of a body of the allies.

Mar. 4. Captain Maitland of the Royal regiment of artillery, under the orders of the Preſidency of Bombay, with 850 Europeans, artillery and infantry, and 1500 Sepoys, together with the Sunderland and Newcaſtle (part of Admiral Pocock's ſquadron) and the company's arm'd veſſels commanded by Captain Watſon, made himſelf maſter of the caſtle of Surat, by compoſition: previouſly to this, he had diſlodg'd the troops of the place from the French garden, after a warm diſpute of four hours, and had made a ſucceſsful attack upon the Outer-Town. Surat is one of the moſt frequented cities in the eaſt, and from the concourſe of Indian pilgrims who make it their road to the tomb of Mahomet, it has been call'd " the gate of Mecca." The government of the caſtle is independent of that of the city, and held by an appointment from the Great-Mogul : the company obtain'd that appointment, ſometime after the reduction of the caſtle, from that Mogul, who was murder'd by his Vizier juſt before the laſt revolution at Delli. The loſs of the company, in kill'd and wounded, did not amount to 100 Europeans; but that, from deſertion, was more conſiderable.

F *Mar.* 6.

Mar. 6. The Pruſſians took poſſeſſion of Fulda.

Mar. 7. Maſſulipatam, in Golconda, was inveſted by Colonel Forde.

Mar. 15. The Pruſſians enter'd Schwerin in the Dutchy of Mecklenbourg.

Mar. 17. The Imperialiſts retook Hirſchfeld.

Mar. 19. La Mignone, a French frigate of 20 guns, 143 men, the Chevalier de Turſainville commander, was taken by the Æolus of 32 guns Captain Elliot; the Æolus afterwards exchang'd ſome broadſides with the Blonde of 32 guns, but the latter eſcap'd into the Road of Baſque.

Mar. 21. The Allies diſarm'd the garriſon of Fulda.

Mar. 25. Lieutenant General Beck diſlodg'd the Pruſſians from the poſt of Grieffenberg, on the frontier of Sileſia, took a magazine, and made Baron Duringſholen, and about 800 Pruſſians, priſoners of war.

Mar. 26. The Pruſſian General Knobloch took poſſeſſion of Saalfeldt, after a very briſk cannonade.

Mar. 27. The Duc de Chartres Eaſt-Indiaman, outward bound from Port L'Orient to Pondicherry, pierced for 60 guns, and mounting 24 French twelve pounders, carrying 294 men, was taken by the Windſor of 60 guns captain Faulkner. Her loading conſiſted of gunpowder, cordage, flour,

ſail-il-cloth, and wines. Three other ships of force were in company with the Duc de Chartres, but eclin'd the engagement, and made off with full til.

Mar. 28. General Linstaedt drove the Austrians rom Hoff.

Mar. 28. The Danae, a French frigate of 40 guns, 330 men, was taken by the Southampton Captain Gilchrist, and the Melampé Captain Hoham, after a brisk engagement. Captain Gilchrist vas shot through the right shoulder with a pound pall, and put on shore at Yarmouth.

Mar. 31. The hereditary Prince of Brunswick, attack'd, above Melrichstadt, the regiment of Hohenzollern Cuirassiers, and the battalion of Wurtzburghers; these he broke, with only two squadrons of Prussian Hussars; many were kill'd on the spot, and 185 taken prisoners.

Mar. 31. The Duke of Holstein dislodg'd the French from Freyenstecnau, and made one Captain, one Lieutenant, and 56 private men prisoners.

April 1. The hereditary Prince of Brunswick took the magazines at Meinungen, and made the garrison of that place, consisting of two batallions of Cologn and Munster, prisoners of war. The same day a battalion of the regiment of Nagel in Waingen, shar'd the fate of the garrison of Meinungen. The regiments of Savoy and Pretlack were defeated at Tann, by the Hanoverian hunters, and Hessian Hussars, and two rich standards taken.

April 4.

April 4. The Count de Florentine of 60 guns, 403 men, the Sieur de Montay commander, was taken by the Achilles of 60 guns, the Honourable Captain Barrington, after a close engagement of two hours, in which the French lost 116 men kill'd and wounded; amongst the latter was the Captain, who receiv'd a musquet ball through his body, of which he died two days after.

April 7 and 8. Colonel Forde took Massulipatam, in Golconda, by storm. The French had 100 Europeans kill'd during the siege, and 409 made prisoners. Above 150 pieces of cannon were taken, with a great quantity of ammunition.— The French detach'd from Pondicherry four hundred men, in the Haarlem of Bristol, under M. Moracin, to the support of their army in Golconda commanded by M. de Conflans; but this supply did not arrive till a few days after Massulipatam had been in the hands of the English. Being reduced soon afterwards to two hundred men by various distresses, they went to Cockanara; where some of them landed, and were defeated by Captain Fisher, who took 26 prisoners (among whom were ten officers,) and kill'd many more; upon which the rest that were in the vessels, sail'd for Pondicherry, and several of these were drown'd.

April 8. The post of Ulriestein, at the source of the Hom, was taken by the Prince of Holstein.

April 10 and 11. The fort of Peenamunde in Pomerania surrender'd to General Manteuffel: upwards of 200 men were made prisoners; 24 pieces of cannon and 4 mortars taken.

April 13.

April 13. Major Brereton, who fucceeded to the command of the troops in the Eaft-Indies on the departure of the Colonels Lawrence and Draper for England, took Conjeveram with the lofs of four officers: he receiv'd himfelf a contufion in his knee; Major Monfon, in reconnoitring, had a wound from a ball (which enter'd near his ear, pafs'd through his cheek, and came out near his nofe) without being afterwards attended with any fenfible inconvenience; Major Caillaud was alfo wounded in the cheek.

April 13. Prince Ferdinand of Brunfwick, march'd up to the right of the French army commanded by the Duc de Broglio, on the eminences of Bergen, between Francfort and Hanau; but after three vigorous attacks in the fpace of two hours and an half, he drew off to fome rifing ground, behind which he remain'd fome time; and afterwards amufing the enemy with a frefh difpofition of his forces, he made his retreat in the night to Windechen, without difficulty. The Prince of Ifenbourg was flain, deeply regretted; and the Generals Gilfoe and Schulembourg were wounded. The whole lofs of the Allies in kill'd, wounded, and miffing, amounted to 2337. The lofs of cannon and men was nearly equal between the two armies. Prince Ferdinand march'd from Windechen, and reach'd Ziegenhayne on the 23d.

April 15. General Hulfen, with the lofs of 70 Pruffians kill'd and wounded, attack'd the Auftrians in front and rear at the pafs of Pafsberg, drove them out of their intrenchments, made General Renard, 51 officers, and 1800 private men prifoners, and took 3 pair of colours, 2 ftandards, and 3 pieces

3 pieces of cannon. The Auſtrians ſet fire to their magazines at Saatz, to prevent their falling into the hands of the Pruſſians. About the ſame time, another body of Pruſſians forc'd the paſs of Peterſ-walde, deſtroy'd the magazine at Auſig, burnt the boats upon the Elbe, and ſeiz'd the meal and forage which the Auſtrians had left at Loboſchutz, Lieutmeritz, and Budin.

April --- General Fouquet took Sacgrendorf, Ingerndorf, & Troppau, and made 223 men, in the latter, priſoners of war.

April 20. M. de Blaiſel defeated a battalion of grenadiers, between Munſter and Queckebom; diſpers'd, or took priſoners, two ſquadrons of the regiment of Finckenſtein ; and obtain'd ſome other inconſiderable advantages over the allied army.

May 1. Colonel Crump landed in March with 600 men, between the towns of St. Anne and St. Francis, on Grande Terre, and deſtroy'd the French batteries and cannon ; on the 30th of that month, General Barrington attack'd the poſt of Goſier with 300 men, carried the intrenchments and battery, and demoliſh'd them, together with the town. This laſt detachment forc'd their way to Fort Louis (in which there was an Engliſh garriſon) and took poſſeſſion of a battery of three 24 pounders. Captain Blomer on the firſt of April, ſallied out of Fort Louis, and ſpiked up an eighteen and a twelve pounder upon a battery of the enemy nearly compleated. On the 12th of April, Brigadier Clavering, with 1300 regulars and 150 of the Antigua volunteers, landed near Arnonville on the Guadalupe ſide ; and, after forcing ſtrong intrenchments

ments and overcoming great difficulties in his march, he oblig'd the French to abandon the Fort of Petit Bourg, 'though fortified with lines and a redoubt fill'd with cannon. On the 15th Captain Stile, with 100 men, deftroy'd a battery at Guoyave, and nail'd up feven pieces of cannon. Brigadier Crump, at the fame time, burnt an immenfe quantity of provifions landed by the Dutch at Bay Mahaut, where he found the town and batteries abandon'd. Brigadier Clavering on the 20th, attack'd the French on the Heights of St. Marie's, and in fpight of a conftant fire of cannon and mufquetry, forc'd them to retire in great confufion, abandoning all their artillery. The next day the army enter'd the Capefterre, a fpot the richeft and moft beautiful in the Weft-Indies, water'd by good rivers every mile or two, with a port belonging to it, where the whole navy of England might ride fafe from hurricanes. In the whole of thefe expeditions, 50 pieces of cannon were taken. On the firft of May, an honourable capitulation was granted to the troops and the inhabitants; immediately afterwards, a reinforcement of 600 regulars, 2000 buccaneers, and 200 ftand of fpare arms for the inhabitants, arriv'd from Martinico, under convoy of M. Bompart's fquadron; on hearing the capitulation was fign'd, they reimbark'd.

—— The Falcon bomb was loft on fome Iflands, in a cruize about Guadaloupe, but the crew and a few ftores were faved. —— The Ifland of Marigalante furrender'd on the 26th of May upon the fame conditions as Guadalupe and Grandeterre.

May 2. The Hardi of 20 guns, 150 men, and the Hermione of 26 guns, 170 men, two French frigates richly laden with indigo and the fineft fugars,

gars, were taken by the Dreadnought, Seaford, Wager, Peregrine, and Port-Antonio.

May 8, Prince Henry of Pruſſia, oblig'd General Maguire, after a ſharp diſpute at Aſch near Hoff, to retire with loſs towards Egra.

May 11. The Pruſſian Lieutenant General Platen, attack'd the regiment of Croneck and the Palatine dragoons, under the command of General Riedeſel; and, after great reſiſtance, made them priſoners of war.

May —— Major Monſon having gain'd ſome ſlight advantages over M. de Lally by his judicious behaviour, the latter withdrew to Trevatoor, canton'd his army, and went himſelf to Pondicherry.

May 16. Prince Henry of Pruſſia enter'd Bamberg without oppoſition.

May 16. The Glaſgow of 20 guns Captain Wilkinſon, had a ſmart engagement with the Oiſeau frigate of 26 guns, which eſcap'd into St. Pierre. The Glaſgow was obliged to put into Leghorn, and refit. Captain Wilkinſon was afterwards appointed to the command of the Jerſey.

May 18. Captain Colby in the Thames of 32 guns, and Captain Harriſon in the Venus of 36, took the Arethuſa frigate of 32 guns (pierced for 36) and 270 men, the Marquis de Vaudreuil commander, eſteem'd the beſt ſailing frigate in the French navy.

May ——

May — The Pruffian General Knobloch made himfelf mafter of Cronach by a brifk cannonade.

May — The Swedes retook Damgarten.

May 30. The Vanguard of the army of the Empire under Count Palfy, was defeated by the Pruffians between Berneck and Gefrees, at a little diftance from Hoff.

June 5. The Allies took Erbefeld, kill'd and wounded many of the garrifon, and made 83 prifoners, among whom were the Chevalier da Montort the Commandant, and eight other Officers.

June 6. Clermont's voluntiers took poft at Ziegenhayn, where they found 3 pieces of cannon.

June 8. General Imhoff abandon'd Fritzlar; and oon afterwards the French took poffeffion of Cafel, Munden, Gottingen, and Eimbeck.

June — The French enter'd Paderborn; fome onfiderable magazines of the Allies, in different)arts, fell into their hands, as they advanc'd.

June 30. The French took the caftle of Ritberg, a place of importance, by a coup de main.

July 1. The French regiments of Turpin and Berchini, were defeated by five fquadrons of Pruffian Huffars; 150 were kill'd and taken, and the eft difpers'd.

July 6. Rear-Admiral Rodney burnt, at Havre le Grace, part of the magazine of ftores for the flat-bottom'd boats, overturn'd and damag'd many of thofe boats, and fet the town on fire feveral times, during a continued bombardment of 52 hours.

July 7. The Hanoverian Chaffeurs furpriz'd a French poft at Neven-kirchen, kill'd a Captain and about 15 men, wounded feveral others, and brought into camp 2 officers and 46 private men prifoners, all belonging to the Voluntaires of Clermont. About the fame time, Lieutenant Colonel Freytag, with a body of the Hanoverian Chaffeurs, fell upon the regiment of the Voluntaires d' Alface near Munden, put many to the fword, oblig'd others to attempt the paffage of the Wefer in Boats, where they were drown'd, and made the Commander of the corps, 28 officers, and 280 private men prifoners.

July —. The poft of Grieffenberg having been retaken by the Pruffians, General Laudohn attempted to difpoffefs them of it; but was repuls'd by General Seydlitz with the lofs of about 300 men kill'd or taken prifoners; the Auftrian General penetrated afterwards into Silefia, by Mark-Liffa and Seidenberg.

July 9. Minden was taken by affault. 1500 of the Allies were made prifoners of war. 20 iron cannon, 2 of brafs, 20,000 facks of oats, 40,000 of wheat, and 70,000 of meal, fell into the hands of the French.

July 11. The Count des Salos, Colonel of a French regiment of horfe, was made prifoner at Holtfhaufen, with 300 troopers of his detachment; 100 more were kill'd on the fpot.

July 11 and 12. The Marquis D'Armentiers loft 100 men kill'd, and 1400 wounded, in a fruitlefs attempt upon Munfter.

July — Colonel Count Hoerdt deftroy'd, beween the 7th and 16th, moft of the Ruffian magazines from Pofen to the Viftula, amounting in all to 61,254 bufhels of different forts of grain.

July 20. Captain Markham of the fhip Elizabeth, of 8 four pounders, 2 fmall ftern chafe guns, and 14 men, engag'd the Revenge, a French fnow privateer of 16 fix pounders, 20 fwivels, and 180 men. The action lafted upwards of four hours, when the Revenge fheer'd off.

July 23. General Wedel, who fucceeded Count Dohna in the command of the army againft the Ruffians, attack'd General Count Solticoff in the Defile of Kay near Zulicau. After an obftinate difpute, the Pruffians were oblig'd to yield to the fuperiority of their enemy, affifted by every advantage of ground; they retreated with the lofs of 1700 kill'd, prifoners, and deferters; and 3000 wounded, whom they brought off: 3 twelve pounders, 2 obufiers, and 10 field pieces, were taken: General Woberfnow, an Officer of great ability, fell in the field of battle, and General Manteuffel was wounded. On the fide of the Ruffians, about 1500 were kill'd, among whom was Lieutenant General Demicou, and 3000 wounded: after the action, the Ruffians took poffeffion of Croffen, and Francfort upon the Oder.

July

July 24. The French abandon'd their lines at Ticonderoga, and set fire to the fort, on the approach of Major General Amherst.

July 24. Lieutenant Colonel Massey, under the orders of Sir William Johnson, (who succeeded to the command on the death of General Prideaux) with the light infantry, picquets of the line, two companies of grenadiers, part of the 46th regiment, and the Indians, was attack'd, near Niagara, by 1200 French collected from Detroit, Venango, and Presque Isle, together with a number of Indians, the whole commanded by Messieurs Aubry and de Lignery. The Brittish troops in front, and the Indians in flank, gave the enemy such a warm reception, that in an hours time their entire force was compleatly ruin'd: the commanders, and all the officers, to the number of seventeen, were made prisoners, many private men kill'd, and the rest dispers'd among the woods.

July 25. Sir William Johnson took possession of Fort Niagara; the garrison of 607 men, exclusive of officers, surrender'd with the honours of war, and were convey'd to New York.

July 25. The Citadel of Munster surrender'd to the Marquis d'Armentieres, and the garrison of 3100 men with Lieutenant General de Zastrow the Commandant, capitulated to be prisoners of war till ransom'd or exchang'd.

July 28. M. de Schlieffen, under the orders of General Dreves, made himself master of Osnabruck, where the Volontaires de Clermont lost some men, and two pieces of cannon.

July

July 31. The British army, commanded by Major General Wolfe, and under him by the Brigadiers Monckton, Townshend, and Murray, landed upon the isle of Orleans in the river St. Laurence, on the 27th of June. The fleet employ'd in this important expedition, was under the orders of Vice-Admiral Saunders, who had two Rear Admirals with him, Mr. Durell and Mr. Holmes. On the 28th, seven fire-ships from Quebec were tow'd aground, without doing the least damage to the ships or transports. On the 29th, four battalions under Brigadier Monckton, drove the French irregulars from their post at Point Levi on the south shore. General Wolfe order'd batteries of cannon and mortars to be erected on that point, which (though across the river) destroy'd the lower town entirely, and did considerable damage to the upper. On the night of the 9th of July, the army pass'd the North Channel, and incamp'd near the left of the French, the river Montmorenci running between the two camps. The enemy occupied the shore of Beauport; from the river St. Charles (which falls into that of St. Laurence near Quebec) to the falls of the river Montmorenci abovemention'd, and were intrench'd in every accessible part. On the 10th, a party of Indians defeated Captain Dank's company of Rangers, and almost disabled it for the rest of the campaign. Some few days afterwards, Colonel Carleton landed with a small party, at the Point de Trempe above Quebec, brought off some prisoners, and return'd with little loss. On the 28th at midnight, the French sent down a raft of fire stages, which succeeded no better than the fire ships. On the 31st of July, General Wolfe determin'd to attack the intrenchments of the enemy on a commanding eminence;

minence; Brigadier Monckton receiv'd orders to land with his corps from Point Levi, and the Brigadiers Townshend and Murray were directed to be ready to pass the ford below the falls of Montmorenci: a great deal of time was unavoidably lost, by an accident of the boats grounding upon a ledge, that ran a considerable distance off the shore; this difficulty being remov'd, 13 companies of grenadiers, and 200 of the second royal American battalion, got first on shore; but the grenadiers, by some mistake, not forming themselves as they were directed, and running on impetuously towards the intrenchments, in the utmost confusion, were check'd by the enemy's first fire, forc'd to shelter themselves in or about a detach'd redoubt, near the water's edge, which the French had abandon'd, and not being able to form under so hot a fire from the intrenchments, were oblig'd to be call'd off; this repulse and delay, the approach of night, a sudden storm coming on, and the tide beginning to make, compell'd the General to desist from so difficult an attack, which was attended with the loss of 182 kill'd, 650 wounded, and 17 missing; in all, 849.

August 1. About 5 o'clock in the morning, the whole French army under the Marshal de Contades, was form'd in order of battle on the plain of Minden. The Duke of Broglio's reserve came close to the Weser. The cavalry, occupied the heath in the center. The infantry, on the left, extended to the marsh near the village of Hahlen. — Prince Ferdinand's army was dispos'd of in the following manner; General Wangenheims's corps was posted, on the left of the whole, near the village of Thonhausen almost close to the Weser. The cavalry of the right wing of the main army, in which

which were all the British horse under Lord George Sackville, took up their ground between Hartum and Hahlen. The infantry of the right wing (on the left of the cavalry) compos'd of the British batalions and the Hanoverian guards, were drawn up behind a fir wood. The left wing of the main army, was posted at Stemmeren. — Between seven and eight o' clock, the two Brigades of British foot, consisting of the following regiments, viz. the 12th Napier's, 20th Kingsley's, 23d Huske's, 25th Home's, 37th Stuart's, 51st Brudenel's, headed by the Major Generals Waldegrave and Kingsley, together with the Hanoverian guards, and Hardenberg's regiment, march'd forward to charge the left of the enemy's cavalry; and notwithstanding the opposition of the two batteries, the repeated attacks of all the cavalry, a fire of musquetry well kept up by the French infantry, and their being expos'd in front and flank, these astonishing battalions totally routed the whole body of the French cavalry, and oblig'd the Saxons who came to their assistance, to retreat. — The regiments du Corps and Hammerstein, (Hanoverian horse) the Prussian regiment of Holstein, and the Hessian horse and grenadiers, distinguish'd themselves prodigiously, and repuls'd the attack on the left of the army. — The batteries erected by the Count de la Lippe Buckenburg in the front of Thonhausen, made great havock among the Swiss and the grenadiers of France. About nine the French began to give way, at ten they fled in disorder, and their retreat was cover'd by the Duke of Broglio. The British artillery perform'd wonders in this action. The British cavalry did not engage. 25 pieces of cannon, 10 pair of colours, & 7 standards were taken. The loss of the French, in kill'd, wounded, and prisoners, amounted to

7000

7000 men. That of the allies, to 2800, of which number the British troops made 1394.

Aug. 1. The Hereditary Prince of Brunswick attack'd and defeated the Duke de Brisac, in the mountains of Coveldt. The French lost many of their men, who were made prisoners, together with five officers of distinction. Six pieces of cannon were taken. Messieurs Killmansegg, Dreves, and Bock, contributed greatly to this second victory, by the admirable manœuvres of the troops under their command.

August 2. Minden surrender'd to the allies at discretion. A great number of wounded officers, and 1533 private men were made prisoners; and a considerable magazine was taken.

August 2. The king of Prussia attack'd the rear guard of the Austrians under General Haddick, as they were upon their march to join the Russians, made 1200 prisoners, and took all the ovens, and 300 waggons loaded with flour, together with 50 of powder, which were immediately destroy'd. On the 3d, the prisoners made upon Haddick's corps amounted to 1600.

August 4. The Marquis d'Armentieres raised the blockade of Lipstadt.

August 4. Major General Amherst took possession of Crown Point, which the French had abandon'd on the first instant. A considerable quantity of ordnance and military stores was found at this post, and at Ticonderoga.

August 5. The city of Leipsic surrender'd to the army of the Empire.

Aug.

August 5. Lieutenant General Urff, furrounded and took prifoners about 800 of the enemy at Detnold, and made himfelf mafter of the heavy baggage of the French army and the military cheft of the Saxons. Among the papers found on this ocafion, there was the famous letter of the Duke le Bellifle to Marfhal de Contades, declaring the nability of the French to carry on the war without great contributions drawn from the countries of the llies, and advifing the Marfhal to make a downight defart before his line of winter quarters.

August — The French burnt their forts at Veango, Prefque Ifle, and La Buef, and retir'd to Detroit.

August 6. The Allies march'd to Bielveld, where hey found a confiderable magazine.

August 9. The Allies made 400 prifoners at Palerborn, and took another magazine; thofe at Munfter, Dulmen, and Warendrop, were dtftroy'd by the French.

August 10. The army of the Empire took poffeffion of Halle, Naumbourg, Zeitz, and Halberftadt.

August 12. The Crefcent Captain Collingwood, ngag'd two French frigates, the Amethyfte of 32 guns and the Barclay of 20; but being difabled in ner rigging, the former efcap'd; the latter was aken, and carried into Baffeterre.

August 12. The King of Pruffia attack'd Count Soltikoff at Cunnerfdorf, about eleven o' clock in

G the

the morning. For almoſt ſix hours, he drove the
Ruſſians from their poſts and intrenchments, with
prodigious ſlaughter; but making a deſperate attempt, with his wearied troops, on their laſt fortified eminence near the Jews Burying Ground, his
infantry were twice repuls'd with vaſt loſs; his cavalry met with the ſame bad fortune. Night ſaved
the ſhatter'd remains of his army. General Put-
kammer was kill'd in the field; moſt of his Generals, and inferior Officers were wounded; almoſt
his whole artillery taken. By a Ruſſian account,
publiſh'd ſome time after the battle, the loſs of the
Pruſſians amounted to 13316 men, excluſive of the
wounded. The Pruſſians on the contrary, including 11,119 wounded, eſtimated their total loſs at
18604 men. The numbers of the two armies were
diſproportion'd; that of Pruſſia fell ſhort of 50,000
effective men. The Ruſſians, including a large
body of Auſtrians under General Laudohn, exceeded 80,000; of theſe, 2571 were kill'd and
10,722 wounded. The Empreſs of Ruſſia has order'd a thankſgiving to be annually obſerv'd, for
perpetuating the memory of this dreadful victory.

Auguſt 15. Luckner's Huſſars routed a conſiderable detachment of the French at Volckmiſſen.

Auguſt 17. The Duke of Holſtein took an entire battalion of the grenadiers Royaux, ſword in
hand in ſight of the French army.

Auguſt 18 and 19 — Admiral Boſcawen, with the
fleet under his command, burnt the Ocean of 80
guns, the Redoutable of 74, and took the Centaur
of 74, the Temeraire of 74, and the Modeſte of
64, off Cape Lagos. M. de la Clue, who commanded the French ſquadron, died of his wound
ſom-

some time afterwards. The Namur's mizen maſt, and both topſail yards, being ſhot away, Admiral Boſcawen was obligʼd to ſhift his flag to the Newark. The French had near 500 men killʼd, and 1800 taken, on board the ſeveral ſhips. The Captains Bently and Stanhope were knighted by his Majeſty for their good behaviour in this action.

Auguſt 19. The Allies took Caſſel with 400 men in garriſon, 1500 wounded, and a conſiderable magazine.

Auguſt 19. The Pruſſians were permitted to evacuate Torgau, leaving behind them their grand magazine, military cheſt, heavy artillery, hoſtages, priſoners of war, and deſerters.

Auguſt 21. Wittenberg capitulated to the army of the Empire, and its garriſon joinʼd the Pruſſian forces. Major General de Horn was put under arreſt by the Kingʼs order, to be tried by a courtmartial, for ſurrendering that place.

Auguſt 23. Lieutenant Colonel Freytagg took Ziegenhayn, and made the garriſon of three or four hundred men priſoners of war.

Auguſt 28. Colonel Wunſch retook Wittenberg by capitulation.

Auguſt 28. The troops under the hereditary Prince attackʼd Fiſcherʼs corps at Wetter, diſlodgʼd it from that poſt, killʼd many men, and made 400 priſoners of war.

September 1. A detachment of the garrison of Stettin surpriz'd a body of 400 Swedes, and kill'd or took prisoners the greatest part of it.

Sept. 2. The hereditary Prince surpriz'd the French at Neider-Weimar, made several prisoners, and took two pieces of cannon.

Sept. — Brigadier Murray landed at De Chambaud on the North Shore, above the town of Quebec, and burnt a French magazine, in which were some provisions, ammunition, and all the spare stores, clothing, arms, and baggage of the army.

Sept. 4. Dresden surrender'd to the army of the Empire under the Prince de Deux Ponts, after having been three years in the hands of the Prussians.

Sept. 4. The King of Prussia dislodg'd a considerable detachment of Russians from Muhlrose, where several hundreds were taken prisoners.

Sept. 4. The French abandon'd their strong camp at Marpurg, and took the route of Giessen; having march'd backwards, since the first of August, about 200 English statute miles.

Sept. 6. General Imhoff rais'd the siege of Munster.

Sept. 8. General Wunsch attack'd the army of the Empire near Torgau, (which the Prussians had retaken some time before) broke their left wing entirely, took their whole camp, and seven pieces of cannon, pursued them for an hour towards Eulenburg,

lenburg, and made upwards of 400 men prisoners of war.

Sept. 10. Vice-Admiral Pocock, the third time, attack'd and defeated M. d'Aché. The French fleet consisted of three ships of 74 guns, one of 70, four of 64, three of 60, two frigates and two store-ships; in all 15. The English had one ship of 68 guns, one of 66, one of 64, three of 60, one of 58, two of 50, three frigates, and one fire-ship; in all 13. Such a force had never before been seen in the Indian Seas. The French had a superiority of 192 guns and 2365 men, besides a great advantage in the size of their ships. The engagement lasted from two in the afternoon till four; when the French rear first, and soon after the center, began to give way; then the van made sail, stood on, and bore away with the whole squadron. M. d'Aché having begun the action before the Weymouth and Sunderland could close, and get properly into the engagement, those two ships were depriv'd, by the nature of that disposition, of an equal share in the glory of the day. The enemy afterwards reach'd Pondicherry, where they landed 400 European seamen, 200 coffrees, about two or three lacks of roupees, and the diamonds taken in the Grantham Indiaman, to the value of two lacks more. The loss of the French in the action, amounted to near 1500 kill'd and wounded; that of the English, to 569. Captain Michie of the Newcastle, Captain Gore of the Marines, the Lieutenants Redshaw and Elliot, were among the kill'd. Captain Somerset of the Cumberland, was wounded in one of his ankles; and Captain Burton receiv'd a contusion in his head. All the officers and seamen behav'd with the utmost gallantry, and maintain'd the honour of their country and the antient reputation of the British flag. The Moras of 50 guns, was said to have been broken up by the French, before this engagement.

Sept. 10. The Swedish squadron attack'd the twelve Prussian vessels near the isle of Usedom, and took eight of them. Usedom surrender'd, and the garrison of 600 men were made prisoners of war.

Sept. 11. The Castle of Marpurg capitulated, and the garrison of 857 men, officers included, surrender'd prisoners of war; a great quantity of provisions and ammunition was found in the place.

Sept. — The Swedes made themselves masters of Templin, near Berlin.

Septemb. 13. Leipsic was retaken by General Wunsch, and three battalions made prisoners of war.

Sept. 13. The British army landed, an hour before day-break, on the North Shore, within a league of Cape Diamond, and about a mile and an half above the town of Quebec; having gain'd the top of the hill, that was of a very steep ascent, and without any path wide enough for two persons to go a-breast, (which oblig'd the troops to pull themselves up by the stumps and boughs of trees that cover'd the Declivity) General Wolfe then saw the French army, under the Marquis de Montcalm, crossing the river St. Charles; he immediately form'd his line; and both armies drew up in order of battle, a little before ten, on the heights of Abraham. The British artillery consisted of one gun

gun only, which was admirably ferv'd; the French had two twelve pounders with them. The battle was brifk and animated for fome time; but the Britifh troops having referv'd their fire till they came within forty yards, and continuing it with vivacity, the enemy were oblig'd to give way in every part. The brave General Wolfe fell at the head of Bragg's and the Louifburg grenadiers, as they were advancing with their bayonets. Brigadier Monckton receiv'd a wound, about the fame time, at the head of Lafcelles's, which oblig'd him to quit the field. M. de Montcalm fell in the front of the oppofite battalions; and Brigadier Senezergues, the fecond in command, receiv'd a mortal wound. The grenadiers, Bragg's, and Lafcelles's, prefs'd on with their Bayonets; Brigadier Marray, advancing brifkly with his troops, compleated the route on this fide; The Highlanders, fupported by Anftruther's, drove part of the enemy with their broad fwords into the town, and part to their bridge on the river St. Charles. Brigadier Townfhend, upon whom the command now devolv'd, having already prevented the French from flanking the left of the army, where he was pofted, repair'd at this time to the center; reftor'd order to the troops whom the hurry of fuccefs had put into fome confufion; watch'd the motions of M. de Bougainville, who with a frefh corps of 1500 men from Cape-Rouge, feem'd to have a defign upon his rear; and render'd the victory fecure. Two pieces of cannon were taken. The French loft about 1500 men kill'd and wounded, chiefly regulars; that of the Englifh was comparatively fmall, amounting to no more than 58 kill'd, 596 wounded, and 3 miffing; In all, 657.

Sep-

Sept. — Prince Henry of Pruſſia made himſelf maſter of the Auſtrian magazines at Gorlitz, Gabel, Zittau, and Bomiſch-Friedland, on the frontiers of Bohemia; and Major-General Stutterheim took about 700 priſoners.

Sept. 18. The town of Quebec ſurrender'd to Vice-Admiral Saunders and Brigadier Townſhend. The garriſon of near 1000 men, officers, ſoldiers, and ſeamen, capitulated to be imbark'd for the firſt port in France. A great quantity of artillery and military ſtores, was found in the town, and the intrenchments along the Beauport ſhore.

Sept. 21. General Wunſch with the vanguard of the Pruſſian army, gain'd a conſiderable advantage near Neuſtadt, over the army of the empire commanded by the Prince de Deux-Ponts; whilſt General Rebentiſch, at the head of five battalions and fifteen ſquadrons of the right wing, was engag'd with the Auſtrians under General Haddick near Stroiſchen : the Pruſſian cavalry were twice repuls'd by that of the Auſtrians; the infantry ſtood their ground with great firmneſs, and remain'd on the field of battle : but General Finck, the commander in chief, having reaſon to think that the Prince de Deux-Ponts, or General Haddick, intended to renew the engagement next day, order'd General Rebentiſch to return, at midnight, into the firſt line. The Pruſſians took one piece of cannon, and loſt five of their own, when their cavalry were repuls'd the ſecond time. General Finck ſtill remain'd in his Camp at Corbitz near Dreſden, on the 24th, when the army of the Empire was retiring to Keſſeldorf. The loſs of the Pruſſians in theſe two engagements amounted to about 1000 men;

men; that of the Auſtrians and Imperialiſts, in kill'd, wounded and Priſoners, exceeded 4000.

S. pt. 25. Prince Henry of Pruſſia left his camp at Hermſdorf near Gorlitz, in the evening of the 3d, and took his route by Rothenburg to Hoyerſwerda; where, after a march of eleven German miles, he ſurpriz'd General Vehla, kill'd 600 Auſtrians in the field and in the woods, made near 500 priſoners, among whom was the General himſelf with upwards of 20 Officers, and took three pieces of cannon.

Sept. 26. Major Brereton took Trivatoor (in the Eaſt Indies) and made, one Captain with 22 men of the Lorrain regiment, and 8 Huſſars, priſoners of war.

October 1. Major Brereton order'd the Majors Monſon and Caillaud to attack Wandewaſh-Pettah (a Pettah is a Village belonging to, and commonly ſurrounding, every Indian Fort) at one end with 500 men; while Major Gordon made another attack, at the ſame time, with 200 men between the Fort and the Pettah: the former met with little reſiſtance in entering the Pettah; but the latter was only able to carry 20 men in with him, his party having been broke by the fire of the enemy. At day-break, the French charg'd the Engliſh with vigour, and, after a diſpute of near two hours, oblig'd them to abandon the Pettah with the loſs of four guns and 202 men (among whom were eleven Officers) in the action and retreat. The French ſuffer'd equally in point of numbers; but the loſs of ſo many Officers of approved valour and merit, was an eſſential advantage to the enemy. The Engliſh return'd to their cantonment at

Conje-

Conjeveram. The French soon afterwards laid siege to Tagada near Trichinopoly; and, having entirely routed Lieutenant Raillard, who came with a small party to its relief, obtain'd possession of the fort, which Serjeant Hunterman surrender'd upon honourable terms. After this success, the French attack'd and carried Seringham, which was gallantly defended by two companies of Sepoys, who were cruelly treated for their bravery.

October 13. The French having a little fleet on Lake Champlain, consisting of a new vessel of 16 guns, a schooner of 10, and three sloops of 8, with swivels in all of them; General Amherst was oblig'd to defer his expedition against Mr. Bourlemaque on the Isle au Noix, till he should be able to command that Lake. On the 11th of October, the General and the troops imbark'd in four Columns on board the batteaus, under convoy of a radeau of six 24 pounders, and a brigantine of 18 guns and 20 swivels, and a sloop of 16 guns and 22 swivels, the whole commanded by Captain Loring. The French, on the 13th sunk two of their sloops in five fathom water, and ran the third a-ground, to prevent their falling into Captain Loring's hands. Contrary winds, and the approach of winter, oblig'd General Amherst to abandon his enterprize against the Isle au Noix, after he had obtain'd this superiority upon the Lake.

October 14. M. des Essars in the Condé of 64 guns, together with a frigate of 22, and two other vessels, attack'd and took Gombroon, a defenceless factory about 15 degrees west of Surat. Gombroon is an European name for Bunder-Abbassi, which was built by the great Shaw Abbas Sophi of Persia, after he had, with the assistance of the English

lish, taken Ormus from the Portuguese, and
ruin'd it. By the 4th and 6th articles of capitulation, M. d'Estaing, then on board the Condé,
made his own exchange, and set himself at liberty
from the parole which he gave at Madrass, and
which ran in the usual form, "not to serve directly or indirectly against the English, during the
present war, or till he should be regularly exchang'd." This gentleman, in the same ship, destroy'd all the English settlements on the coast of
Sumatra, in the course of the following year: of
which exploit, a very magnificent account was
publish'd in the Amsterdam Gazette.

October 23. Colonel Luckner attack'd a strong
post of the French at Neider-Brechen, kill'd one
Lieutenant Colonel, one Major, two Captains, between 40 and 50 inferiour officers and private
men; made an officer and 71 private men prisoners; and took 99 horses, together with 112
waggons loaded with forage.

October — The Swedes were driven from Passewalk and Demmin by General Manteuffel, who
seiz'd their military chest at the latter place.

October 29. Baron Gemminghen, who commanded the rear-guard of the Duke d'Aremberg's
troops, was defeated near Pretsch, by the Generals
Rebentisch and Wunsch, under the orders of Prince
Henry. The Austrians lost part of their tents, a
large quantity of baggage, and some cannon in the
engagement; Baron Gemminghen, 20 officers,
and 1200 private men were made prisoners. The
next day General Finck made more prisoners at
Dabem.

November

November 5. The Swedes abandon'd Anclam, and repafs'd the Peene.

Nov. 20. M. de Gayon, having obtain'd on the 20th the terms he demanded from the Count de la Lippe, march'd out of the town of Munfter on the 21ſt, and General Imhoff enter'd it on the 22d.

Nov. 20 and 21. At Maxen, not far from Struppen, in the neighbourhood of the famous camp of Pirna; Marſhal Daun ſurpriz'd, ſurrounded, and made priſoners 12,762 Pruſſians, including Officers and Generals; took 24 ſtandards, 96 colours, 3 pair of ſilver-kettle drums, one of braſs, and 70 pieces of cannon of different bores. The Auſtrians loſt about 1000 men. The names of the nine Pruſſian Generals were, Finck, Rebentiſch, Wunſch, Platten, Lindſtaedt, Moſel, Bredow, Faſult, and Gerſdorff.

Nov. 20. The French fleet under Marſhal Conflans, (having been reinforc'd by draughts from M. Bompart's ſquadron, which arriv'd on the 8th of November, after the violence of the wind had driven Sir Edward Hawke into Torbay) ſet ſail on the 14th, from the harbour of Breſt. M. Conflans diſcover'd Commodore Duff's ſquadron of frigates at four o' clock in the morning of the 20th, but chaſing it in a line, Sir Edward Hawke appear'd in ſight time enough to prevent its capture. About half an hour paſt two in the afternoon, the engagement began between the two fleets, to the ſouthward of Belliſle. About four, the Formidable of 80 guns 1000 men, ſtruck after a deſperate reſiſtance. A little after this, the Theſeé of 74 guns 815 men, a new ſhip, uninjur'd by the fire of the

Brit-

British fleet, rowl'd several times in deep plunges and sunk on her broadside. The Superbe of 70 guns 800 men, which had likewise receiv'd no injury in the action, sunk instantly like a stone; out of the crews of these two ships, 50 only were saved. By day-break, on the 21st, the Resolution of 74 guns Captain Speke, was discover'd dismasted on a large sand bank call'd "the Four." The Essex of 64 guns Captain Obrian, having been order'd to slip, and pursue the French Heros of 74 guns, and the Soleil Royal of 80 guns (which under cover of the night had anchor'd among the British fleet, and then cut, and run ashore, to the westward of Croizie) also unfortunately struck upon the same bank. Both these ships were irrecoverably lost, and their remains set on fire. About fourscore of the Resolution's company, in spite of the Captain's remonstrances, made rafts, put off, and were driven out to sea: one Lieutenant, with a boat's crew, belonging to the Essex, was driven on the French shore: the rest of the crew, in both ships were preserv'd. On the 22d, the Soleil-Royal and the Heros were destroy'd; the former by the French, the latter by the English. Seven or eight of the French line of battle ships got into the river Vilaine; the remainder put out to sea the night of the action, and afterwards retir'd into one of the ports in the isle of Aix, from whence they were brought into the river Charante. The Heros having struck to the Magnanime, before she was destroy'd; Lord Howe demanded the crew, as his prisoners, at the Duc d'Aiguillon's table: the fact was acknowledg'd, but the discussion of so nice a point, was left to their respective Sovereigns. Only nine of the British ships had any share in this victory. The Juste, a French ship of 70 guns, was afterwards lost in that narrow and dangerous passage

sage between the Four and Croizie; of 800 men, a tenth only was saved. The French fleet consisted of 25 ships, four of which were frigates; the English, of 33; ten of which were frigates from 50 to 28 guns. His Majesty to recompence this important service, granted a pension of 2000 pounds per annum to Sir Edward Hawke, for his life, and for the lives of his two sons, and the survivor of them; and Sir Edward afterwards receiv'd the unanimous thanks of the House of Commons.

Nov. 24. The Calcutta Captain Wilson, Duke of Dorset Captain Forrester, and Hardwick Captain Sampson, having demanded, of the Dutch Commodore, an English snow, and four or five sloops, which he had arbitrarily stopp'd in the river Bengal, and that demand not being complied with, began a bold and resolute engagement with the seven Dutch ships under the Commodore's orders. After an action of two hours, the Commodore struck, with three other ships; the remaining three ran down the river, and fell into the hands of the Royal George and the Oxford Indiamen

Nov. 24. Colonel Forde, with 350 Europeans, 1500 Sepoys, 20 Gentlemen of the independent Company mounted, 50 Persian horse, and about 30 Volunteers, intending to halt at Chandanagore; was fir'd upon by the Dutch troops, which had occupied that place; the Colonel immediately dislodg'd them, kill'd near 50, and pursued the rest to the walls of their own Fort Chincura: he took upon this occasion four field pieces and all their baggage.

Nov. 25. The Dutch army, compos'd of Europeans and Buggesses, having advanc'd from their ships near to Chincura, Colonel Forde met them

in

n a neighbouring plain, gave them battle, and put
hem to flight in such a manner, that very few ef-
ap'd being kill'd or taken prisoners. In confe-
[uence of this victory, a treaty was concluded beween the English and the Director and Council of
Chincura, to the advantage of the former.

Nov. 30 The hereditary Prince of Brunswick,
and Prince Charles of Bevern, defeated, near Fulda,
three battalions of grenadiers, and the regiment of
Wernick, being part of the army of the Duke of
Wirtemberg. A considerable number of these battalions was cut to pieces, the rest threw down their
arms, and were made prisoners of war, with all
their officers; the hereditary Prince took from
them, two pieces of cannon, two pair of colours,
their baggage, and best cloathes, in which they
were dress'd that day for a feu de joye.

Nov. 30. The garrison of Wondivash (in the
East Indies) consisting of 5 subaltern Officers, 63
private Europeans, and 500 Sepoys, surrender'd
prisoners of war to Colonel Coote; 49 pieces of
cannon were taken, with a great quantity of Ammunition.

Dec. 4. The Mermaid of 24 guns struck on Wal-
ker's, Key, one of the most northern of the Baha-
mas, and was lost; the crew were saved.

Dec. 3 and 4. Lieutenant General Beck, under
the orders of Marshal Daun, attack'd and defeated
a considerable body of Prussians, near Meissen,
commanded by General Diercke; many of the
Prussians were cut to pieces; Major Gen. Diercke
himself, 55 Officers, and the three battalions of
Haufen, Canitz, and Bernbourg, besides dragoons
and

and Huffars, were made prifoners; 8 pieces of cannon, 61 brafs drums, all the baggage, and a confiderable number of horfes were taken.

Dec. 10. The fort of Carangoly (in the Eaft Indies) furrender'd to Colonel Coote upon honourable terms; five out of nine guns were difmounted.

Dec. — The Hunter and Efther cutters, ftation'd off Havre de Grace, were taken by a French frigate that came out of Havre for that purpofe.

Dec. 25. The hereditary Prince of Brunfwich arriv'd at Chemnitz in Saxony, with a body of 10 or 12,000 men, detach'd from the army of Prince Ferdinand, to the affiftance of the King of Pruffia.

Dec. 26. Governour Littleton concluded a treaty of peace and friendfhip, at Fort Prince George in South Carolina, with Attakullakulla or the little Carpenter, Deputy of the whole Cherokee Nation, and other principal Cherokees, which that Nation foon afterwards violated in the moft open and fhameful manner.

Dec. 29. Colonel Luckner with his Chaffeurs, cut to pieces or made prifoners, a body of 400 French volunteers, (excepting 22 men only, who efcap'd) and took one piece of cannon.

Dec. — M. Scheiter pafs'd the Rhine, furpriz'd a French Detachment, burnt a large magazine, and took the whole baggage of the Swifs regiment of Jenner, without any lofs on his fide.

Supplies granted by Parliament for the fervice of the year 1759.

Twelve million, feven hundred forty nine thoufand, eight hundred and fixty pounds.

A lift

war, from the 31st of December 1758 to the 31st of December 1759.

January.	guns.	men.	captors.
The Machault of Granville	24 nine pounders.	240	taken by the Juno Captain Phillips.
The St. Michael of Dunkirk, with a ransomer on board.	6	50	by the Saphire.
A privateer	6	}	by the Antigua sloop.
A privateer	12		
The Marquis de Marigny of Granville	20	194	by the Montague Captain Parker.
February.			
The Moras of St. Maloe	22	202	by the Unicorn Captain Graves.
A privateer			by a man of war, and sent into Cork.
The Hardi Mendiant of Dunkirk	8	60	by the Mountague Captain Parker.

	guns.	men.	captors.
La Mouche of Havre	8	80	by the Coventry and Thames.
March.			
The Cabriolet of Dunkirk	6	58	by the Jamaica sloop.
A privateer of St. Maloe	22 nine pounders.	250	by the Adventure of 32 guns Captain Moore.
La Maria Catherine	8		by the Amazon Captain Norton.
April.			
A cutter, of Dunkirk	8	60	by one of his Majesty's cutters.
Marquis de Barail of Dunkirk	14	104	by the Brilliant and Deptford.
The Carilloneur of Dunkirk	8	60	by the Grace cutter and the Rochester's boats.
Conquerant of Cherburg	6 carriage 10 swivels	29 }	by the Tamer frigate Capt. Hughes.
Chasseur of Dunkirk	6 carriage	42	

	guns.	men.	captors.
Dispatch of Morlaix	10 carriage 8 swivels	30	by the Diligence sloop Capt. Eastwood.
Basque of Bayonne	22 carriage	210	by the Brilliant Captain Parker.
Le Vieux of Bourdeaux	8 carriage	36	by the Surprize Captain Antrobus.
Le Velour from St. Domingo	24	110	by the Favourite of 20 guns, of a much inferiour weight of metal, Captain Edwards commander; the engagement continued for 2 hours and an half. Captain Edwards had been Lieutenant of the Tartar.
May.			
A privateer	8 carriage 6 swivels	52	by the Liverpool Captain Knight.
La Dunkerquoise of Dunkirk	8 carriage	52	by the Stag Captain Angel.
The Countess of Serfe of Dunkirk with two ransomers, pierc'd for 22 guns	18	187	by the Adventure Captain Moore.

June.	guns.	men.	captors.
The Bona Esperanza			by the Penguin.
A privateer			by the Adventure.

July.

Lanouvelle Hirondelle of Dunkirk with one ransomer	6 carriage 6 swivels	35	by the Liverpool Captain Knight.

Two Dutch ships, of about 350 tons each, loaded with 73 tons of biscuit, 51 quarters of beef and pork, 200 barrels of powder, and a vast quantity of cannon ball, and bombs taken by the Success.

August.

Two privateers		by the Antelope and Jamaica sloop.
A privateer, M. Palanqui commander		by the Lively Honourable Frederick Maitland.

The Favourite sloop from Pondicherry to Mauritius was taken by the Royal George Indiaman Captain Beamish, and carried into Madrass; she had two Colonels and a Captain on board, and 40,000 rupees (2s 4d to 5d each) in specie.

September.	guns.	men.	captors.
The Mercury schooner, a tender to the Brest-fleet	4	36	taken from under Cameret-fort by the boats of Sir Edward Hawke's squadron.
The Aimiable Granadina of Port au Prince	13	70	by the sloop Mars (a tender to the Marlborough) James Paterson commander; after an engagement of an hour and an half.
Two French Privateers			run ashore at Guadalupe, and burnt by the Fortune sloop of 10 guns, commanded by Mr. Rott first Lieutenant to Commodore Moore.
October.			
A privateer	6		driven ashore at Point Noir in Guadaloupe, by the Antigua sloop.
November.			

The Senecterre, Duke de Fronsac, and Soleil-Royal, struck on a sand bank in St. Lawrence river, below Quebec, and were lost.

December.	guns.	men.	captors.
A cutter of Boulogne			taken by two of his Majesty's cutters.
The Chesaria of 500 tons, with six guns unmounted in her hold	18	100	by the Rippon. —— she sail'd from a place twenty leagues above Quebec
The Infernal	10		carried into Barbadoes by the Amazon.

1760.

January — AN advanc'd post of the Allies at Herborn, consisting of a Captain and 100 men, was obliged to submit to the French after a vigorous resistance.

Jan. 7. M. de Derenthal reliev'd the Castle of Dillenbourg, made 40 French officers and 700 private men prisoners, and took seven pair of colours, with two pieces of cannon.

Jan. 7. Major Keith's Highlanders and Luckner's Hussars, attack'd Baufremont's dragoons in the village of Eybach, kill'd and dispers'd great part of them, made about 80 prisoners, and took near 200 horses with the baggage of the regiment. The Highlanders greatly distinguish'd themselves on this occasion.

Jan. 11. The Marquifs of Granby bomb-ketch, was run down by the Bird tender, to the east-ward of the island of May in the Firth of Forth, and sunk immediately to the bottom.

Jan. — A French East-Indiaman, taken about two years before by the Protector, a ship belonging to the English East-India Company, was condemn'd in Doctors Commons as a lawful capture.

Jan. 22. Colonel Eyre Coote defeated Lieutenant General Lally near Wondivash. The French force

force was compos'd of 2200 Europeans, 300 Cofferies or Caffres from Madagascar, and between 9 and 10,000 black troops. The English amounted to 1700 Europeans and 3500 black troops. The French, in their own account, own'd the loss of 800 men kill'd and wounded, 200 of whom the Conquerors buried in the field. Among the prisoners were Brigadier General Bussy, Le Chevalier Godeville quarter master general, Lieutenant Colonel Murphy, of Lally's regiment, Le Chevalier de Poete Knight of Malta (who afterwards died of his wounds) three Captains, five Lieutenants, and two Ensigns. Twelve pieces of iron cannon, and ten of brass were taken, together with a quantity of shot, and all implements belonging to the train. The loss of the victorious army amounted to 192 Europeans and 70 Blacks kill'd and wounded. The gallant Major Brereton died of his wounds. M. Lally blew up a large magazine of powder in his retreat, and soon afterwards recall'd all his troops from Seringham, consisting of near 500 European horse and foot. After this victory, Colonel Coote detach'd Captain de Vasserot to lay waste the bounds of Pondicherry, who brought off a booty of 4000 head of cattle.

Jan. 27 and 28. —— Count Fersen, the Swedish General, surpriz'd the Prussians in the suburb of Anclam, drove them into the town, and enter'd it with them, took General Manteuffel prisoner with about 300 men, kill'd 13, wounded 12, and made himself master of 3 pieces of cannon. Major General Stutterheim collected the scatter'd Prussians, and obliged the Swedes to retire.

Jan. 30. Le Chevalier de Tilly surrender'd Chittipet to Colonel Coote. Four Officers, 127 Europeans,

)eans, and 300 Seapoys were made prisoners; and nine guns taken, with a quantity of ammunition. About this time Captain Wood invested Arcot, got possession of the Pettah, routed Zulapherzing's Forces, and took his whole camp.

Jan. 30. Captain Smith, with a detachment, intercepted a party of the enemy going from Arcot to Gingey, and took one Captain of the Lorrain regiment, 3 Commiſſaries, 10 Europeans, 50 Seapoys, and 2 pieces of braſs cannon 8 pounders.

Jan. 30. By a liſt publiſh'd on this day in Antigua, it appear'd that the ſquadron under Commodore Moore, from the 30th of Auguſt 1757 to the 26th of December 1759, had taken 53 French privateers, drove 3 aſhore, and retaken 24 Engliſh veſſels.

Feb. 2. Timmery ſurrender'd to Major Monſon; one Serjeant, 20 Europeans, 60 Seapoys, and ſix pieces of cannon were taken.

Feb. 10. Arcot ſurrender'd to Colonel Coote. 3 Captains, 8 Subalterns, 236 Europeans, and between 2 and 300 Seapoys, were made priſoners of war, 4 mortars, and 22 pieces of cannon were taken, together with a great quantity of all military ſtores. The very day that Arcot ſurrender'd, 27 Huſſars deſerted, with their horſes and arms, and came over to Colonel Coote; not long afterwards, the whole body of European cavalry, in the French King's ſervice, follow'd that example. In this whole expedition from the 30th of November to the 10th of February incluſive, the French loſt 1081 Europeans kill'd, wounded, and priſoners; 27 deſerters, 1360 Seapoys, 114 pieces of cannon

in

in iron and brafs, 4 mortars, and a very confiderable quantity of ammunition.

Febr. — The Falmouth, a ſhip belonging to Admiral Cornifh's ſquadron, obliged the Haerlem to run aſhore, two leagues to the northward of Pondicherry. — The garriſons of Permacoil and Alemparvé, furrender'd Priſoners of War.

Febr. 15. In the night, the Ramilies of 90 guns, 734 men Captain Taylor, daſh'd to pieces, in a violent ſtorm, againſt a rock between the Start Point and Plymouth. One midſhipman aud 26 ſeamen were ſaved; the Captain and all the reſt of the crew unfortunately periſh'd. — The Hawke cutter with one officer and 12 men was loſt in the ſame terrible ſtorm.

Febr. 20. The Auſtrians, under General Beck, attack'd the Pruſſians, under General Czetteritz, near Torgau; the loſs in this affair was of no great importance, but the Pruſſian General had the misfortune to be taken priſoner, with two ſquadrons of light cavalry.

Febr. 21. The caſtle of Carrickfergus capitulated to Brigadier General Flobert at the head of 1000 French troops; and Lieutenant Colonel Jennings ſurrender'd himſelf priſoner of war, together with four companies of Major General Strode's regiment. Colonel Jennings bravely repuls'd the enemy in their firſt attack upon the Caſtle, which they endeavour'd to take by aſſault; but the place being abſolutely untenable, and the ſoldiers in want of ball, he was obliged to propoſe terms of capitulation. M. Flobert was wounded in the leg, and left at Carrickfergus when the troops reimbark'd ark'd. Colonel Jennings receiv'd the thanks of the Irish House of Commons for his bravery and conduct.

Febr. — The Thames Captain Richard Saunders, from Leghorn to London, valued at 100,000 pounds sterling, was taken by the Fulvie privateer of Dunkirk and her consort, each of them pierc'd for 22 guns and mounting 18, after an engagement of two hours.

Febr. 29. Captain Elliot in the Æolus of 32 guns 220 men, together with Captain Clements in the Pallas of 36 guns 240 men, and Captain Logie in the Brilliant of 36 guns 240 men, attack'd and took the Marshal Bellisle of 44 guns 545 men (troops included) Captain Thurot, La Blonde 32 guns 400 men Captain La Kayce, and the Terpsichore 26 guns 300 men Captain Defrauaudais: the engagement was between the Mull of Galloway and the Isle of Man, and lasted upwards of an hour and an half. The French had near 300 kill'd and wounded; the English, no more than 5 kill'd and 31 wounded. Captain Elliot and his gallant companions receiv'd the thanks of the Irish House of Commons for this important Service. M. Thurot, who fell in the action, was an excellent seaman, a brave officer, and a generous enemy!

March 12. Major Podewills, with 300 Prussian Dragoons and Hussars, surpriz'd 1400 Cossacks at Grenfwalde, kill'd a Colonel, Lieutenant Colonel, and 80 men, made 30 prisoners, and brought away 50 horses.

Mar.

March 15 and 16. General Laudohn, with a considerable force, attack'd, near Newstadt, the Captains Blumenthal and Zittzwitz, with the regiment of Manteuffel, and a squadron of the dragoons of Bareith, under their command. Five cover'd waggons laden with baggage, and 18 carts with meal and oats, fell into the hands of the Austrians, who suffer'd nevertheless in the engagement, losing 28 officers and near 1000 men kill'd and wounded; the total loss of the Prussians did not exceed 200 men. The Austrians abandon'd Newstadt on the 17th.

March 16 and 17. A body of light troops of the army of the Empire, under the orders of General Luckzinski, surpriz'd at Zeitz, and carried off, 8 officers and 100 private men of a Prussian regiment of Carabineers.

March —. The Tartar's prize, a frigate of 20 guns, founder'd in the Mediterranean, but the officers and crew were taken up by a Danish ship, and carried into Malta.

March 28. The Penguin frigate of 20 guns, Captain Harris, was taken and sunk, off Vigo, by the Malicieuse of 36 guns and the Opale of 32.

April 2. The Condé East-Indiaman of 36 guns and a frigate of 18 with 800 men under the Count d'Estaign, oblig'd the crew of the Denham Indiaman to set fire to her, and afterwards destroy'd the English settlements on the coast of Sumatra.

April

April 4. The Biddeford of 20 guns, Captain Skinner, and the Flamborough of 24 guns, Captain Kennedy, engag'd the Opale of 32 guns, 250 men the Marquis d'Ars commander, and the Macieufe of 36 guns 250 men M. de Goimpy commander. The battle lafted between three and four ours, when the French frigates fled with all the ſil they could make. Captain Skinner was unforunately kill'd in the action, and his Lieutenant Mr. Knollys died of his wounds foon afterwards. Mr. Stace the Mafter, fought the ſhip till the enemy made off. This engagement did great honour to the Britifh Marine.

April 5. Carical in the Eaſt-Indies, a ſmall penagon, but of great ſtrength, and built exactly on he plan of Liſle, ſurrender'd to the land and ſea Officers under Rear Admiral Cornifh and Major Monfon.

April 28. The regiment of M. D'Apchon, together with ſome Volunteers, attack'd Colonel Freyagg in Vacha, who was obliged to abandon that own; but taking poſt upon a riſing ground, he kept the French in play, till two battalions of grenadiers came to his Affiſtance; the French then retir'd, but were purfued for three leagues, attack'd and drove from Geifa, where they had intended to quarter that night.

April 28. The Chevalier de Levis, at the head of 10,000 French and Canadians, and 500 Indians, was attack'd by Brigadier General Murray, with 3000 men only, near Quebec. The action lafted an hour and three quarters, when General Murray was oblig'd to retreat, after having loſt 259 kill'd,
13 pri-

13 prisoners, and 832 wounded and missing. Lieutenant Colonel Burton, Major Dalling, and Captain Ince, were mention'd with honour in the General's account of this battle. All the officers and soldiers did their Duty. The French, by their own confession, had 2500 men kill'd and wounded. The cannon, which could not be brought off, were nail'd up. The severity of the climate, and the scurvy, had already destroy'd 1000 of the garrison, and rendred 2000 more totally unfit for any service.

Apr. 29. The Prince of Wales, a rich ship from Genoa and Leghorn, valued at 50,000 pounds, was taken by a French frigate.

May 2 and 3. — Two hundred pick'd men of the Prussian army, who were sent to mark out a camp near the Elbe, were taken prisoners by General Lasci, after a gallant defence.

May 5. The Prussians abandon'd Nossen, and set fire to their magazine; but the Austrians came up time enough to save part of it.

May 16 and 17. In the night of the 28th of April, the French open'd trenches against the town of Quebec; but retir'd with precipitation between the 16 and 17th of May, on the arrival of part of the British fleet. They left behind them, their camp standing, all their baggage, stores, magazines of provisions and ammunition; 34 pieces of battering-cannon, (4 of which were brass twelve pounders) 10 field pieces, 6 mortars, 4 petards, a large quantity of scaling ladders, and intrenching tools beyond number. The day before this retreat, Captain Schomberg of the Diana and Captain Deane

Deane of the Loweſtoffe, had been order'd by Commodore Swanton, to attack two frigates, two arm'd ſhips, and many ſmaller veſſels, which lay above the town. The French fled in the greateſt confuſion; the Pomona frigate was driven on ſhore above Cape Diamond; the Atalanta ran herſelf aſhore, and was burnt at Point au Tremble, about 10 leagues above Quebec; Moſt of the other ſhips and veſſels were likewiſe driven aſhore, or effectually deſtroy'd. The Loweſtoffe, in purſuit of theſe frigates, was loſt upon ſome unknown rocks, but the officers and men were ſaved. In conſequence of theſe ſucceſſes, a nation of Indians ſurrender'd themſelves to the Engliſh, and enter'd into an alliance with them.

May 24. The French garriſon, of 500 men, under Brigadier Waldener, at Butzbach, were defeated by Colonel Luckner; four officers and 100 private men were made priſoners; the reſt were either cut to pieces, or diſpers'd.

May 29. A company of grenadiers of the regiment Dauphine, were made priſoners of war by the Black Huſſars of the allies, in a ſlight ſkirmiſh near Fulda.

June 1. Colonel Montgomery and Major Grant deſtroy'd Eſtato, Sugar-Town, and every village and houſe in the lower Nation of the Cherokees.

Jun. 1. By an account collected from Lloyd's liſts, it appear'd, that between the firſt of June 1756, and the firſt of June 1760, the number of ſhips taken by the French amounted to 2539, including 78 privateers: of this number 321 were retaken. During the ſame ſpace of time, the number

ber of ships taken by the English amounted to 944, of which 243 were privateers.

June — The Russian General Tottleben made 200 Prussians prisoners of war near Coslin, and routed two independent battalions.

June — General Wolferidorf, under the orders of General Laudohn, took possession of the almost impregnable lines of Landshut, and of the fortress of that name, which were abandon'd by General Fouquet.

June 17. General Fouquet repossess'd himself of Landshut, and all the neighbouring heights.

June 17 and 18. General Laudohn with a body of 12000 volunteers, made a general assault upon the town of Glatz, but was repuls'd by Colonel D'O, who commanded in that fortress, with considerable loss.

June — The Prussians under General Forcade obliged the Russian General Tottleben to retire, after a smart engagement; but the latter being reinforc'd by part of the vanguard of the army destin'd for Pomerania, General Forcade was attack'd in his turn, and defeated, with the loss of 500 men kill'd, besides prisoners and deserters.

June 23. General Laudohn, at the head of near 50,000 men, attack'd the Prussians under General Fouquet, near Landshut; and drove them from their different posts, in which they were strongly intrench'd: the action began at a quarter before two in the morning; in less than an hour, the Austrians carried the intrenchments on the eminences

ences of Buckberg and Doctorsberg; the line of ommunication between those eminences was afterwards forced; and the Prussians, having been successively dislodged from their remaining posts, were at last obliged to lay down their arms in the field about eight o' clock in the morning, and ask for quarter. 7800 men (almost the whole of the Prussian army that surviv'd the engagement) were made prisoners of war, and 49 pieces of ordnance of different bores, 9 haubitzers, 24 ammunition waggons, 34 pair of colours, 2 standards, one pair of silver kettle drums, fell into the hands of the conquerors. The Austrians acknowledged only the loss of 767 kill'd, 2087 wounded, and 351 missing. General Laudohn, in his particular detail of this victory, distinguish'd the merit and services of his Generals and Officers in so handsome a manner, that he deserv'd to be as much esteem'd for his modesty, as he had been admir'd for his military abilities.

June 30. The castle of Marburg surrender'd to the French, and the garrison of near 400 men were made prisoners of war.

July 1. Between the 24th of June and the 1st of July, Colonel Archibald Montgomery, with a detachment of the royal regiment of foot, the Highland regiment, and a part of the South-Carolina provincials, march'd to the town of Etchoey in the middle settlements of the Cherokee nation, and return'd back again to his camp at Fort Prince George, being, in all, 160 miles: on the 27th of June he engag'd with, and repuls'd, the Indians who oppos'd themselves to his march. The dangerous passages through narrow defiles, and gaps of mountains, might have enabled an handful of

I   men

men to resist the efforts of a whole army; but in spight of these difficulties, Colonel Montgomery destroy'd the Cherokee settlement at Etchoey (in which he found 500 bushels of Indian corn) with the loss only of 20 men kill'd and 77 wounded.

July 3. A fire broke out in the dockyard at Portsmouth, and destroy'd the rope-house, spinning-house, hemp-house, and one of the storehouses. This accident was suppos'd to have been the effect of lightning.

July 8. Captain Byron in the Fame, together with the Dorsetshire, Achilles, Scarborough, and Repulse, destroy'd, in Chaleurs Bay, the Machaux frigate of 30 guns, two large storeships, nineteen sail of smaller vessels, two batteries, and two hundred houses.

July 10. The hereditary Prince of Brunswick engag'd a very considerable body of the French army on the heights of Corbach; but, after a vigorous dispute, was oblig'd to retire in some confusion. General Count Kielmansegge, Major General Griffin, and the two battalions of Brudenel and Carr, greatly distinguish'd themselves in this affair: the hereditary Prince, putting himself at the head of a squadron of Blands (commanded by Major Mill) and Howard's Regiment of dragoons, charg'd the enemy so furiously and effectually with these brave troops, that he enabled his infantry to make a safe retreat: he receiv'd a slight wound in the shoulder. Twelve pieces of cannon, four haubitzers, and thirty ammunition waggons fell into the hands of the French, whose loss in kill'd and wounded was computed at 700 men. The total loss

loſs of the Allies, in kill'd, wounded and miſſing, amounted to 824.

July 16. The caſtle of Dillingbourg, after an honourable defence, ſurrender'd to the French; and the garriſon, conſiſting of near 250 men, were made priſoners of war.

July 16. The hereditary Prince of Brunſwick ſurpriz'd and defeated a body of the French under Major General Glaubitz, near the village of Erxdorf at ſome diſtance from Ziegenhayn. Two battalions of Royal Baviere, three of Anhalt, together with the Major General himſelf and the Prince of Anhalt Coethen, were made priſoners of war; five pieces of artillery, one hautbitzer, and all their arms and baggage, were taken. Elliot's regiment of light-horſe under Major Erſkine, behav'd with remarkable intrepidity. The whole number of priſoners amounted to 177 officers and 2482 private men. The loſs on the part of the Allies, did not exceed 85 kill'd, 95 wounded, and 6 miſſing.

July 18. The Allies evacuated Paderborn, of which the French took poſſeſſion.

July — A French frigate of 28 guns and 180 men, bound to Quebec with ſtores, was loſt on the iſland of Flora, and all the men, except about 28, were drown'd.

July 22. — Between the ſecond and ſeventh of July, the King of Pruſſia, having march'd with his army to Koningſbruck, Lichtenberg, and Marienſtern, paſs'd the river Sprehe near Groſs-Dobrau, and occupied the camp at Doberſchutz about half a German mile from Bautzen, making a feint to
puſh

push forward into Silesia: on receiving intelligence that Marshal Daun had gain'd two marches upon him, he struck his tents at eight o' clock in the evening of the eighth, repass'd the Sprehe near Bautzen, and on the 13th, fix'd his head-quarters at Grunau, behind the Great-Garden near Dresden; as the King approach'd the Elbe, he was join'd by General Hulsen with his corps from Meissen. From the 13th to the 19th, the King besieged Dresden vigorously; but Marshal Daun being now arriv'd with his army, and incamp'd within a league of the city, his Majesty drew off his forces on the 22d, and rais'd the siege. In the night between the 21st and 22d, sixteen battalions, sent through the town by Marshal Daun, sallied out upon the Prussians, and, at first, obtain'd some advantage; but were, in the end, repuls'd and pursued with loss.

July 26. The old fortress of Glatz was taken sword in hand, and the new one surrender'd at discretion; the Austrians made themselves masters of a considerable magazine; their total loss, by their own account, did not exceed four officers and sixty-four private men kill'd, seven officers and 138 men wounded.

July 31. The hereditary Prince of Brunswick, General Sporcken, and the Marquis of Granby, attack'd and defeated the reserve of the French army commanded by the Chevalier de Muy, near Warbourg. The Swifs regiment of Lockmann, was severely treated by the British cavalry, which charg'd the enemy's cavalry and infantry, several times, with success, notwithstanding a long march of near five miles upon a full trott. Besides the British cavalry under General Mostyn; the battalion of Maxwell's grenadiers, Colonel Beckwith with his

brigade

brigade of English grenadiers and Scotch Highlanders, and Captain Philips with the artillery, distinguish'd themselves by their conduct and intrepidity. Many of the enemy were drown'd in the Dymel; they left near 1500 men on the field of battle, and ten pieces of cannon; the prisoners exceeded the number of the slain; the French brigades of Bourbonnois, La Couronne, Rochfort, and Planta, with the regiment of Rovergue, and Fischer's corps, were the principal sufferers in this engagement. The total loss of the British forces amounted to 590 men; no return was made publick, of the kill'd, wounded, and missing, in the other troops of the allied army.

August 1. The French under Prince Xavier of Saxony, took Munden sword in hand, where they found a magazine; the garrison, consisting of 350 men, were made prisoners of war. Cassel and Gottingen surrender'd at the same time.

August 4. General Laudohn, after having bombarded Breslau without effect; retired from that city, on the approach of Prince Henry of Prussia.

August 4. General Werner attack'd, and defeated, a body of 2000 Austrians under General Caramelli, kill'd great part of the Arch-Duke Joseph's regiment of dragoons, and made 7 officers, with 370 private men, prisoners.

August 9. The garrison of Fort Loudon, march'd out of that place with their arms and amunition, according to capitulation; but the next day the treacherous Cherokees, to the number of 700, surrounded them, pour'd in vollies of small arms, and showers of arrows, from every side, and obliged them

them to surrender at discretion. All the officers, (except Captain Stuart) and between 30 and 40 private men were kill'd, many wounded, and the rest carried into a miserable captivity.

August 10. Major General Luckner made a French detachment at Nordheim, consisting of 332 men, prisoners of war. The same day Colonel Donnop attack'd a body of 2000 volunteers of the French army, in the wood of Sababourg, from which he dislodg'd them with the loss of near 500 men, and 3 pieces of cannon, which were taken by the Prussian hussars.

August 11. The Castle of Ziegenhayn surrender'd to the French, and the garrison of 750 men were made prisoners of War.

Aug. 15. The King of Prussia decamp'd on the 3d, from the borders of the Elbe, and having reach'd Lignitz on the 10th, he found the Austrians posted in a very advantageous situation, occupying all the ground between Parchwitz and Cossendau; Marshal Daun was in the center, General Laudohn on the right, and General Beck on the left. The King march'd in the night of the 11th, in hopes of turning the enemy, and reaching Javer; in this march, he discovered a new corps of the Austrians under General Lasci, which afterwards join'd Marshal Daun, in spight of the King's dispositions to prevent that junction. On the 13th, his Majesty return'd to the camp at Lignitz, where he heard that Count Czernichew had laid a bridge over the Oder at Auras, and was to pass that river the same day with 24000 Russians. Time press'd, and the danger grew more formidable every moment. By one judicious movement, the
King

King preserv'd his whole army; on the 14th, he quitted Lignitz, and possessed himself of the heights of Pfaffendorf; he receiv'd intelligence, near two o' clock the next morning, of General Laudohn's march, by Bennowitz, towards those heights: the King immediately divided his army into two bodies; the right remain'd upon the ground, which was well defended by batteries to prevent the approach of Marshal Daun, while the left fell upon Laudohn's corps about three o' clock in the morning, and drove it, fighting, almost to the river Katzbach. In this critical action, the Austrians lost 82 pieces of cannon, 23 pair of colours, and 10,000 men. The King of Prussia's total loss fell short of 2000. Immediately after the battle, his Majesty pass'd the defile of Parchwitz, and the next day moved forwards to Neumarck. The Russians retir'd over the Oder. The Austrians, in their own account of this action, confess'd that they had 6043 men kill'd, wounded, and missing, and 68 pieces of cannon taken.

August — Anclam and Demmin were evacuated by the Prussians.

August 20. Lieutenant General Hulsen defeated the Prince of Deux Ponts and General Haddicke, near Strela. The Prince of Nassau Usingen Colonel of the regiment of Deux Ponts, 39 officers, and 1214 private men were taken prisoners; upwards of 2000 Austrians were kill'd and wounded in this engagement. The Prussians took one piece of cannon, two pair of colours, and two standards; their loss did not exceed 15 officers and 658 private men. The enemy made themselves masters of one three pounder; and two other broken and dismounted

mounted pieces of cannon, were oblig'd to be left behind.

August 25. The French drove the Hanoverians out of Gottingen.

August 26. The Coſſacks under General Tottleben, attack'd the Pruſſians under General Goltze, cut to pieces a ſquadron of the Huſſars of Dingelſtadt, and obtain'd other conſiderable advantages.

Auguſt — The Eurus frigate, Captain Bateman, was loſt in the river St. Laurence, but the crew were all ſaved.

Auguſt — The tender, belonging to the Dublin man of war, was loſt in the Weſt-Indies, with 100 choſen men on board, who all periſh'd.

September — The corps under General Luzinſki, took poſſeſſion of Halle.

Sept. 4. Lord Howe in the Magnanime, together with the Prince Frederick and Bedford, attack'd and reduced a fort on the Iſle Dumet, garriſon'd by a company of 54 men of the regiment of Bourbon; he found, in the fort, nine pieces of cannon of 18 and 22 pounders.

Sept. 6. The hereditary Prince, at two o' clock in the morning, ſurpriz'd the voluntiers of Dauphiné and Clermont in the town of Zierenberg, kill'd and wounded a conſiderable number of them, brought off two pieces of cannon, and made 42 officers with 300 private men priſoners; among the officers, were M. de Norman Brigadier, who commanded the volunteers of Dauphiné and M. de
Co-

of thofe of Clermont. The Al-
han ten men kill'd and wounded
neral Griffin was wounded in the
)net of one of his own men, ow-
r miftake, occafion'd by his talk-
language, to a prifoner who re-
firelock. The confequeuces of
elt by the General, many months
England.

al Amherft having oblig'd M.
nder the poft and fort of Ifle
Galette, on the 25th of Auguft;
iving abandon'd the Ifle au Noix
at month, upon the approach of
under the command of Colonel
real capitulated on the eighth of
arrifons of that place, Trois Ri-
uartieres, the ifland of St. Helen,
he troops in the field, agreed to
as and to be tranfported to Old
ence of his Britannick Majefty,
:o ferve during the prefent war.
varlike ftores and provifions; and
country were to be given up *bonâ*
: of the Roman Religion was al-
Canada. Brigadier General Gage
ohnfon commanded under Gene-
; remarkable, that General Mur-
ips from Quebec, landed below
7th of September; and the next
iland, from the Ifle au Noix,
1 Shore, oppofite General Am-
iting, in this manner the whole
the Englifh, againft Montreal.

Sept.

Sept. 12. The corps under General Beck, was attack'd and defeated by the left wing of the Pruffian army, and purfued by their cavalry almoft as far as Striegau; on this occafion between 7 and 800 Pandours were made prifoners of war.

Sept. 12. The Count de Stainville defeated a body of 4 or 5000 men of the allied army near Munden upon the River Orcke. Colonel Ferfen, and many of the cavalry, were made prifoners, and 8 pieces of cannon taken; the reft of the troops, under the command of Major Bulow (who had fucceeded in his expedition againft Marburg, made fome prifoners, and taken a confiderable booty) fecured their retreat under favour of the night.

Sept. 17. The Pruffian General Neuwied, occupied the heights of Gerfdorf, having driven away the Auftrian fquadrons which poffefs'd them; He afterwards attack'd and repuls'd fome battalions of grenadiers, which march'd againft him, and took 300 men prifoners, together with 16 pieces of cannon.

Sept. 18. General Werner, by a march of eleven days from Glogau, rais'd the fiege of Colberg. The Ruffians retir'd with the greateft precipitation, abandoning tents, cannon, ammunition, baggage, forage, and provifions in very great quantities, to the Pruffians.

Sept. 19. Marfhal Broglio and Prince Xavier of Saxony, attempted to furprize General Waggenheim in his camp at Lawentzhagen; but that able General made good his retreat, notwithftanding his inferiour numbers, with the lofs only of 150 men

...en kill'd, wounded, and prisoners, and 4 pieces ... cannon.

Sept. 23. M. de Luckner beat a detachment of ...e French cavalry near Norten, and took prisoners ...ne Lieutenant Colonel, several subalterns, and ...07 dragoons.

Sept. — Colonel Belling surpriz'd a body of ...000 Swedes in the neighbourhood of Prentzlow, ...nd made 2 officers, 6 subalterns, and 250 private men, prisoners of war.

Sept. — The Temple and Griffin, part of the ...quadron under the orders of Sir James Douglass, ...ut out seven vessels from the Grenades, (amongst ...hich was his Majesty's sloop Virgin, taken, in ...pril last, by the French) after silencing the batteries which defended them; these ships, in their ...assage from the Grenades to Antigua, fell in with ...nd took thirteen other vessels laden with provisions for Martinico.

Sept. 27. Torgau surrender'd to the army of the ...Empire under the command of the Prince de ...Deux Ponts, and the Prussian garrison of 2400 ...men were made prisoners of war.

October 2. The army of the Empire, gain'd a ...onsiderable advantage over the corps of Prussians, commanded by General Hulsen, near Wittenberg.

October 3. General Werner attack'd the Swedish ...orps under General Ehrenschwerdt, at or near ...'asewalch, made 16 officers and 500 private men ...risoners, and took 6 pieces of cannon.

October

October 3. The castle of Cleves capitulated to the troops of the hereditary Prince of Brunswick; and M. de Barral, with about 500 men, was made prisoner of war.

October 4 and 5. The Prussian Garrison evacuated Leipsick, and march'd by Halle, to Magdeburg.

October — The Lyme man of war founder'd in the Baltick, and the carpenter, with about 22 men perish'd.

October 9. The city of Berlin capitulated to General Tottleben, and agreed to pay 200,000 crowns the next day, as a gratuity to the troops, and to give letters of exchange for the sum of 1,500,000 crowns, demanded by the Russians under the title of a contribution. Three incomplete battalions, amounting to 1200 men, were made prisoners of war. Independent of the sums abovemention'd, the damage done to the city, and its neighbourhood, by this irruption of the enemy, was very considerable.

October 13. Wittenberg capitulated to the Count de Guasco under the Orders of the Prince de Deux Ponts. Two Battalions of Plotho, and one of Grollman, were made prisoners of war. Thirty one pieces of cannon, and a quantity of ammunition were found in the place.

October 14. The corps of Fischer, detach'd from the French army under the command of the Marquis de Castries, obliged an advanc'd post of Hanoverians to retire from Rhineberg, with the loss of 180 men.

October 16. The hereditary Prince of Brunſwick [at]tack'd the army of the Marquis de Caſtries, [w]hich was conſiderably ſuperiour in number to his [o]wn, and advantageouſly poſted in a wood near [th]e convent of Campen. The action continued [w]ith great briſkneſs for four hours; when the [P]rince finding it impoſſible to force the wood, gave [or]ders for a retreat about nine o' clock in the morn[in]g: this was happily executed, without a briſk [p]urſuit from the enemy. The Major-Generals Grif[fi]n and Elliot, and Lieutenant Colonel Harvey, [w]ere wounded. Lieutenant Colonel Pitt, and Lord [D]owne, were wounded and taken priſoners; the [la]tter died of his wounds. On the part of the [F]rench, Lieutenant-General Segur, Brigadier-Ge[n]eral Wangen, ſeveral officers, and ſome hundred [p]rivate men, were made priſoners; two pieces of [c]annon and one pair of colours, taken. The diffi[c]ulty of the ground did not permit more than five [F]rench regiments to engage: theſe were the regi[m]ents of Normandie, Auvergne, la Tour du-Pin, [B]riqueville. and Alſace; they took from the Al[li]es one piece of cannon, and fourteen ammunition [w]aggons. Both the Marquis de Caſtries and the [h]ereditary Prince were ſlightly wounded in the en[g]agement. The French own'd the loſs of 841 [k]ill'd and 1795 wounded; the Engliſh acknow[l]edg'd no more than 247 kill'd, 925 wounded, and [1]42 priſoners.

October 18 and 19. The Sirenne Commodore [M]'Cartie of 32 guns and 280 men, ſtruck to the [B]oreas Captain Uvedale, of 28 guns and 170 [m]en, after an engagement of three hours. — The [V]aleur Captain Talbot, of 20 guns and 160 men, [ſ]truck to the Lively, the Honourable Captain

Mait-

Maitland, of 20 guns, and 160 men, after an action of an hour and an half. Both thefe were King's frigates. — The Prince Edward, a merchant frigate, Captain Dubois, of 32 guns and 180 men; and the Fleur de Lis, a King's frigate, Captain Diguarty, of 32 guns and 190 men, were burnt and deftroy'd by the Hampfhire, Captain Norbury, of 50 guns and 350 men. — All the four frigates were failing from Cape Francois, and were loaded with indigo and fugar. His Majefty's three fhips acted under the orders of Rear-Admiral Holmes.

October 25. King George the 2d died fuddenly, between 7 and 8 o' clock in the morning, in the 77th year of his age, and the 34th of his reign; the oldeft Prince that ever fate upon the Englifh Throne, and the oldeft crown'd Head in Europe, excepting Staniflaus King of Poland Duke of Lorrain and Barr.

October 26. The Conqueror of 74 guns, ran on St. Nicholas's Ifland, and was loft.

October — General Hulfen and Prince Eugene of Wirtemberg, made 500 men of the Duke of Wirtemberg's troops prifoners at Cothen, and obliged the Duke himfelf to retire to Leipfic.

October — Wittenberg and Leipfic were recover'd by the Pruffians; and 400 Pandours ferving in the army of the Empire, were made prifoners of war.

November 2. The Pruffians attack'd 1000 Horfe under General Brentano near Lang-Reichenback
be-

between Schilda and Torgau, and made 400 Prisoners.

Nov. 3. The King of Pruffia, having previoufly taken or difpers'd St. Ignon's regiment of dragoons, in a wood near Torgau, gave battle at Slpitz to the Auftrian grand army under the command of Marfhal Daun. The Marfhal prefented a front defended by 200 pieces of cannon, which play'd brifkly upon the Pruffians; the victory was difputed with obftinacy and bloodfhed from about a quarter after two in the afternoon, till near eight in the evening; during which time, the advantage was, for the moft part, with the Auftrians: but between ten and eleven, the Pruffians, under General Ziethen, made an attempt to poffefs themfelves of the little eminences of Siplitz, which entirely commanded the army of the enemy; in this they fucceeded, and fortified the ground in fuch a manner, as to prevent every effort of the Auftrians to diflodge them. Under thefe circumftances the latter were obliged to abandon the field of battle at day-break, and leave Torgau to the Pruffians, who enter'd that fortrefs early in the morning. The King of Pruffia receiv'd a flight contufion on the breaft by a mufket-fhot in the engagement; Marfhal Daun was wounded, and forced to be carried off the field of battle; and to leave the command of the army to General O Donnel.

The

The Austrian account of the loss on both sides in the action near Torgau.

Austrians.

Kill'd ——	Generals	2
	Inferiour Officers and private men	1541
wounded ——	Generals	5
	Officers	5
	Inferiour Officers and private men	3649
prisoners and missing —— }	Generals	4
	Officer	1
	Inferiour Officers and private men	5619

37 —— pieces of cannon taken by the Prussians.

Prussians.

(exclusive of the kill'd and wounded.)

Prisoners. ——	Generals	2
	Colonels	2
	Officers	95
	private men near	4000

taken { 39 colours
2 standards
8 pieces of cannon (which were afterwards left behind in the retreat) } by the Austrians.

The Prussian account of the loss on both sides in the same action.

Prussians.

Kill'd		2500
wounded		4900
prisoners	Generals	2
	many Officers	
	private men	1500

Austrians.

(exclusive of the kill'd and wounded.)

Prisoners	Generals	4
	Officers	212
	private men; upwards of	8000

taken by the Prussians — 50 pieces of cannon.

From these different accounts it may be concluded with too much probability, that the total loss on both sides, in this very destructive battle did not fall short of thirty thousand men.

Nov. 19. The Prussians took possession of Landhut, which the Austrians had previously abanlon'd.

Nov. — The Epreuve, a French frigate of 200 ons, 14 guns, and 136 men, was taken by the Niger.

Nov. 29. Major General Breidenbach, at the ead of two Hanoverian regiments, the Brunswick

wick guards, and a detachment of cavalry, attack'd the poſt of Heidemunden upon the Werra, and carried the town; but not being able to make himſelf maſter of an intrenchment which cover'd the paſſage of the river, he retired at midnight after the loſs of 161 men, officers included.

Nov. 29. M. de Luckner, having in vain cannonaded and attack'd the caſtle of Arnſtein, defended by M. de Vertuil, was obliged to retire with his corps towards Friedland.

Dec. 16. A large magazine of hay and ſtraw at Prague was accidentally ſet on fire, and intirely conſum'd. This magazine was intended to have ſupplied the Auſtrian army, for the greateſt part of the winter.

Dec. 21. The cargo of the Prince Edward merchant-ſhip, from Leghorn, taken by the French, was ſold at Toulon; the utmoſt value of ſhip and cargo together could not amount to more than 5000 pounds ſterling, though the French accounts pompouſly rais'd it to 568,750 pounds.

Dec. 23. Count Broglio with 10,000 men, attempted to ſurround a body of between three and four thouſand of the Allies under M. de Luckner, in the town of Heilingeſtadt; but the road leading to Witzenhauſen not being inveſted, the Hanoverian General made his retreat, by that village, to Scharffenſtein; in this affair, the French loſt 300 men; the Allies had only ſome few men wounded, and not a ſingle horſe kill'd or taken. The French troops of the right, miſſed their way, and did not come in time to their point of attack,
which

which occasion'd the miscarriage of this well-concerted Design.

Supplies granted by Parliament for the service of the year 1760.

Fifteen millions, five hundred three thousand, five hundred sixty four pounds, fifteen shillings, and nine pence half-penny.

A list of many considerable privateers, &c. and arm'd merchantmen, taken by his Majesty's ships of war, from the 31st of December 1759 to the 31st of December 1760.

January.	guns.	men.	captors.
The Fame privateer			carried into Leghorn by the Ambuscade Captain Basset.
A privateer of	10		carried into Barbadoes by the Crescent and Barbadoes frigates.
A privateer of	14		
February.			
A shallop privateer			taken by a man of war.
A privateer sloop			by the Hampshire Capt. Norbury.
March.			
A privateer of St. Maloe	6		by the Jason.
Fox privateer of Dunkirk	12		by the Roast Beef arm'd ship.
Ocean of St. Maloe	1 four pounder 8 swivels	22	by the Cumberland cutter and the custom house boat of Plymouth.
Le Chevalier Barro of Bayonne	20	146	by the Repulse.

	guns.	men.	captors.
A privateer of	36	400	by some of the men of war bound to Quebec.
A shallop privateer of	6		drove on shore by two cutters near Callais, where she bulged.
A privateer of	12		sent into Antigua by the Echo.
A privateer of	14	120	sunk by the Levant, and the crew perish'd.
April.			
Le Chevalier de Grosselle	2 carriage 4 swivels	24	taken by the Launceston.
The Hazard of Brieux.	8 swivels	26	by the Peggy sloop.
The Villeginie of St. Maloe	12 carriage 6 swivels	60	by the Antelope. This privateer had done considerable mischief to the British trade.
Count de Nancy of St. Maloe	4 carriage	39	by the Vengeance.
A privateer			overset in a fresh gale, and went to the bottom, after having been chas'd by the Minerva.

	guns.	men.	captors.
Le Soliel of Bourdeaux of 360 tons	12	70 fold. 45 fail.	taken by the Adventure, Lieutenant Norwood.
The Margaret of Rochelle	8	58	by the Orford.
A frigate of	26		reported to have been taken by the Juno off Bilboa.
The Providence of St. Maloe	4	32	by the Lynn.
A schooner privateer	4 carriage 6 swivels	38	by the Rochester.
Le Chauve Souris of Cherburg		17	by the Kingston.
Mercury of Rochelle	10 carriage 10 swivels	90	by the Carcass sloop.
Cutter privateer	4 carriage	48	by the Dispatch sloop and Grace cutter.
Pallas of Bayonne	14	100	by the Fame and Achilles.
Brocanteur from St. Domingo, worth 10,000 pounds.	18 (fourteen thrown overboard)	36	by the Niger.

	guns.	men.	captors.
A ship of 400 tons			driven on shore by the Pallas on the black rock off the entrance of the Bay Douverne; the ship, cargo, and crew, were lost.
May.			
Temeraire, a new sloop of St. Maloe	4 carriage 6 swivels	38	taken by the Lynn.
A privateer	8 carriage		by the Venus.
A privateer			by the Speedwell.
A privateer	2		by the Tamer.
A privateer			by the Mars.
Victory of St. Maloe	24		by the Rainbow and Thetis.
Jason of St. Maloe	8	52	by the Niger.
A privateer	1	15	by the Cruizer cutter.
Sampson of Bayonne	24		by the Juno.
A privateer			by the Dover cutter.
A privateer			chaced by the Melampe off Ushant, overset, and went to the bottom.

	guns.	men.	captors.
St. John privateer.	14	47	brought into Port Royal by the Cerberus and Lively.
Contabre privateer	8 carriage 10 swivels	52	taken by the Antigua, Captain Innes.
June.			
A privateer			taken by the Tartar.
Filou of Dunkirk.	6 carriage 6 swivels	34	by the Esther cutter, Lieutenant Pinfold.
A privateer, the Hardi of St. Maloe	2 carriage 2 swivels	26	by the Basilisk.
Free Mason of Dunkirk	4 swivels	15	by the Hornet Captain Johnstone.
A privateer	14 carriage		by the Active.
A privateer schooner	4 six pounders 12 swivels		by the Prince of Orange in Tadusac river.
A privateer	8 carriage	50	by the Antigua sloop.
A pettiaugre	8 swivels	9	by ditto.
A privateer	10 carriage		by the Crescent.
A privateer	6		by the Emerald.
A privateer			by the Esther cutter.

Manderony privateer			by the Hind Captain Bond.
Menette of Bourdeaux	4 carriage, 8 swivels		by the Æolus; she founder'd soon after she was taken.
A privateer	14 carriage		cut out out of Roseau and Grand Ance in Dominica, by the Montagu and Belliqueux.
A privateer			
A privateer			
A sloop			
A privateer	1 carriage, 2 swivels		taken by the Leveret tender Lieutenant Bell.

July.

Revenge privateer	8 carriage	44	by the Arethusa frigate
A privateer of Dunkirk	10	52	by the Deal Castle.
Heureux privateer of Dunkirk	2 carriage, 2 swivels	27	by the Fowey.
L'Heureux Retour of Marseilles	8 carriage	56	by the Valeur.
A privateer			by the Echo frigate
Three privateers	14		by the Echo and Levant frigates.

August.	guns.	men.	captors.
La Catherina privateer	7 swivels	23	by the Basilisk sloop.
A privateer with 12 ransomers			by the Ranger sloop.
St. Antoine of Granville	2 carriage 4 swivels	25	by the Launceston.
Duc d' Ayen	7 carriage	65	by the Hazard sloop.
A vessel commanded by M. la Broquerie	12 ten pounders 4 swivels	100	by Colonel Williamson with five row gallies, off La Galette.
La Pic privateer	4 carriage 6 swivels	25	by the Antigua, Captain Bagster.
L'Esperance schooner	6 carriage 8 swivels	37	by the Antigua, Captain Bagster.
September.			
Count de Guiche privat.	8 carriage	54	by the Flamborough Cap. Kennedy.
Elizabeth of St. Maloe	6 carriage 6 swivels	41	by the Tweed.
St. Antony privateer	8 carriage		by the Crescent.
Intrigue privateer	10		by the Belliqueux.

	guns.	men.	captors.
La Fleche privateer	3 carriage 6 swivels	22	by the Antigua, Captain Nott.
Le Modeste privateer	8 carriage		by the Antigua Captain Nott.
Phenix of Morlaix	12 carriage 12 swivels	120	by the Actæon Captain Ourry.
Countefs d'Ayen privateer	8 carriage 8 swivels	62	by the Alarm cutter.
A privateer sloop			by the Renown, off Cape Nicholoa.
Bien Aimé of Dunkirk	12 nine pounders 14 swivels	112	by the Thames, Captain Colby.
Tavignon privat. pierc'd for 26 guns, mounting	18 carriage		carried into St. John's Newfoundland, by two frigates.

October.

A privateer.   taken by the Tweed, Captain Paston.

November.	guns.	men.	captors.
Angelique of Bayonne	6	60	taken by the Hero.
A privateer	16	200	driven on shore between Cape Barfleur and la Hogue, and effectually destroy'd, by the Actæon.
Determine of Nantz.	1 carriage 3 swivels	20	taken by the Torbay.
D'Igoville of P. L'Orient	14 carriage 6 carriage	123	by the Torbay.
A privateer	6 swivels 12 musquetoons 30 small arms	17	by the Burton arm'd sloop, in the river St. Laurence.
A privateer	10 carriage		by the Levant.
Two privateers			by the Hero.
A schooner	6 carriage		by Capt. Dobson in a sloop mann'd with forty soldiers from Quebec.
A large sloop from St. Eustatia to Martinico.	12	60	by the Emerald Captain Middleton.

	guns.	men.	captors.
A privateer	10		
A privateer	8		all three by the Emerald.
A privateer	8		
A privateer	8		both by the Echo.
A pettie augre	10 swivels		

December.

	guns.	men.	captors.
Fortune privateer of Bayonne	6 carriage	50	taken by the Hero.
A cutter privateer	10	52	by Admiral Rodney's squadron.
Grivois of St. Maloe	10 carriage, 10 swivels	80	by the Actæon
A privateer of Dunkirk	10 carriage	54	by the Anson cutter.
Favourite of St. Maloe	6 carriage	60	by the Diligence sloop Captain Osborne.
A brig privateer			sunk by the Actæon.
Two French Turkey ships			carried into Leghorn by an English privateer.

	guns.	men.	captors.
Phœnix privateer	18	125	taken by the Quebec, Captain Levison Gower.
Vainquer	10 carriage 16 swivels	90	⎫ taken by the boats of the Trent and Boreas in Cumberland Harbour, commanded by Lieutenants Millar and Stewart.
Mackau	6 swivels	15	⎭
Guespe	8 carriage	86	destroy'd by the French, to prevent her from falling into the hands of the officers before-mention'd.

N.B. *The reader may perhaps have observ'd, that some few events are mention'd in this work, which, in strictness of speech, have no immediate connection with the subject of it; but as they seem'd to regard the trade and commerce of these Kingdoms, it is hoped the insertion of them will be easily excused.*

CHRONOLOGICAL ANNALS

OF THE

WAR.

PART THE SECOND.

INTRODUCTION.

THE extraordinary and unexpected Turn of political Affairs since the Close of the Year 1760, makes it necessary to prefix a short Preface to this second Part. A Congress having been appointed, with the Consent of all the Powers concern'd, to be held at *Augsburg*, for terminating the War in *Germany*, and for re-establishing a General Peace; *Great Britain* and *France* agreed to discuss their particular Interests in a distinct and separate Negotiation. The Duke *de Choiseul*'s Letter to Mr. *Pitt*, and the *French* King's Memorial, both of the 26th of *March* 1761, carried all the Appearance of Candor and Sincerity. A Counter-Letter and Memorial were return'd, on the Part of *Great Britain*, upon the 8th of *April*. In the latter End of *May*, M. *Bussy* arriv'd at *London*, and Mr. *Stanley* at *Marly*, with plenipotentiary Powers from their respective Courts. In the Course of the Negotiation, the Difficulties seem'd to be reduced to three Points. First, A Recompence for the Captures made upon the *French* Merchants before the Declaration of War; 2dly, The Restitution of *Wesel* and *Gueldres*, with the Territories

ritories dependant on them, to the King of *Pruſſia*; and 3dly, The withdrawing all Aſſiſtance in Men or Subſidies, mutually and *bonâ Fide*, from their Allies in *Germany*. The firſt was ſtrongly inſiſted upon by *France*, and as peremptorily refuſed by *England*; the ſecond was demanded by *England*, and rejected by *France*; for the third, it was no eaſy Matter to find a Temperament, which would equally ſatisfy both Parties. By the other Articles, it was propos'd, on one Side or the other, — That *England* ſhould retain all *Canada* according to its moſt extenſive Limits, including the Courſe of the *Ohio*. — That Lines ſhould be traced out, marking the Nations to be accounted neutral and independent, between *Canada*, *Carolina*, and *Louiſiana*. — That the *French* ſhould exerciſe the Right of fiſhing and of drying Fiſh on the Coaſt and Banks of *Newfoundland*, agreably to the 13th Article of the Treaty of *Utrecht*; and that the Iſles of *St. Pierre* and *Michelon*, without any Fortification or military Eſtabliſhment, ſhould be ceded to her for the Uſes of her Fiſhery. — That the Works added to the Port of *Dunkirk*, ſince the Commencement of the War, ſhould be effectually demoliſh'd. — That there ſhould be an equal Partition of *Tabago*, *St. Lucie*, *Dominica*, and *St. Vincent*, commonly called the *Neutral Iſlands*. — That *Senegal* and *Goree* ſhould be guarantied to *Great Britain*; in Return for which the Settlements of *Anama-*

INTRODUCTION.

...oo and *Akra* on the Coast of *Africa* should ...e guarantied to *France*. — That the *French* ...nd *English East-India* Company should en- ...er upon an immediate Treaty concerning ...heir mutual Differences, to be adjusted and ...oncluded at the same time with the Treaty ...etween the two Nations. — That *Minorca* should be restored to *Great Britain*, with all the Artillery &c. found in Fort *St. Philip* at the time of its Surrender. — That *Bellisle*, *Guadalupe*, and *Marigalante*, should be given up in like Manner to *France*. — That the Landgraviate of *Hesse*, County of *Hanau*, and Town of *Gottingen*, should be evacuated and restored to their respective Sovereigns.—That the *French* King should declare he never had any Intention of keeping Possession of *Nieuport* and *Ostend* after the Conclusion of a General Peace. — But the determin'd Firmness maintain'd on each Side, in Reference to the three difficult Articles already specified, rendered all the rest ineffectual. The Negotiation was finally broke off towards the Close of *September* 1761, and the two Ministers return'd to their respective Courts. Some time afterwards the *French* Ministry publish'd their historical Memorial of this Negotiation, which may be consider'd as an Appeal to their own People, and to *Europe*, against the Court of *London*. A similar Step was taken by *France* in 1709. By the 37th Article of the famous Preliminaries, debated at the *Hague* in that Year, *Lewis* the XIV was required to assist the Allies in compelling the *Spaniards* to abandon King *Philip*, and to come under the Obedience of King *Charles*; M. *de Torcy* agreed to this Article, but the King refused to ratify it; He said "If he must make War, "he had rather make it upon his Enemies, "than upon his Children;" and he then address'd, for the first Time, a circular Letter to his Subjects, calculated to excite their Resentment, their Honour, and even their Compassion itself; This Letter wrought powerfully upon the *French* Nation. The Politicians of those Days thought, that M. *de Torcy's* humiliating Journey to the *Hague* was made only with a Design to expose the Haughtiness of the Allies in rejecting the Concessions of *France*, and to animate his languishing Countrymen with new Zeal in the Prosecution of the War. *Voltaire*, in his Age of *Lewis* the XIV, is of the contrary Opinion; and asserts that Peace was the single Object of M. *de Torcy's* Views. The same Variety of Sentiment seems to have taken Place in Regard to the late Negotiation: Some have concluded that all the Concessions on the Part of *France*, were Nothing but a pretended Display of Moderation to conciliate the Affections of *Europe*, whilst a Demand was strenuously insisted upon, which no victorious People could submit to with Honour; such was the tenth Article of the Ultimatum of *France* relative to the Captures made before the Declaration of War, to which if the

Court

Court of *London* had consented, it had avow-
ed national Perfidy and Violence before all
Europe. Others notwithstanding were per-
suaded, that the *French* Offers were perfectly sincere, and dictated by public Distress.
Be this as it will; the Facts which I now
proceed to mention lead me to think, that
a Peace at that particular Period would have
been unfortunate, if not destructive, to *Great
Britain*; and would have restor'd to *France*
at least 20,000 Sailors, to have been employed in a new War, in which She might have
almost instantly engaged herself as the Ally of
Spain. In the fifth Article of the *French*
Memorial, dated the 15th of *July* 1761,
there are these Words " *England* shall enter
' into Possession, as Sovereign over the Island
' of *Tabago*, in the same Manner as *France*
' over that of *St. Lucie*, saving at all Times
' the Right of a third Person, with whom
' the two Crowns will explain themselves, if
' such a Right exists." This was the prepa-
ratory Step to an Introduction of the *Spanish*
Demands into the Negotiation, which were
fully open'd in the private Memorial of *France*
of the same Date, and were reduced to these
three Articles; First, The Restitution of some
Captures made upon the *Spanish* Flag. 2dly,
The Privilege of fishing on the Banks of
Newfoundland. 3dly, The Demolition of the
English Settlements in the Bay of *Honduras*.
M. *Bussy* represented to Mr. *Pitt*, that it
would be very dangerous to determine the

Fate of the neutral Iſlands, without attending to the Claims of *Spain*, with which the Catholic King had recently acquainted the Court of *Verſailles*, but which might be eaſily relinquiſhed, if the other three Articles were adjuſted to the Satisfaction of that Monarch. This blending of the Concerns of *Spain* with the ſeparate Treaty between *Great Britain* and *France*, though ſurprizing at that time to the Court of *London*, was afterwards clear'd up; when it appear'd, that the Courts cf *Verſailles* and *Madrid* had, even then, been negotiating a Family Compact, in full Contradiction to the Spirit of the Treaty of *Utrecht*, and in expreſs Violation of the Rights of Commerce which *Great Britain* ought to enjoy. This famous Compact was ſigned at *Verſailles* on the 15th of *Auguſt*, and ratified on the 8th of *September*, twelve Days before Mr. *Stanley* broke off the Negotiation with the Duke *de Choiſeul*. By It, the whole Houſe of *Bourbon* was to act as one Man; a perpetual League, offenſive and defenſive was eſtabliſh'd againſt all the World; a reciprocal Naturalization was to take Place between the Kingdoms of *France*, *Spain*, and the two *Sicilies*; all the commercial Nations were to be informed, that they were no longer to expect the ſame Privileges in Trade which they formerly poſſeſs'd, but which were now conferred excluſively upon the Subjects of the three contracting Powers; No Prince, who did not deſcend in the Male Line from the

Auguſt

August House of *Bourbon*, was ever to be admitted into this Family Compact; the mutual Guaranty of the Dominions of *France* and *Spain* was agreed to; with a Declaration, that it extended only to those Dominions, of which *France* should be in actual Possession at the General Peace. It is sufficiently evident from the whole Tenor of this Compact, that any Treaty between *Great Britain* and *France*, made at that Juncture, must have been delusive, if not momentary; unless the Dignity and Interests of the former had been tamely sacrificed to the Demands of *Spain*. On the 18th of *September*, Lord *Temple* and Mr. *Pitt*, deliver'd their Advice in Writing to his Majesty relative to the Conduct of *Spain* and the Measures to be pursued in Consequence of it; that Advice, being not conformable to the Sentiments of the rest of his Majesty's Servants, was rejected; upon which, they resign'd their respective Employments. Previously to this Resignation, Mr. *Pitt*, in his Letter of the 28th of *July*, had directed Lord *Bristol*, in the King's Name, to demand of Mr. *Wall* a full and explicite Explanation of the Tendency of the *Spanish* Armaments, and of the Views of that Court in Relation to *Great Britain*. Mr. *Wall* acquainted Lord *Bristol*, that *France* had made a voluntary Offer of assisting *Spain* with all her Force, in Case of a future Rupture between the Courts of *London* and *Madrid*; and that the King his Master had received so

friendly

friendly an Offer with Cordiality; but that *Spain* was not looking out for an Occasion of quarrelling with *Great Britain* in the Time of her greatest Glory and Power; on the contrary, She was desirous of cementing a mutual Friendship. Lord *Bristol* wrote, in his Letter of the 28th of *September*, that he was press'd by Mr. *Wall*, to give the strongest Assurances at home, of their Readiness to adjust their Differences with Us, if We would only abandon our recent Settlements on the Coast of *Honduras*, to save the *Spanish* Puntondor, or Point of Honour. Lord *Egremont*, in two Letters of the 28th of *October* gave Directions, by the King's Order, to Lord *Bristol*, to demand a Communication of the Treaty of *Versailles*, or, at least, of those Articles of it, which had any immeditate or distant Reference to the Interests of *Great Britain*; and to couch that Demand in the most polite and friendly Terms, not so much urging his Arguments, as insinuating them. Before the Receipt of these, Lord *Bristol* inform'd Lord *Egremont*, in his Letter of the 2d of *November*, of a great Alteration in Mr. *Wall*'s Style and Sentiments; who said, We were intoxicated with our Successes, and had therefore refused the reasonable Concessions offered Us by *France*; that We intended in the first Place to ruin the *French*, and then to crush the *Spanish* Power; that he would be the first to advise his Master not to let his Subjects fall without Arms in their Hands;

that

that it was high time for *Spain* to open her Eyes, and not to suffer a Neighbour, an Ally, a Parent, and a Friend, to receive rigid Laws from an insulting Conqueror; that the Court of *Versailles* had communicated to that of *Madrid*, punctually and minutely, every Step taken at *Paris* and *London* during the Negotiation for Peace; and that his Catholic Majesty had judg'd it expedient to renew his Family Compacts with the most Christian King. This animated Discourse was occasioned by the Advice which *Spain* had receiv'd of Mr. *Pitt*'s Resignation, and of the Motives which produced it. The whole Court was immediately in a Ferment, having always consider'd themselves as the aggriev'd Party, and never imagining that the *English* would be the first to propose or begin the War. In Answer to this Letter, Lord *Bristol* was order'd to insist, in the King's Name, on an immediate, clear, precise, and categorical Answer from the *Spanish* Court to this Question, "What were their Intentions relative to *Great Britain*?" At the same time his Lordship was directed, to avoid all Harshness in the Manner, while he maintain'd a becoming Firmness in the Matter of the Demand; and to act, *fortiter in Re, suaviter in Modo*. If he did not receive proper Satisfaction, he was then to come away from *Madrid* without taking Leave. In Obedience to these Orders, Lord *Bristol* waited upon Mr. *Wall*, with whom he had a cool and candid Conference;

that

that Minister himself acknowledged the Caution We had used, in declining the Attack of those *French* Settlements which had any Connection with the Territory of *Spain*, and agreed with Lord *Bristol* concerning the public Nature of what had pass'd in the *British* Councils on the Change of the Ministry; but yet he declar'd that the Copy, which he had already given, of his own Dispatch to the Count *de Fuentes*, was the only Answer he was at Liberty to make to his Lordship's Enquiries. In this Copy, Mr. *Wall* used these Words " You know how easy it would be for " the King to give a positive Answer, but his " own Dignity hinders him from it; consider- " ing this Demand as a necessary Condition " for entering upon a Negotiation with *Spain*, " on Differences which, they own, have sub- " sisted a long time." Upon the whole, Mr. *Wall* strongly express'd his Wishes that some Temperament might be found out for adjusting their mutual Disputes; and he promis'd to lay before the King, faithfully and minutely, the Disposition and Sentiments of his *Britannic* Majesty. Two Days after Mr. *Wall* acquainted Lord *Bristol* in a second Conference, that the King of *Spain* was sensible of all the Assurances of Friendship and Marks of Attention, which had been convey'd through his Means; but that his Catholic Majesty did not think it expedient to give any other Answer with Regard to the Treaty, than that which had been communicated in the Dispatch

patch of the Count *de Fuentes*: Lord *Bristol* then found himself obliged, to apply, in Form, for that full categorical Answer, which the Court of *London* had order'd him to demand; and he press'd Mr. *Wall*, with Address and Energy, to go in Person to his Catholic Majesty, and to enlarge upon all those Arguments in Favour of his Demand, which he had employed with him in their several Conferences. On the tenth of *December*, Mr. *Wall* inform'd Lord *Bristol* by Letter, that since he had demanded in Writing a positive and categorical Answer to this Question " If *Spain* " thought of joining herself with *France* a- " gainst *England*?" and had declar'd at the same time that he should look upon the Refusal as a Declaration of War, and, in Consequence, leave the Court of *Madrid*; he was therefore to acquaint him, that the Spirit of Haughtiness and of Discord which had dictated that inconsiderate Step, and which, for the Misfortune of Mankind, still reign'd so much in the *British* Government, was what made, in the same Instant, the Declaration of War, and attack'd the King's Dignity; that he might retire when, and how, it was convenient to him, which was the only Answer his Majesty had order'd him to give. A Copy of this Letter was receiv'd in *London* on the 24th of *December*; the next Day, the Count *de Fuentes* deliver'd his Memorial to Lord *Egremont*; in which, Mr. *Wall*'s Words were recited, the Conduct of
the

the Minister *Pitt* was arraign'd, who (it was falsly and indecently said) still appear'd to hold the Reins of Government by another Hand, and a Declaration was made in the Name, and by the express Order of the King of *Spain*, that the Treaty in Question contain'd Nothing in it which had the least Relation to the present War. Thus the ever-memorable Puntondor of the *Spanish* Court, precipitated the two Nations into the Calamities of a War, the Events of which will be found in the following Collection. Lord *Egremont* answer'd the Count *de Fuentes* on the 31st of *December*, with the Spirit that became a Minister of a beloved Monarch, whose Honour had been insulted by the Terms of that Memorial, and with the Moderation due to the Character of great Sovereigns. In Regard to the public Declaration of his Catholic Majesty, made when it could no longer be of Use to either People, his Lordship justly observ'd, that the Terms in which the Declaration was conceived, spared the *British* Nation the Regret of not having receiv'd it sooner; for the Demand was, " If the Court " of *Spain* intended to join the *French* our " Enemies — to make War on *Great Britain* " — or to depart from their Neutrality?" But the Answer related only to one Treaty of the 15th of *August*, without explaining, in any Manner, the Intention of *Spain* towards *Great Britain*, or the further Engagements She might have contracted in such a Crisis.

On

INTRODUCTION. 173

On the 2d of *January* 1762, the King in Council signed a Declaration of War against *Spain*.

It may not be improper to remark in this Place, that the War between the Empress Queen and the King of *Prussia* commenc'd, on the former's evading an Explanation of the Tendency of her military Preparations, and refusing to give an Assurance to the latter, that he should not be attack'd by her, during the then present (1756) or in the Course of the succeeding Year. The Court of *Berlin* made three Applications to that of *Vienna*, for obtaining this Explanation and Assurance; To the first, it was answer'd, that considering the violent general Crisis in which *Europe* was at that time, the Empress Queen's Duty, and the Dignity of her Crown, requir'd her to take sufficient Measures for her own Security, as well as for the Safety of her Friends and Allies; On the second, the Court of *Vienna* eluded the Demand, denying only the Existence of a supposed Concert against the King of *Prussia*; But when the third Application was made, the Empress Queen flatly refused any further Explanation.

Among the several Evils which the present War has brought upon Mankind, *this* probably may be reckon'd of the most lasting Consequence, that the Law of Nations has been publickly invaded with a violent and
wanton

wanton Cruelty: Many learned Men have compos'd large Treatises upon this Law, in Hopes of circumscribing the interested Ambition of Princes within those Limits of general Equity, which even they themselves would be asham'd to pass, in a Matter of particular Right. But cool Precepts of moral Honesty, seldom find Admission into the Cabinets of Princes. An absurd and an infamous Distinction seems long to have taken Place, between the Morality of the Governors and the Governed: The very same Conduct which would fix an indelible Stain of Infamy upon the latter, too often reflects a Lustre upon the former, that dazzles a vulgar Eye. To this State-Casuistry we are greatly indebted for all political Injustice; of which there never was a more flagrant and outrageous Instance, than in the Behaviour of the King of *Spain* to his *Portugueze* Majesty. All the Arguments advanc'd in the *Spanish* Memorials to palliate the Invasion of *Portugal* are a daring Insult upon Common-Sense, and betray a Weakness of Judgment, almost equal to the Iniquity of the Measure which they were intended to support. Instead of confuting what so effectually confutes itself, I shall now only lay before the Reader a compendious Account of the Claims which his Catholic Majesty may perhaps make upon his Brother in Law, and of the principal Events which happened in the celebrated War between the two Nations, on the Duke of *Bra-*
gança's

INTRODUCTION.

gança's afcending the Throne of *Portugal* under the Name of Don *John* the fourth. Don *Henry*, Cardinal-Archbifhop of *Evora*, came to the Crown upon the Death of the unfortunate Don *Sebaſtian*, and reign'd a Year and an half: He was the laſt of the Royal Blood of *Portugal* in the male Line. The Title to the Succeſſion lay between the Iſſue of MARY and CATHERINE, Daughters of Prince EDWARD the Son of King EMANUEL, and between *Philip* the 2d of *Spain*, Son of the Princeſs ISABELLA the Daughter of that King. MARY was married to the Duke of *Parma*, from whom the preſent King of *Spain* is maternally deſcended; but the General Aſſembly of the States of *Portugal* paſs'd a famous Law at *Lamego*, in 1139, by which it was enacted, that the eldeſt Daughter of the King, in Caſe of Failure of Iſſue Male, ſhould have the Right of Succeſſion in her, if ſhe married a *Portugueze* Nobleman; but if ſhe married a Prince or Nobleman of any foreign Nation, ſhe ſhould then forfeit all that Right. The Reaſon of this Limitation is thus explain'd: "BECAUSE our People ſhall not be "obliged to obey a King who is not a *Por-* "*tugueze* by Birth; ſince they were our own "Subjects and Countrymen who gave Us a "King, without any foreign Aſſiſtance, by "their own Valour, and at the Expence of "their Blood." This is a fundamental Law of *Portugal*, and *Philip* the 2d admitted the Validity of it, when he himſelf inſiſted that
a *Spani-*

a *Spaniard* was no Foreigner. CATHERINE, the younger Sister of *Mary*, became the Wife of the Duke of *Bragança*, from whom the present King of *Portugal* is lineally descended. Such was the State of the several Claims. Whoever had the fairest Pretensions, *Philip* had indisputably the greatest Power. His Wealth; His establish'd Character for political Abilities; and, above all, his Situation; enabled him to take Possession of *Portugal* in the Close of 1580; and that Kingdom remain'd in his Family till 1640, when the Tyranny of the *Spaniards*, and the Spirit of the *Portugueze*, rais'd the Duke of *Bragança* to the Throne. The Battle of *Montijo* in 1644; that of *St. Miguel* in 1658; the vigorous Attack made upon the *Spanish* Lines before *Elvas* by the Marquis of *Marialva* in 1659; all these, were Proofs of the Resolution and Fortune, with which the *Portugueze* Troops acted, in the Assertion of their recover'd Freedom. The *Spaniards*, exhausted by the Success of *France*, having ended their War with that Nation by the Peace of the *Pirennes*, were left at Liberty to bring their whole Force against *Portugal*. The Actions of *Canal* and of *Amexial* in 1663, were still favourable to the *Portugueze*; but General *Schomberg* (afterwards Count of *Mertola* in *Portugal*, Marshal of *France*, Duke *Schomberg* in *England*, and Duke of *Leinster* in *Ireland*) was the Person who put a Period to the flattering Expectations of *Spain*.

He

INTRODUCTION. 177

he came, with 4000 *French* Troops, into *Portugal*; which were hir'd in the Name of that King, and paid, in Reality, by the King of *France*. With this choice Body of experienc'd Soldiers, he join'd, in 1665, the *Portugueze* Forces under the Marquis of *Marialva*, gain'd a complete Victory, at *Montes Claros*, over the *Spanish* Army commanded by the Marquis of *Carracena*, and fix'd the Throne in the House of *Bragança*. The Firmness, Constancy, and Zeal of the *Portugueze*, were conspicuous in the whole Course of this War, which lasted 28 Years. The Marquis of *Marialva*, their fortunate General, who was one of the Nobles that proclaim'd King *John*, desir'd his Heart might be placed near the Body of that Monarch, where it was accordingly deposited with this Inscription.

> *Hic, ubi* Lusiadum *jacet Instaurator in Urnâ,*
> **Pignus habet positum Cor,** Marialva, *suum;*
> *Usque suum sequitur Regem* Marialva *sepultus,*
> *Ut Vitam credas,* NON *periisse* FIDEM.

It is easy to imagine how very difficult a Work it must prove, notwithstanding almost any Advantages, to force the Necks of such a People into a Yoke which they have once shook off; and to bring those again into Subjection, who are equally animated by a Detestation

M

testation of their Enemy, and a Remembrance of their former Glory.

Another great Event, which happen'd in the Beginning of the Year 1762, occasion'd a remarkable Alteration in the Affairs of *Europe*, and was attended with serious Consequences. This was the Death of the Empress of *Russia*. By a Treaty concluded at *St. Petersburg*, on the 30th of *September* 1755, She had engaged to maintain 40,000 Foot and 15,000 Horse for the Defence of *Hanover*, during the Space of four Years, and to take upon herself alone the whole Charge of their Subsistence. In Consideration of this expected Succour, it was stipulated, that she should receive 100,000£. *per Annum* in Advance whilst her Troops remain'd upon her own Territory; and 500,000£. *per Annum* as soon as they should be drawn out into actual Service. At this Time We were afraid of the King of *Prussia*: In the Fluctuation of political Councils we shifted our Plan, and enter'd into a close Alliance with that Monarch. Thus the Treaty of *St. Petersburg* became a blank Paper. But the Empress of *Russia*, fixed in her Resolution, invaded the *Prussian* Dominions as the Ally of the Empress Queen of *Hungary*, which she was not able to invade as the Ally of *Great Britain*. The Death of this powerful and fortunate Princess deliver'd the King of *Prussia*, who was reduced almost to the last Distress, from a formidable

and

nd determin'd Enemy. *Peter* the third, her Succeſſor, adopted, not only a different, but an oppoſite, Syſtem. Soon after his Acceſſion, he agreed to a mutual Exchange of Priſoners without Ranſom, and to a general Suſpenſion of Arms; He offer'd to ſacrifice his own Conqueſts to the Re-eſtabliſhment of Peace, and invited all his Allies to follow his Example. By the Accounts which were publiſh'd of his early Proceedings, he ſeem'd, at leaſt, to attend to the domeſtic Happineſs of his Subjects; for he conferr'd upon his Nobility the ſame Independence which that Order enjoys in the other Monarchies of *Europe*; and he lower'd the heavy Duties upon Salt in Favour of the Commonalty. Thus gratifying both the greateſt and meaneſt of his People, he appear'd to thoſe at a Diſtance to be ſtrengthening himſelf in the Hearts of the *Ruſſians*, and to be ambitious of a Popularity equal to that which had been beſtow'd upon any of his Predeceſſors.

This was only the Judgment of Perſons at a Diſtance; thoſe who were nearer the Scene were hardly able to perceive any Thing but a blind Precipitation in Affairs of Moment, blended with a Zeal for Trifles. The diverſified Errors of his Government made it believed, that he was meditating the Deſign of ſetting aſide the Great Duke *Paul*, in Favour of the depoſed Prince *Ivan*. A Deſign of ſuch Nature muſt have ariſen either from extreme Madness, or from some Family-Suspicion; which it would not become me to insinuate. He had hardly made Peace with *Prussia*, before he threatened *Denmark* with a War, on Account of his Pretensions to Part of the Dutchy of *Holstein-Schleswick* in *Germany*. He drove every Thing before him with an extravagant and thoughtless Rapidity. Instead of courting the Affections of his Guards, who had made and unmade the Monarchs of *Russia*; Some of these he slighted, All, perhaps, he affronted, by taking a ridiculous Pleasure in the Uniform of his *Prussian* Regiment, and by placing an idle Confidence in his *Holstein* Troops. He was obliged to communicate with the *Greek* Church, yet he insulted the Rites of it; and distinguish'd the Fast-Days by a large Piece of Beef. He had not the Virtues of the private Man to compensate for the Defects of the Prince. His Propensity to the Northern Vice of Intemperance in Drinking betray'd him into a Discovery of his ill-concerted Measures; whilst an open Disregard of the Empress his Consort confirm'd her Apprehensions of Danger, and taught her to consult her own Security. The memorable Event of this fatal Conduct is known to all the World. Among the Conspirators were, the Empress, and the Velt Marshal *Rosamowsky* Hetman of the *Cossacks*, whom the Emperor had, a little time before, declar'd Colonel of one of the Regiments of Foot Guards. The Empress,

press, in her famous Manifesto publish'd after her Husband's Death, brought a Variety of Accusations against him; she charg'd him with Ingratidude to the Empress *Elizabeth* his Aunt; with Incapacity; an Abuse of Power; a Contempt of Religion and Law; a Scheme to remove the Grand-Duke from the Succession; to settle it in Favour of a *Stranger*; and even to put herself to Death.

Thus We have seen a soverign Prince of *Holstein*, great Nephew of *Charles* the twelfth, Grandson of *Peter* the first, and Heir of those rival Monarchs, once elected Successor to the Crown of *Sweden*, actually ascending the Throne of *Russia*, hurl'd down, after a short Reign of six Months, from all his Greatness, by the Intrigues of a Woman and the Resentments of a standing Force, supported by the Concurrence of an offended Nation; leaving an important Lesson to absolute Princes, of the Instability of human Grandeur, and of the certain Danger of an establish'd military Power under a weak and capricious Government. This very unhappy Monarch died within eight Days after his Deposition. The *Suspicion* of the World, warranted by historical Examples, has concluded that his Death was violent: Indeed it has been reported, that whilst he was Great Duke, a Minister of State declared in Words to this Effect, That Nothing could cure him but a black Dose: Nevertheless, I would willingly hope such a Suspicion was ill grounded. A deposed Prince may be hated; but a murder'd one is pitied, and excused. The Dictates of Policy are attended to, when those of Humanity are forgot: And surely it is not highly improbable, that Vexation and Anguish of Mind, preying upon a disorder'd Constitution, might bring on that Distemper which carried him to his Grave.

It does not appear, that the Interests of the King of *Prussia* have greatly suffer'd by this sudden Revolution. If the *Russians* are no longer his Friends, neither are they any longer his Enemies; and in his critical Situation, the very ceasing to act against him, is to act for him.

That the Reader may entertain a clearer Idea of the former Revolutions, and of those which may hereafter take Place, in this unquiet Empire; I have subjoin'd a genealogical Table of the royal Family of *Russia*, from 1613 to the present Time.

Pedigree of the Imperial *Russian* Family.

Feodore Romanow, furnamed *Philaretes*, Patriarch of *Ruſſia*, married to *Scheromotow*.

I. **Michael Foedorowitz** married *Eudocia Streſchnew*; He was elected Czar in an Aſſembly of the principal Boyars in 1613, and deſcended in the female Line from the ancient Czars.

Maria Ilychna Miloſlawſki, ── II. **Alexius Michaelowitz**, Czar in 1645. ═ *Natalia Kiritowna Nariſkin*, his firſt Wife. his ſecond Wife.

| III. **Foedore Alexiowitz**, Czar in 1676. He died without Iſſue. And appointed his Brother *Peter* to ſucceed him in the Empire. | IV. **Ivan Alexiowitz**, Czar in 1682, and aſſociated with *Peter* in the Government by the Strelitzes. He married *Proſcovia Fuderowna Sultikof*. | *Eudocia Foedorowna .Lapuchin* his firſt Wife. | IV. **Peter Alexiowitz** the Great. Czar in 1682, with his Brother *Feodor*, afterwards ſole Emperor of all the Ruſſias. | V. *Martha Thaiſenbauſen*, a young *Livonian* Priſoner, taken at *Marienburg*, with whom he publickly declared his Marriage in 1710. Afterwards **Catherine** the firſt, Empreſs in 1725. |

Catherine Iwanowna, married the Duke of *Mechlenburg*.

Anne of *Mechlenburg*, married Prince *Antony Ulric* of *Brunſwick Bevern*.

VIII. **Ivan** the ſecond, Emperor in October 1740, and depos'd Dec. 6. 1741. This Prince has two Brothers and two Siſters.

VII. **Anna Iwanowna**, married the Duke of *Courland*. Empreſs in 1730. She died without Iſſue.

Alexis Petrowitz, the Czarowitz, who died in the Life-time of his Father. He married *Charlotta Louiſa* of *Brunſwick Wolfenbuttle*.

VI. **Peter Alexowitz** the ſecond, Emperor in 1727.

Anna Petrowna, elder Siſter to the Empreſs *Elizabeth*, married the Duke of *Holſtein*.

X. **Peter** the Third, Emperor *January* 1762, depoſed by his Wife, July 9. 1762. He married *Catherine Alexiowna* of *Anhalt Zerbſt*.

XI. **Catherine** the Second, Empreſs in July 1762.

Paul Petrowitz, the Great Duke.

IX. **Elizabetha Petrowna** Empreſs in 1741.

CHRONOLOGICAL ANNALS
OF THE WAR.
PART THE SECOND.

1761.

January 2. General Manfberg having been attack'd by the Count de Broglio and M. de Stainville in the town of Duderftadt, retir'd to the neighbouring heights, where he maintain'd himfelf till the next day, when he was affifted by the Generals Kielmanfegge and Luckner, who drove the French from the town, and purfued them as far as Witzenhaufen. The Allies loft 190 men; and the French, by their own Accounts, 600: among whom, three complete companies of grenadiers were made prifoners.

Jan. 8. A detachment of 150 horfe, and 2 companies of grenadiers, under the command of the Vifcount de Belfunce, march'd out of Gottingen, attack'd a poft of the Allies near Gibelhaufen, and made about 100 men prifoners, among whom were four officers.

Jan. 8. The Unicorn of 28 guns, 200 men, Captain Hunt, engaged the Veftal, a French frigate of 30 guns (twelve, nine, and fix, pounders) and 220 men, M. Boifbertelot commander. The action lafted near two hours; in which both the Captains were mortally wounded. Lieutenant Symons, after his Captain was difabled, fought the fhip with courage and conduct, took the Veftal, and

and was rewarded with the command of the Mortar sloop. The Vestal, had many men kill'd and wounded; the Unicorn only five kill'd; six dangerously, and four more slightly, wounded.

Jan. 10. Captain James Smith of the Seahorse of 20 guns and 160 men, fought with the Opale frigate of 36 guns and 350 men, the Marquis d'Ars commander, at the distance of 34 leagues S. W. from the Start; after a warm engagement of an hour and a quarter, in which the ships were board and board three different times) the enemy left the Seahorse with great precipitation, upon the approach of the Unicorn. The loss of the Opale amounted to near 150 kill'd and wounded, among the former of whom was the Captain; that of the Seahorse consisted in eleven kill'd, and thirty eight wounded, many of the latter very dangerously. Captain Smith was afterwards detain'd at home, to be prefer'd to the command of a larger ship the first opportunity.

Jan. 10. The Venus of 36 guns, 240 men, Captain Harrison, engaged the Brune, a French frigate of 32 guns and 316 men; for upwards of two hours; when the Juno of 32 guns coming up, and firing a few guns, the Brune struck; having had 19 kill'd and 39 wounded. The Captain, first Lieutenant, and Master of the Venus, with 15 private seamen, were wounded; but four only were kill'd. Two sailors were wounded on board the Juno.

Jan. 13. The Annemame and Sardoine, King's frigates, arm'd for war by the merchants, carrying each 14 guns and 130 men, and prime sailors, were taken by the Mars and Orford.

Jan. —

Jan. — Ten thousand Russians under Count Tottleben, enter'd lower Pomerania, and took possession of New Stetin and Burwalde.

Jan. 15. The Mogul's Troops, said to have consisted of 80,000 men, headed by Shah Zadda, and supported by a small number of French troops under M. Law, were totally defeated, near Patna, by Major John Carnack at the Head of 500 Europeans, 2500 Seapoys, and 20,000 black Troops, with 12 pieces of cannon. M. Law, and most of the French, were taken prisoners.

Jan. 15. Pondicherry, the capital of the French settlements on the coast of Coromandel, surrender'd at discretion to Colonel Eyre Coote. An amazing quantity of artillery and amunition was found in the fort, and on the works; among which there were no less than 81 serviceable pieces of brass, and 436 of iron ordnance. The sum total of the Prisoners (inclusive of the King's troops, company's troops, and inhabitants) amounted to 2072. All these were reduced to the extremity of famine, having devour'd every Animal from an elephant to a mouse. Camels, dogs, and cats, had been for some time their common food. Even rats sold for 13 pence a piece. Before they surrender'd they ate, by dint of boiling, their leathern jars (call'd Dame Joan's) used for keeping oil and butter. The joy arising from this important conquest, was damp'd by the misfortune which happen'd to our fleet in a storm on the first of this month. The Duke of Aquitaine and the Sunderland of 64 guns each, founder'd; only one man from the former, and eight from the latter, were saved. The Newcastle of 50 guns, and Queenborough of 20, together

ther with the Protector fireship, were drove on shore and lost; but the people, the ordnance, and great part of the stores and provisions were preserv'd. In the preceding Year, the Cumberland of 54 guns was lost off Goa. During the blockade of Pondicherry, the boats of the fleet, under Captain Newson of the South-Sea-Castle, cut out the Balleine a frigate of 36 guns, and the Hermione ship; and the Medway and Newcastle took, from under the guns of the Danish Fort at Trincambar, a ship call'd La Compagnie des Indes; she was pierced for 54 guns, and had escaped out of the harbour of Pondicherry.

Jan. 20. The Griffin Indiaman, homeward bound through the straights of Sapy, struck upon a rock, and was lost; the crew were saved.

Jan. 23. Captain Hood in the Minerva of 32 guns and 220 men, fought with, and took the Warwick of 34 guns (pierced for 60) M. le Veger de Belair commander, having 295 men on board, 74 of whom were soldiers. She was bound to the Isle of France and Bourbon, with provisions, ammunition, and stores, and had 14 men kill'd and 32 wounded in the action. The Minerva had the same number kill'd, and 34 wounded; three of the latter died soon afterwards. The Minerva suffer'd also considerably in all her masts, from the consequences of this sharp engagement.

Jan. 24. The Felicité, a French frigate of 32 guns, Captain Donell, bound to Martinico with a cargo worth 30,000 pounds sterling, was attack'd, drove on shore on the coast of Holland, and entirely destroy'd by the Richmond of 32 guns and 220 men, Captain Elphinston. The French Commander fell

fell in the engagement, and near 100 of his crew were kill'd or wounded. The action lasted two hours, when the enemy fled from their quarters, left their ship, and escaped. The Hermione, consort to the Felicité of the same force and value, was lost coming out of Dunkirk.

Jan. 26. Prince Xavier of Saxony beat up the quarters of the Prussians at Sondershausen, and carried off part of Wunsch's battalion from Ebeleben. General Luckner pursued the French in their retreat beyond Langensaltzen, took one of their magazines at Deiswitz, and made the guard of two officers and thirty men prisoners of war.

Jan. 27. The French, under M. de St. Victor, surpriz'd the post of Stadbergen. Major Delaune, who commanded the garrison compos'd of part of Lane's battalion, was kill'd in his chamber.

Feb. 10. M. Louet surrender'd the fort of Mahe, on the coast of Malabar, to Mr. Hodges commander at Tellicherry, and to Mr. Munro commander of the King's and Company's troops employed in that expedition.

March — The Ajax East-Indiaman, homeward bound, of 750 tons 26 guns, and 100 men, with a valuable cargo on board worth 200,000 pounds sterling, was taken by the Prothée of 64 guns captain Cornei commander.

Mar. 13. The Entreprenant, pierced for 44 guns, carrying only 26 (twelve and six pounders) with 203 men, arm'd for war and merchandize, and loaded with various goods for St. Domingo, was taken by the Vengeance Captain Nightingale
of

of 28 guns (nine and four pounders) and 200 men. The engagement continued, at three different times, for three hours and a quarter. The Entreprenant had 15 men killed, and 24 wounded; the Vengeance, 6 kill'd and 27 wounded, moſt of them dangerouſly.

Mar. 26. The Chevalier d'Origny made a battalion of the Britannic legion priſoners at Wolfſhagen, where he took one piece of cannon and a magazine. The ſame day the French Royal Legion made 300 Engliſh priſoners at Alsfelt, who had been left there for their recovery. — A battalion of Hanoverians, that block'd up the caſtle of Arolſen, was, for the moſt part, taken or deſtroy'd.

Mar. 27. Colonel Colignon abandon'd Nordheim to the French garriſon of Gottingen, and loſt 220 men, with two pieces of cannon, in his retreat.

From *Febr.* 11. to *March* 27 and 28. incluſive. The allied army, on the 11th of February began their march to the attack of the French poſts. The principal events of this attack, in the courſe of ſeven weeks, are thrown together in the following account. Fritzlar capitulated to the hereditary Prince of Brunſwick. Lieutenant General Breidenbach was kill'd in an unſucceſsful attempt upon Marpourg. Guderſberg ſurrender'd to Lord Granby. The Generals Sporcken and Sybourg gave a ſignal defeat to the Saxons near Langenſaltzen, made 5000 priſoners, and took ſome cannon. Lieutenant General D'Oheim defeated M. de Maupeou's advanc'd guard near Sachſenberg, and made that General priſoner. At Roſenthal, Fritzlar, and Melſungen, a large quantity of meal and forage

was

was deftroy'd. A confiderable magazine was found at Ober-Morfchen; 80,000 facks of meal, 50,000 facks of oats, and a million of rations of hay, were taken or ruin'd at Hirfchfeld. At Fulda the French burnt a magazine of hay, and the Allies took a very great magazine of flour and oats. Another large magazine was found at Eyfenach. Count la Lippe open'd the trenches before Caffel in the night of the firft of March. The garrifon of Caffel fome days afterwards made a fuccefsful falley on the befiegers, enter'd the trenches, and nail'd up one piece of cannon, carried off four mortars, and deftroyed the works of the grand battery. The French fet fire to their magazines at Friedberg. Luckner pufh'd his corps as far as Afchaffenbourg, of which he took poffeffion. From this time, every thing went retrograde. A detachment from the garrifon of Gottingen obliged the Hanoverian garrifon of Duderftadt to furrender prifoners of war. Major General Baron Clofen, under the orders of M. Broglio, defeated the hereditary Prince of Brunfwick near Grunberg, made near 2000 prifoners, and took 12 or 13 pieces of cannon. M. de Monchenu beat a party of the Allies juft above Ziegenhayn, took 400 prifoners, befides fome Officers of diftinction. In the night between the 27th and 28th of March, the Allies raifed the fiege of Caffel; after which, the French went into quarters of cantonment in Heffe, and the Allies into their own behind the Dymel. The feveral French magazines, which were taken or deftroy'd before the Allies repafs'd the Dymel, amounted, according to fome valuations, to feven millions of florins.

Mar. 30. The Count de Broglio, having march'd out of Caffel with his garrifon, attack'd the rear guard of the Hannoverians with fuccefs, took four pieces of cannon, several ammunition waggons, and many prisoners.

April 1. The Oriflame of 40 guns mounted, twenty six of which were 12 pounders, and fourteen 18 pounders, with upwards of 370 men, was taken by the Isis commanded by Lieutenant Cunningham, after a running engagement of four hours and an half. The Isis had only 4 men killed, and nine wounded; Captain Wheeler who commanded her, was kill'd in the beginning of the action. The loss of the Oriflame, in killed and wounded, amounted to between 40 and 50; she sailed remarkably well, and had received a thorough repair.

April 2. The Imperialists, to the amount of 6 battalions and 800 horse, under the command of two Generals, were attack'd, routed, and dispers'd, by the Prussian Generals Schenkendorff and Sybourg, near Saalfeld. One Colonel, one Major, twenty nine officers, and 800 private men were made prisoners; four pair of colours and six pieces of cannon were taken. Ziethen's Hussars, under Major Hundt, particularly distinguish'd themselves.

April 2. The Berten, an East-Indiaman, bound from Port L'Orient to the Isle of France and Pondicherry, pierced for 64 guns, mounting 28, and manned with 353 men, of whom 93 were soldiers, laden with ordnance, naval stores, merchandize, and 24000 dollars in specie, was taken by the Hero Captain William Fortescue and the Venus Captain Harrison. The entire cargo of this prize, was valued by her Captain at 90,000 pounds sterling.

April 3.

April 3. The Kings of Great-Britain and Pruſſia accepted the propoſal of the belligerant Powers, contain'd in their declaration of the 26th of March, for opening a congreſs at Augſburg, in order to negotiate a general peace.

April — The Pheaſant, a French frigate of 16 guns 125 men, was taken by the Albany ſloop Captain Brograve; the Pheaſant threw 14 of her guns overboard in the chace.

April 6. A Pruſſian detachment attack'd a corps of Imperialiſts under General Guaſco, near Plaven in the Voigtland, and took one Colonel, eight officers, 150 men, four pieces of cannon, and all the baggage. The Pruſſians loſt the brave Major Hundt of Ziethen's Huſſars, one Lieutenant, and 30 private men.

April 7. Between the 14th of February and this day, the garriſon of Gottingen alone made 1600 of the Allies priſoners of war.

April 8. Major General Hodgſon and Commodore Keppel attempted to diſimbark the Britiſh troops at St. Andro near Point Lomaria; but the French were ſo ſtrongly intrenched on each ſide of the hill, which was exceſſively ſteep, and the foot of it ſcarp'd away, that after repeated efforts they were oblig'd to deſiſt. Major General Crawford and Brigadier Carlton exerted themſelves with ability on this occaſion, and the latter was wounded in the thigh. One of the flat-bottom'd boats landed ſixty of Erſkine's grenadiers, commanded by Captain Oſborne, who gain'd the top of the hills by a very difficult aſcent; but being attack'd as
ſoon

soon as they were form'd, by a numerous force, they were routed before it was possible to send them any effectual assistance; twenty of this party were brought back from the rocks by the boats. The loss of the British troops, in kill'd, wounded, and prisoners, amounted to 434.

April 13. The Austrian General Reid attack'd the Prussian line, which was form'd before Miltitz, forced that post, kill'd and wounded 100 men, and made 40 prisoners.

April 21. A magazine of hay which the French had form'd at Wesel, accidentally took fire, and was consumed. It consisted of 1,250,000 rations, and was valued at two millions of livres.

April 22. Beauclerk's grenadiers under Captain Paterson, boldly climb'd up a rock, and made good their landing upon Bellisle against 300 of the enemy, till the remainder of the corps under Brigadier Lambert were enabled to come to their assistance. The rest of the troops afterwards landed without difficulty. Captain Paterson lost his arm in this gallant service. Mr. Lambert was strongly recommended by General Hodgson to his Majesty's favour, for the conduct and spirit which he shewed on this memorable occasion. The French lost three brass field pieces, and some of their wounded were made prisoners.

April — The Speedwell cutter of eight guns, station'd off Oporto, was taken by two French men of war on the coast of Spain, and sent into Vigo.

April 23. A detachment of 3000 men from the garrison of Gottingen attack'd a battalion of the British legion in the village of Feldhaven near Uslar, and made 100 prisoners. They were afterwards dislodged from that post by the Hanoverians, who took above 50 dragoons.

May 5. General Luckner with 100 Hussars came up with 300 horse of the garrison of Gottingen, entirely routed them, made one officer and thirty troopers prisoners, and took sixty one horses. — Captain Brinsky attack'd them the same day, on their return, with 100 Hussars and 50 of the Brunswick cavalry, drove them before him into Gottingen, and made three officers and 53 dragoons prisoners; the Vicomte de Belsunce their commander narrowly escaped being taken in the pursuit. The village of Spielen beyond the Fulda was taken by Captain Riedesel with 100 men of the Brunswick Hussars, and the garrison of 50 men were kill'd or made prisoners, with little loss on the part of the Allies.

May — The Austrians abandon'd Freyberg on the approach of Colonel Kleist, who took 84 men and 100 horses.

May — The King of Prussia took an Austrian magazine of meal at Bautzen.

May 17. Colonel Kleist attack'd part of General Guasco's corps at Schellenberg, and took 118 men together with three officers.

May 21. General Beck attack'd a body of Prussians on the Queiss near Greiffenberg, kill'd and wounded

wounded 600 men, took near the same number prisoners, and made himself master of four pieces of cannon.

May — One hundred horse of the Allied army took, near Nordheim, a French Lieutenant Colonel, 34 dragoons, and 40 horse. M. de Belsunce himself narrowly escaped.

June 6. Lord Rollo and Colonel Melvil, supported by the squadron under Commodore Sir James Douglass, landed their troops on the island of Dominica, attack'd and drove the French from four different intrenchments, one above another, upon the face of a steep hill, and made M. de Longprie the Commandant, and M. de Couche the second Officer, prisoners of war. Having thus taken the island by assault, Lord Rollo granted the inhabitants a protection till his Majesty's pleasure should be further known. Dominica is well wooded and water'd, and supplied the French with quantities of coffee, cocoa, and cotton; the soil in many places is rich, and the land very high, which makes it capable of producing excellent sugar-cane, if properly cultivated.

June 7. The citadel of Palais surrender'd to General Hodgson and Commodore Keppel. The Chevalier de St. Croix and his garrison obtain'd all the honours of war, and were transported to the Continent at the Expence of his Britannick Majesty. The British prisoners were declar'd to be free from the moment of the capitulation, but the French prisoners were to be exchang'd according to the cartel of Sluys. It is difficult to ascertain the exact loss of the British troops in this long and well-disputed siege. Some accounts make th
kill'

kill'd amount to near 2000 men. The Captains Bell, Wightwick, and Collins, of the Marines, were promoted to the rank of Majors in the army, for their gallant behaviour. The number of French troops in the citadel, when it was invested, amounted to 2600, of whom 922 were kill'd, wounded, or made prisoners, during the siege.

June 13. The Hampshire and Centaur, part of Rear Admiral Holmes's squadron, took the St. Anne, pierced for 64 guns, having on board six 24 pounders, twenty six 12 pounders and eight 8 pounders, with 389 persons. She was commanded by M. D'Aguillon, and her cargo consisted of indigo, coffee, and sugar, to the value of one million of French livres.

June 16. General Luckner took 84 oxen under the walls of Gottingen, drove back the garrison, kill'd and wounded 100 men, and made one Captain and 14 private men prisoners.

June 17. M. Scheiter cross'd the Rhine with only 36 horse, and in the space of 93 hours, set fire to the French magazines at Xanten, and other places, and plunder'd a great quantity of baggage. The magazines which he destroyed, amounted to 1,635000 rations of hay and straw, near 6000 sacks and several thousand rations of oats.

June — The French made 245 prisoners at Luhnen and Kamen, and took two pieces of cannon.

June 20. Two thousand Austrians surpriz'd a flying camp of the Prussians near Schweidnitz, made

200 prisoners, and carried off 300 horse with some other booty.

June — Marshal Broglio took possession of Warbourg and Paderborn; General Sporcken lost a small number of men and some cannon in his retreat from the former place.

June 28 and 29. The detach'd corps of M. Broglio's army, made between four and five hundred of the Allies prisoners of war, and took 19 pieces of cannon with 4 haubitzers.

From *June* 10 to *June* 30. inclusive. Lieutenant Colonel Grant of the 40th regiment of foot, with the troops under his command, penetrated into the middle and back settlements of the Cherokees, burnt 15 towns, destroy'd above 1400 acres of corn, beans, and pease, and drove 5000 people into the woods and mountains, where they would be necessarily reduced to great distress for want of subsistence. — His loss in this expedition amounted only to one subaltern, one serjeant, and nine private men kill'd, four subalterns, one drummer, and forty seven private men wounded.

July — Le Beaumont, a French East-Indiaman bound for the Isle of Bourbon, of 600 tons, 22 guns nine pounders and 280 men, was taken by the King George privateer of 24 guns twelve and nine pounders and 240 men Captain Reid commander, after an obstinate engagement of seven hours, in which the former had upwards of 60 men kill'd and the latter 25.

July 8. General Ziethen reconnoitred the Russian army, skirmish'd with an advanced post, kill'd

200 men, and afterwards retreated in good order to his camp at Storkneft in Poland.

July 13. A body of French troops under the command of M. Chabot, intending to furprize M. Luckner, near Samle, was attack'd and defeated by that General; 150 men were made prifoners, and 200 horfes taken.

July 14. The Captains Kampen and Engel, Captain Lieutenant Sanders, and Lieutenant Muller, with 220 horfe in different detachments, burnt upwards of 30 carriages of bacon and provifions, deftroy'd or gave away a prodigious quantity of bread and meal, took 700 horfes, ruin'd 2000 more, and in their return to the allied army made prifoners 250 recover'd men of the enemy's troops.

July 15 and 16. Marfhal Broglio decamp'd on the 15th at day-break from Erwite, and attack'd Lord Granby's camp in the evening with great brifknefs: his Lordfhip fuftain'd the efforts of the enemy with refolution and fuccefs, till the arrival of Lieutenant General Wutgenau, who had received orders to march to his fupport. The French being now taken in flank, they could no longer withftand the firmnefs of thefe Generals, with whom Prince Ferdinand was in perfon, but were driven back into the woods, after a fire of artillery and fmall arms which lafted till late in the night. The action was renewed at three the next morning, and continued till nine; M. Wutgenau's corps, againft which the French made redoubled attacks, maintain'd its ground with intrepidity; at laft M. Broglio appear'd to have a defign of planting fome batteries upon an eminence, oppofite to Lord Granby's camp, which was not inclosed within the lines: to prevent the bad consequence of such a design, Prince Ferdinand order'd the nearest troops to advance upon the enemy, which they did with such courage, that the French soon gave way, and retreated precipitately, abandoning their dead and wounded. Maxwell's battalion of grenadiers took prisoners the regiment of Rouge, consisting of four battalions, with their cannon and colours. Upon the news of this defeat on the right, the left of the French army under the Prince de Soubise, which was opposed to the hereditary prince, desisted from the attack; 200 men, commanded by Major Limburg, defended the village of Scheidingen, on that side; against all the attempts of the enemy. The loss of the French in kill'd, wounded, and prisoners, was computed at about 5000 men; nine pieces of cannon and six pair of colours were taken. The brigades of the King, Auvergne, Belsunce, and Nassau, suffer'd the most. The Duke of Havre and his son in law the Marquis of Cirrac, the Marquis of Rouge Lieutenant General and his son the Colonel, were kill'd: their loss in Officers was very considerable. This battle was fought in the field of Kirch-Denckern, near Hiltrup, and at no great distance from Ham. The Allies had 311 men kill'd, 1011 wounded, 192 made prisoners, and three pieces of cannon taken.

July 17. The Achilles of 64 guns and the Buffon of 32, were taken at the distance of 19 leagues from Cadiz, by the Thunderer of 74 guns Captain Proby, and the Thetis storeship Captain Moutray, after a bloody combat of half an hour, in which the Thunderer had 17 men kill'd and 113 wounded, 17 of whom died soon afterwards; Captain Proby was slightly wounded in the hand. The
French

French frigate did not strike till after the Modeste had come up, and fired some guns into her. These two ships carried upwards of 900 men between them. The Captain of the Achilles was gently censur'd, the Lieutenant degraded from his Nobility and imprison'd, and the Ensign shot, for their behaviour in this engagement.

July — A great convoy of provisions was destroy'd by Colonel Freytag, between Cassel and Warbourg; the Brunswick Hussars ruin'd two French magazines upon the Werra, and Major General Luckner, in his retreat from Neuhaus near Paderborn (which he had forced on the 17th) had a smart engagement with the enemy, and made 150 prisoners.

July 18. Marshal Butterlin having detach'd some regiments of Hussars from his head-quarters at Pristawe, to cut off the retreat of Colonel Lossow, who had been reconnoitring the Russians; the latter fell upon them by surprize, kill'd 20 men, made 2 officers, 14 subalterns, 2 surgeons, and 106 private men prisoners, took 100 horses, and dispers'd the rest.

July 20. Colonel Belling, and Lieutenant Colonel Goltz, gain'd some advantage over the Swedes at Verchen.

July 19 to 21. Colonel Freytag, in a second expedition, destroy'd a great quantity of ammunition and corn belonging to the French, on the Fuld and the Werra, without the loss of a man.

July 21. The Swedes took Demmin, and made 100 men of Hordt's Battalion prisoners of war. At

Malchin, the Prussian Lieutenant Colonel Goltz lost 100 men; and at Damgarten, a Lieutenant and 20 Prussian Hussars were taken prisoners.

July 22. The King of Prussia attack'd General Brentano's cavalry near Munsterberg, and made 150 Fouriers prisoners.

July 28. and 29. Part of Commodore Keppel's squadron under Sir Thomas Stanhope, demolish'd the works and fortifications on the isle of Aix: Captain Chaplin of the Furnace bomb distinguish'd himself on this occasion.

July 30. General Luckner attack'd Marshal Broglio's rear-guard at Lipsprinck, and destroy'd the corps of Volontaires de Broglio.

August 2. The Russians attack'd a Prussian magazine between Welda and the Oder, but were repuls'd with considerable loss.

August 3. The King of Prussia pass'd the Neisse, drove part of the Austrian army as far as Hoff in Moravia, and made 100 prisoners.

August 5. Prince Ferdinand attack'd Lieutenant General de Stainville, who had between 16 and 18 battalions and as many squadrons under his command, and obliged him, after a dispute of three or four hours, to abandon the post of Stadtbergen.

August 6. A convoy of 250 waggons going towards the Weser, was taken by a detachment of Hunters belonging to Colonel Freytag's corps. The desertion, at this time, was very great in the French army.

August

August 7. Thirty men of the allied army under the Chevalier de Donceel, attack'd near Stockern, and difpers'd a guard of 70 Auftrians that was placed for the protection of 65 pontoons, and afterwards burnt the pontoons together with a fmall French magazine.

Auguft. 7. The Subtile, a French frigate belonging to the Eaft India company, of 16 guns 84 men, and of about 300 tons burthen, bound from Mauritius to L'Orient, was taken by the Aquilon Captain Chaloner Ogle.

Auguft 14. Lieutenant General Diemar, with a garrifon of 300 men, gallantly and fuccefsfully defended the fmall town of Horn againft 8000 French and 6 pieces of cannon.

Auguft 14 and 15. General Luckner, having arrived with his corps on the heights near Daffel, detach'd his own regiment towards the right wing of the French, and Colonel Freytag, with all the light horfe, towards their left. The enemy, under the command of M. Belfunce, drew back their forces towards the foreft of Solling, after detaching a large body of horfe and foot to the high road that leads to Eimbeck; this body was inftantly charg'd and totally routed by Luckner's Huffars. In front, General Luckner himfelf attack'd the French, whom he found drawn up in order of battle, but they foon retired and drew nearer to the foreft of Solling; Colonel Freytag obliged their light horfe to difperfe themfelves in the foreft, where they were prefently follow'd by General Luckner: Lieutenant Colonel de Stockhaufen, who had previoufly pofted himfelf in the Solling

with

with his hunters, then engaged with, and defeated, the French infantry, and the Brunswick Hussars pursued them with success. In these different attacks, 44 officers and 759 private men were made prisoners; three pair of colours and 800 horses were taken.

August 15. Some Prussian regiments, among which were those of Finkenstein and Czelteritz, attack'd near Lignitz in Silesia, 30 squadrons of Austrian cavalry and 10 battalions of grenadiers who were on their march to join the Russians; these regiments took a great number of prisoners, and dispers'd the enemy in such a manner, that only 10 squadrons were enabled to effect the intended junction. About the same time, General Knoblock made two regiments of Russian infantry prisoners in their retreat towards the Oder.

August 15. Captain Faulkner in the Bellona of 74 guns, and Captain Loggie in the Brilliant of 36, came up with the Courageux of 74 guns Captain du Gue Lambert, the Malicieux of 32 guns Captain Longueville, and the Hermione of 32 guns Captain Montigney. The Bellona attack'd the Courageux, and the Brilliant the two frigates. After an engagement of three quarters of an hour, the Courageux struck, having lost the amazing number of 240 men kill'd, and 110 wounded. The French frigates bore away from the Brilliant 23 minutes after the Courageux was taken. The Bellona had only 6 men kill'd and 28 wounded; the Brilliant 5 kill'd and 16 wounded.

August 18. The Castle of Waldeck surrender'd to the French.

August 18. The Marquis de Conflans attack'd the rear-guard of a detachment of the allied army, in its march from Munster to the lower Embs, made some prisoners, and took the tents belonging to Scheiter's cavalry, together with 30 baggage waggons.

August 19. General Romanzow took possession of the town of Coslin near Colberg in Pomerania.

August — The Fatalasam, a ship belonging to the East India company, bound from Fort St. George to Calcutta in Bengal, was wreck'd in her passage, and only 27 persons were saved: among those who perish'd were, five lieutenants, two ensigns, two surgeon's mates, one volunteer, sixteen sergeants, one drummer, and 218 rank and file, belonging to the 84th regiment of foot commanded by Colonel Eyre Coote. Major Gordon, Captain Scott, Ensign Ogilvie, and Mr. Browne the Surgeon, escaped on shore, but died with the fatigue of their journey, in attempting to reach Calcutta.

August 25. The Austrian army join'd that of the Russians in Silesia.

August 30. A body of the allied army surpriz'd Dorsten, and made M. Viersét with the first battalion of his regiment, and several piquets, prisoners of war. Next day the light troops took 300 waggons, many equipages, and the different patroles of French horse that were posted along the Lippe.

August 31. The corps, under the Generals Luckner and Freytag, and Colonel Stockhausen, were attack'd by the French, and obliged to abandon several posts in the defiles of the Hartz mountains.

September 3. — The vanguard of the Prince of Soubise's army recover'd Dorsten, made 180 of the Allies prisoners, and took one piece of cannon.

Sept. 15. The Prussian General Platen destroy'd some considerable Russian magazines at Coblin and Gostin, attack'd 5000 waggons at a Convent near the latter place, defeated the convoy of 4000 men, kill'd many, and made 2000 prisoners, including Brigadier General Czerapow, 3 Majors, and 20 inferiour officers. Five haubitzers and 2 pieces of cannon were taken.

September 19. General Romanzow having attack'd and carried a redoubt which cover'd one of the flanks of the Prince of Wurtemberg's Camp, he made another attempt on the Prince's intrenchments, but was repuls'd with the loss of near 3000 men, officers included, and the Prince recover'd the redoubt that was taken the preceeding day.

September — A body of Russians repuls'd the Prussian Lieutenant General Werner near Treptow in Pomerania, and took the General himself prisoner, whilst he was endeavouring to rally the regiment of Wurtemberg which had been put into confusion.

September 22. General Romanzow failed in another attempt upon the Prussian intrenchments before Colberg.

September 24. The Marquis de Conflans made himself master of Embden, where he raised large contributions; 200 English invalids who compos'd the garrison, obtain'd an advantageous capitulation, and embark'd for Bremen.

September — The French enter'd Osnabrug, and levied exorbitant contributions.

October 1. The Austrians, under the orders of M. de Laudohn, made themselves masters of Schweidnitz by a *coup de main*. Lieutenant General Zastrow governour of the fortress, and 3771 men were made prisoners of war. A large magazine of powder blew up in the attack, which did equal damage to the Prussians and the Enemy. 181 pieces of cannon were found in the place. The loss of the Austrians consisted in 279 kill'd 1007 wounded and 140 missing. Of the Russians (who were engaged in this assault) 51 were kill'd and 45 wounded. The grenadiers of that corps particularly distinguish'd themselves.

October — The strong Castle of Scharsfels in the Hartze mountains surrender'd to the French after a siege of eight days, who demolish'd its fortifications; Meppen capitulated to the Prince of Conde on the 3d, in which 500 of the Allies were made prisoners of war.

October 7. Part of the army of the Empire took possession of Halle, but quitted it again on the tenth.

October 10. Wolfenbuttel capitulated to Prince Xavier of Saxony, after a five days siege.

October 11. Three French frigates mann'd six large boats, in hopes of boarding and taking the
Lively

Lively frigate, which lay at anchor in view of the garrison of Belliſle; but a detachment of 85 men, compoſed of Morgan's light infantry, together with ſome Marines, ſet off in four boats, attack'd the enemy with briſkneſs, kill'd 15 men and wounded 19, and brought five of their boats back with them to Belliſle.

October 13. Prince Frederic of Brunſwick attack'd, and forced, the French, in the intrenchments which they had thrown up, at the Paſs of Oelpher, for covering the ſiege of Brunſwick. Many of the enemy were kill'd; and one Major General, ſeveral officers, upwards of 200 private men, and one piece of cannon were taken. In conſequence of this ſucceſs, the French rais'd the ſiege of Brunſwick, and abandon'd Wolfenbuttel.

October 20, 21 and 22. The Ruſſians made furious attacks both upon Colberg and the Prince of Wirtemburg's intrenchments, but without any effect.

October 21. The Ruſſians took two Pruſſian detachments, which ſerv'd as a convoy to a tranſport from Stetin laden with proviſions for Colberg. General de Platen, who march'd to Golnow with a view to protect and cover that tranſport, was obliged to ſend it back to Dam, after which he retir'd himſelf to Stargard. The Ruſſian light troops having, on the 13th, blown up 85 waggons loaded with bombs and gunpowder, and deſtroy'd 100 more fill'd with proviſions and other ſtores, they afterwards made themſelves maſters of the town of Golnow, and burnt the ſuburbs. 40,000 bombs and balls were found in Golnow.

October 24. The Ruffians, detach'd by General Romanzow from Colberg, made themselves masters of Treptow, and obliged General Knobloch with three battalions and a corps of cavalry, amounting to 4000 men, to surrender prisoners of war. The Pruffians also lost six colours and ten cannon.

Octob. 25. The Griffin of 28 guns, captain Taylor, was lost off the Bermuda islands, and 50 of the crew were drown'd.

October 29. The Pruffians were dislodged from Stepnitz by the Ruffians; and General Berg surpriz'd Colonel Combiere at the village of Sanglow near Golnow, whom he made prisoner, together with 36 officers and 1000 men; six pieces of cannon were taken on this occasion. Colonel Combiere commanded the van guard of General Platen's troops, which, to the number of 6000 men, had unfortunately penetrated as far as Golnow.

November 2. The Ruffian General Berg attack'd General Platen between Stargard and Pyritz, but was repuls'd with the loss of 500 men kill'd and wounded.

November 5. Prince Ferdinand form'd a judicious plan for surprizing 15 battalions under the Count de Chabot at Efcherfhaufen. The Marquis of Granby reach'd Wickenfen, on the 5th, to block up the defilé leading from Efcherfhaufen to Eimbeck, having previously forced the Post of Cappelnhagen; the same day General Conway and General Scheele join'd at Halle, in the morning: the Count de Chabot perceiv'd he had no other way to escape but by turning to the right, towards

Stad-

Stad-Odendorp; this road would have been also block'd up by General Hardenberg, if he had not been retarded in his march by the overturning of his pontoons in a hollow way; by this accident the French General was enabled to make his escape to Eimbeck.

November 7. Count Broglio attack'd the Marquis of Granby and General Conway, just as they were beginning to encamp at Foorwohle, after a fatiguing night-march through snow and difficult roads: an advanced body of Chasseurs under Lieutenant Colonel Maxwell, at first very prudently retir'd; but, on being supported, they return'd to the charge with vigour and conduct; the French were repuls'd with great spirit, and driven back almost to their very camp.

November 9. The Marquis of Granby was again attack'd by the Enemy, and he again repuls'd them with considerable loss. Major Fraser distinguish'd himself greatly on this occasion. Marshal Broglio perceiving that Prince Ferdinand had already gain'd his flank, and was partly in his rear, thought fit to decline a general engagement, and abandon'd Eimbeck in the night, and all the adjacent country.

November —— Captain M'Kenzie of Fort-Cumberland arm'd two vessels at Bay Verte, and proceeded with them to Bay Chaleurs, where he broke up a settlement of plunderers that had done considerable mischief to the British navigation in those parts. 240 men, women, and children, were carried away prisoners to Bay Vert, together with or 10 vessels laden with their effects; all their other small-craft was destroy'd.

November — The Ruffians repeated their attack upon the Prince of Wirtemburg's intrenchments, with the fame indifferent fuccefs.

November 13. The Hereditary Prince of Brunfwick attack'd near Katlenbourg, and routed, a large detachment of cavalry commanded by M. de Clofen.

November 15. General Romanzow took the fort of Munde at the entrance of the river Perfante, and cut off all communication by water between Stetin and Colberg.

December 1. A Silefian Gentleman, of the Name of Wargotfch, form'd a plan for feizing the King of Pruffia in the fuburbs of Strehlen, by employing a refolute body of cavalry to fet fire to thofe fuburbs, and then to fecure his Majefty's perfon in the confufion. Wargotfch's fervant detected the confpiracy; for having been fent with a letter from his mafter to a popifh Prieft, by whom it was to be forwarded to an Auftrian Lieutenant Colonel, and having remark'd a particular agitation in the delivery of it, he immediately concluded that the contents were dangerous, and therefore carried the letter to a Pruffian officer in Strehlen. Wargotfch and the Prieft were arrefted, but afterwards made their efcape.

December — The fort of Munden, under Colberg, towards the Sea, was taken by the Ruffians; by the lofs of which, the entry of any Ruffian veffel with provifions, into Colberg, was rendered uncertain and dangerous.

December — The Ruffians made an unfuccefsful attempt to take Colberg by ftorm.

December 10. The nine principal Headmen of the Cherokee nation arrived in Charles Town, and in a few days afterwards the treaty between that nation and the province of South Carolina was finally ratified, in all its forms, by the Lieutenant Governour and thofe nine Indians refpectively.

December 12. The Prince of Wirtemburg was defeated by a detachment of General Romanzow's army.

December 13. The Ruffians gave a vigorous affault to Colberg, and were beat back with confiderable lofs.

December 17. Colberg furrender'd to the Ruffians who loft many men while they lay before the place The brave garrifon, confifting of 79 officers an 3000 private men, were made prifoners of wai 146 pieces of cannon were found in the arfenal 40 pair of colours and 4 ftandards were taken. Cc lonel Heyden acquir'd great honour by his fpirite defence of this fortrefs, during a fiege which lafte upwards of five months. General Romanzow, a cording to the Ruffian account, made 8000 pr foners in the courfe of the campaign, exclufive 5000 deferters.

December 19. An article of this date from W fel, mention'd the deftruction of immenfe mag zines belonging to the allied army in Weftpha and Eaft-Frizeland, during the latter part of tl campaign. The Amfterdam Gazette gave the pu lick a more minute and early account of those which were ruin'd in East-Frizeland, amounting to upwards of two millions of rations. Notwithstanding which, the London gazette firmly and positively denied the truth of that relation, and affirm'd that the loss of their magazines in Westphalia and East-Frizeland was greatly exaggerated, nothing being more certain that the Allies had little of consequence in those parts.

December 26. The French frigate Hermione, of 36 guns, was lost on the bar of Vigo.

December 27. The Boulogne of 20 guns 140 men, M. de St. Romain commander, bound from the Isle of Bourbon to Port L'Orient, laden with coffee and pepper, and valued at 40,000 pounds, was taken by the Venus Captain Harrison.

December 30. The Biddeford of 24 guns Captain Gordon, was lost off the Yarmouth sands. Out of 160 men, only the Lieutenant, Master, Surgeon, Lieutenant of the Marines, and about 70 private men were saved.

Supplies granted by Parliament for the service of the year 1761.

Eighteen millions, eight hundred and sixteen thousand, one hundred and nineteen pounds, nineteen shillings and nine pence three farthings.

A list of many considerable privateers, &c. and arm'd merchantmen, taken by his Majesty's ships of war, from the 31st of December 1760 to the 31st of December 1761.

January.	guns.	men.	captors.
Le Chevalier d'Arthessay of Granville	8 carriage 6 swivels	58	taken by the Hornet sloop.
The Valeur of St. Maloe	4 carriage 14 swivels	28	— by the Swallow sloop.
A privateer of St. Maloe	6 carriage 6 swivels	39	— by the Venus Captain Harrison.
The Maria Theresa of St. Maloe.	10 carriage	75	— by the Aquilon Captain Ogle.
The Revenge cutter privateer of Dieppe, taken after an engagement of an hour and an half.	6 carriage 6 swivels		— by the Hunter arm'd cutter Lieutenant Jarvis.
L'Ecureuil of Bayonne	14 carriage	122	— by the Minerva Captain Hood.
Le Bien Aimé, laden with sugar and coffee	20	85	— by the Trent Captain Lindsay.

	guns.	men.	captors.
The Royal Cantabre of of St. Maloe	4 carriage 6 swivels	65	taken by the Aquilon.
The Count de Valence of Boulogne	10 carriage	70	— by the Stag Captain Angel.
Le Chevert of Dunkirk	18 six pounders	160	— by the Amazon and Solebay.
The Minerva of Dunkirk	6 carriage 4 swivels	42	— by the Vengeance Capt. Nightingale.
The Dutchefs of Gramont of St. Maloe, late his Majesty's sloop Hawke.	12 carriage		— by the Juno Captain Towry.
The Society of St. Maloe.	6 carriage	60	— by the Hornet Capt. Johnstone.
Le Compte de Gramont of Bayonne	20	117	— by the Aquilon Captain Ogle.

February.

A French cutter privateer sunk off Beachy Head, and all the crew drown'd	10		— by the Grace cutter.

	guns.	men.	captors.
The Duke of Mazarine privateer	12	106	taken by the Niger Captain Fitzherbert.
A cutter privateer of Calais	6	46	— by the Arethusa Honourable Captain Vane.
A privateer driven on shore between the seven islands and Brehat, when the crew quitted her, and she bulged soon afterwards.	10		— by the Wasp sloop Captain Yates.
A privateer	14	140	— by the Jersey.
The St. Joseph and St. Antoine.	12	84	— by the Favourite, Captain Pownall.
A large vessel of 400 tons bound from Bourdeaux to St. Domingo	18	75	— by the Blonde, Captain Kennedy.

March.

The Sultan of Bayonne	10	73	— by the Swallow sloop.
The Auguste of St. Maloe	12	67	— by the Vengeance.

	guns.	men.	captors.
The Chamillant	4 carriage 2 swivels	15	taken by the Biddeford, Captain Howe.
The Hazard	6 swivels	22	— by the Albany Capt. Brograve.
A shallop privateer	2 carriage 6 swivels	24	— by the Grace arm'd cutter, Lieutenant M'Bride.
The Hardi of Bayonne	10 carriage	125	— by the Tweed Captain Paston.
The Zephire	12	114	— by the Aquilon.
The Marshal Broglio of Brest	8	80	— by the Unicorn and Tweed.
Le Lutine.	8	68	— by the Alarm Capt. Rushworth.
The Marquis of Chartres of St. Maloe.	6	76	— by the Niger.
A privateer of St. Maloe.	4 carriage 4 swivels	45	— by the Vengeance
April.			
Le Carnival.	4 carriage 10 swivels	64	— by the Æolus Captain Elliot.
The Bienbroynon of Dieppe.	1 carriage 12 swivels	35	— by the Terpsichore, Sir Thomas Adams, Baronet.

	guns.	men.	captors.
The Lion of Bayonne	6 carriage 12 swivels	85	taken by the Venus.
The Augustine	8 carriage 6 swivels	61	— by the Biddeford.
A privateer	22 carriage		— by the Actæon.
The Grand Cyprus of Bayonne	12	116	— by the Blonde.
The Fidelle of Bayonne	4 carriage 17 swivels	45	— by the Milford, Captain Man.
The Admiral of Bayonne	12 carriage 16 swivels	65	— by the Milford.
Two French Turkey ships			— by the Sheerness.
Two large Martinico men outward bound			— by the Firme.
Le Grand Serpent.			— by the Blonde Captain Kennedy,
A privateer	8 carriage	50	— by the Belliqueux.
The Pomona Merchant ship of Bourdeaux.	8	45	— by the Danae Captain Martin.

May.	guns.	men.	captors.
The Marquis de Beringhen of Dieppe	8 carriage 6 swivels	60	taken by the Biddeford.
The Quemper	8 carriage 8 swivels	65	— by the Arethusa Captain Keeler.
A privateer	36 carriage		— reported to have been taken by the Tartar.
The François	8	61	— by the Jamaica Captain Burdon. driven on shore in an attack upon James Fort in the river Gambia.
A snow privateer	16		
The Holy Family bound from Smyrna to Marseilles.			taken by the Pallas.
The St. Anthony of Padua from ditto to ditto.			— by the Vestal.
June.			
The Marshal Duke de Biron of Dunkirk, pierc'd for 20 guns, with ransomers for 4605 pounds.	15 carriage 12 swivels	109	— by the Argo Captain King.

	guns.	men.	captors.
A privateer of Dunkirk.	1 carriage (a nine pounder) 10 swivels	30	taken ⎫
A privateer of ditto	2 carriage	24	destroy'd ⎬ by an arm'd cutter.
The Russian of Bayonne	6 carriage 16 swivels	46	taken by the Fowey Capt. Tonyn.
A ship from Martinico to Naples	13 carriage	57	— by the Repulse Captain Allen.
The St. Gregory from Martinico laden with sugar, coffee, and cotton.			— by the Blonde.
A privateer	18	135	— by the Cygnet Captain Napier.
A small privateer sloop			— by the Favourite.
Six privateers and a stout Martinico ship.			reported to have been taken the beginning of this month, and carried into Jamaica by the Trent Captain Lindsay.

July.

| La Fleur of Dunkirk | 2 | 29 | taken and sunk by the Swan. |

	guns.	men.	captors.
The Loup of Dunkirk, with five ransomers	12 carriage 8 swivels	70	taken by the Badger Captain Scott.
The Triumphant of Cherbourg	2 carriage	18	— by the Cholmondeley cutter.
A rich Domingo ship of 300 tons			— by the Burford.
A ship from Port au Prince of 200 tons, with sugar, coffee, and indigo			— by the Thames frigate.
Le Faucheur with one ransomer	6 carriage 8 swivels	40	— by the Richmond Captain Elphinstone.

August.

The Duc de Noailles	12 carriage		— by the Richmond.
A dogger privateer	10	59	cut out of Dunkirk Road by the boats of the Maidstone and Melampe under the command of Lieutenant M'Bride.
The Aurora of Rochelle	10	75	taken by the Aquilon.

	guns.	men.	captors.
A small privateer.			taken by the Diligence sloop.
The Hazard of Dunkirk	6 swivels	15	taken — by the Fly arm'd cutter
The Maria Theresa of ditto.			destroy'd — Lieutenant Barkley
September.			
The Colibry of Dunkirk, with three ransomers	16 carriage	110	taken by the Danae.
The Benjamin of Granville			— by the Diligence sloop.
A privateer driven ashore near Dunkirk			— by the Leostoffe cutter.
The Amarante of St. Maloe	18	137	— by the Mars.
The Two Brothers	14		— by the Raisonable.
October.			
Twenty two merchant ships at Monte Christi			— by Admiral Holmes's squadron, and carried into Jamaica.
A sloop	15		carried into Antigua by an English frigate.
The Heureux privateer		50	taken by the Hornet.
The Henry of Bayonne	10	58	— by the Dorsetshire.
A privateer	14		— by the Antigua brig.

	guns.	men.	captors.
November.			
The Duc de Noialles	6 carriage 16 fwivels	143	— by the Granada.
A privateer cutter of Havre	8 carriage	37	— by the Liverpool Capt. Knight.
L'Epreveir of Calais	6 fwivels	20	— by the Richmond.
The Erneftine of Dunkirk	10 carriage	67	— by the Syren, Unicorn, and Martin floop.
A floop laden with fugar	10	52	fent into St. John's in Antigua, by the Virgin.
December.			
L'Aimable Gabrielle of St. Jean de Luz	14	108	— by the Efcorte.
A privateer of St. Maloe	12 carriage 12 fwivels	75	— by the Scorpion floop.
The Pierrier of Bayonne	6 carriage	80	— by the Æolus Captain Hotham.

The French took 814 fhips from the Englifh, in the courfe of the year 1761.

1762.

January 5. Elizabeth Empress of Russia died, in the 52d year of her age, and in the 22d of her reign.

January 11 and 12. The French frigate La Zenobie, M. de Sage commander, a new ship, carrying 22 nine pounders, and 210 men, with provisions on board for six months, was wreck'd on Portland Beach, and only 71 men were saved.

January 12. The Prussian Generals Platen and Wunsch, after having taken several places, penetrated within a league of Naumbourg, which the army of the Empire quitted, and retir'd towards Weimar, with the loss of men and baggage. Prince Henry's winter quarters were enlarged by this expedition.

January 16. General Monckton landed his troops without molestation near the Case des Navires in the island of Martinico, between Pointe des Negre and la Case Pilote, at the distance of little more than a league from Fort Royal, the ships of war under Admiral Rodney, having previously silenc'd the batteries that were above the place of landing. The Raisonable of 64 guns was lost, on the 7th upon a little reef of rocks in St. Anne's Bay, as she was leading in for one of the enemy's batteries: all the people and stores were saved.

January 21. M. Reid attack'd the advanc'd posts of the Prussians in Saxony, in which the latter lost near 1000 men in kill'd, wounded, and deserters, together with four pieces of cannon.

January 25. The Chevalier de Vosseil, with a detachment of 65 men, obliged 300 Prussians to lay down their arms. He was afterwards made a Lieutenant Colonel for his bravery and conduct.

January 30. Mr. William Hay first Lieutenant and Commander (in the absence of Captain Martin) of the Danae of 36 guns, engaged a large French ship of force, yard arm and yard arm, for an hour and an half; the latter got off in a shatter'd condition with the loss of numbers kill'd and wounded. Seventy men were kill'd and wounded on board of the Danae.

February 3. An Austrian detachment attack'd L'Abadiés independent Battalion at Gross Parda near Grimm, kill'd the greatest part of it, and took many prisoners.

February 4. The citadel of Fort-Royal capitulated to General Monckton and Admiral Rodney. — Previously to this important event, General Monckton order'd the Morne Tartenson to be attack'd on the 24th of January at day-break. The grenadiers under Brigadier Grant, supported by Lord Rollo's brigade, charg'd the Enemy's advanc'd posts. Brigadier Rufane, with his brigade and the Marines, attack'd the redoubts on the right, along the coasts; 1000 seamen in the flat-bottom'd boats, row'd up, as he advanc'd. The light infantry under Lieutenant Colonel Scott, supported by brigadier Walsh's brigade, possess'd them-

themselves of a plantation on the left, and got
round the French. — The attack was carried on
with such vigour and impetuosity, that the troops
carried the strong post of Morne Tartenson by nine
o' clock. the Enemy retir'd in the greatest confusion to Fort Royal and Morne Garnier; some of
the grenadiers follow'd them to the bridge of the
Town, and brought off a few prisoners. The General, in pursuit of his plan, order'd Walsh's brigade, and the division of grenadiers under Grant,
to take a plantation more to the left; Scott's light-
infantry made themselves masters of an advantageous post opposite to Morne Garnier; Brigadier
Haviland's corps supported them on their right;
Walsh's brigade, and the grenadiers, communicated with the latter; and the Marines cover'd the
road between the two plantations. — This was the
situation of things, when the General found it ab-
solutely necessary to attack the Morne Garnier,
which extremely incommoded him in his preparations for the siege of the citadel Morne Garnier
stands higher than Morne Tartenson, from which
it is separated only by a deep ravine cover'd with a
thick brush, and by a rivulet in the bottom: art
and nature join'd to render it almost impregnable.
The Enemy, on the 27th, prevented General
Monckton in his attempt, and march'd at four in
the afternoon, under the protection of their batteries, against the light-infantry and Haviland's brigade; these repuls'd the French immediately,
pass'd the ravine at their heels, and (being reinforc'd by Walsh's brigade and Grant's grenadiers)
seiz'd the French batteries, and took post. The
Enemy's regulars retir'd into the town and citadel.
The militia dispers'd themselves in the country. The
British troops avail'd themselves of this terror and
confusion, and became entire masters of Morne
Gar-

Garnier by nine o' clock at night. — The citadel being now commanded, the town in the poffeffion of the troops; and Morne Capuchin, at the fmall diftance of 400 yards from the citadel, being afterwards taken; the garrifon to the number of 800 men, beat the chamade on the 3d of February, and furrender'd the next day. The regulars were put on board the fleet, to be fent to France; the other forces were made prifoners of war till the final reduction of the ifland. Thefe feveral attacks coft the French 1000 men, in kill'd, wounded, and prifoners. The lofs of the Britifh troops amounted to no more than 96 kill'd including feven officers, 389 wounded including thirty two officers, and eleven private men miffing. Four, rank and file, died afterwards of their wounds. The gallant failors made no difficulty in carrying mortars and the heavieft fhip's cannon up fteep mountains, and even acrofs the French line of fire. — On the 7th of February, Pidgeon ifland, one of the defences of the harbour, furrender'd; and nine quarters of the ifland capitulated, on terms advantageous to the inhabitants, and honourable to the conquerors. Fourteen ftout privateers were taken in Fort-Royal Bay; and many more, in the different ports of the ifland, were to be delivered up, agreably to the capitulation. The artillery and ftores, taken in this conqueft, were confiderable. — The grenadiers in three divifions, headed by the Lieutenant Colonels Fletcher, Maffey, and Vaughan, together with the light-infantry and rangers under the command of Lieutenant-Colonel Scott, Major Leland, and Captain Kennedy, had the greateft fhare in the courfe of this fuccefs. Indeed all the troops that compos'd this brave army, exerted the fame fpirit, which the feveral corps of it had before fo providentially difplay'd, in the reduction of Louifburg, Crown-Point,

Point, Quebec, Montreal, Guadaloupe, and Bellisle.

February 4. The Actæon Captain Ourry, under the Orders of Admiral Rodney, fell in with off Tabago, and took, a large Spanish store ship of 800 tons burthen, laden with cannon, powder, small arms, and ordnance stores, for la Guayra.

February 9. Prince Lobkowitz dislodg'd the Prussians from Pegau, who lost, on that occasion, about 400 men. The Austrians had only 20 men kill'd, 26 wounded, and 15 missing.

February 11. The Boutin, a French East-India man of 460 tons, 189 men, and 20 guns, was taken by the Blonde Captain Kennedy. She came from the Mauritius, was laden with coffee and some pepper, and afterwards sold for upwards of 23,000 pounds.

February 16. General Monckton took possession of Fort St. Pierre and the rest of the Island of Martinico, in virtue of a capitulation form'd and sign'd on the 13th and 14. — The defection of the inhabitants, by compelling the surrender of the fort saved the town from destruction. 320 grenadiers march'd out with the honours of war, to be embark'd immediately for France: M. le Vassor de la Touche Governor General, Monsieur Rouill Lieutenant Governor, and the staff, were to follow them soon after. In the forts, Royal and St. Pierre, the redoubts, and the batteries, there were found 436 pieces of serviceable cannon of different sizes, and 1463 serviceable barrels of powder, including fill'd cartridges for cannon, together with a proportionable quantity of all other stores, an munition

munition, and implements of war. Few places, so strong and important as Martinico, have been entirely subdued with such an inconsiderable loss on the part of the victors. Soon after this conquest, the island of Santa Lucia surrender'd to Captain Hervey at discretion.

February 19. The Dromedaire, a French East Indiaman, bound from Port L'Orient to the Isle of France, was wreck'd on St. Vincent, one of the Cape de Verd Islands. Out of 150 men, 86 only were saved, among whom there were three officers.

February 20. The Austrians and Imperialists dislodg'd the Prussians from the post of Lomatsch, and burnt a magazine.

March 3. A Spanish ship, taken by the Richmond, Captain Elphinstone, in her passage to the West-Indies, was brought into Madeira. This ship came from the Havannah, and had, on board, 100 tons of Campeachy logwood, 2000 raw hides, and about 70,000 dollars, besides indigo, coffee, and bale goods. She was call'd Il Castill de la Marr, and her Captain offered to ransom her for 60,000 pounds sterling.

March 4 and 5. The Island of Grenada, together with the Grenadillas and their dependencies, surrender'd to Brigadier General Walsh and Commodore Swanton, upon the terms granted to Martinico. This conquest was made without the loss of a man; though the fort, and the intrench'd hills above it, might have been more obstinately defended. Brigadier Walsh afterwards took possession of the island of St. Vincent.

March 11. The St. Prieft, a French Eaft-Indi[a]
man, of 700 tons burthen, carrying 230 men, paf[-]
fengers included, bound from the Ifle of Bourbo[n]
to Port L'Orient, was taken by the Valiant Com[-]
modore Keppel, (one of Sir George Pococke's fqua[-]
dron) and brought into Plymouth, by the Burford
Captain Gambier. Her cargo confifted principall[y]
of coffee and pepper.

March 13 and 14. A Spanifh frigate, call'd l[a]
Ventura, of 26 guns (12 pounders) on one deck
and 300 men, commanded by Captain Don Jofepl[h]
de las Cafas, attacked, and was taken by, the Fowe[y]
of 24 guns (nine pounders) having on board onl[y]
134 men, two of whom were fick and incapable o[f]
fervice, Jofeph Mead Efquire commander. Th[e]
frigate was on her return to the Havannah, fron[n]
whence fhe had been fent with money for the pay[-]
ment of the Catholick King's troops at Porto Ric[o]
and St. Domingo. The engagement began at th[e]
diftance of fix or feven leagues from Cape Tibe[-]
rone, and lafted for about an hour and an hal[f]
when both fhips fheer'd off to repair the damag[e]
they had received; at ten o' clock at night, Caf[p-]
tain Mead bore down a fecond time upon the Ver[-]
tura, and exchang'd a few broadfides with her[,]
but the darknefs preventing him from forming [a]
fatisfactory judgment of her motions and difianc[e]
he made fail to windward, and kept his men [at]
quarters to obferve her, as clofely as poffible, durin[g]
the night. On the dawn of the next morning, th[e]
engagement was renewed for the third time, whe[n]
the Fowey went as near to the Ventura as fhe cou[ld]
do, without falling on board of her: the difpu[te]
was long, and well maintain'd; at laft, about ha[lf]
an hour paft eight, the Spanifh frigate ftruck h[er]

colours; she was reduced almost to a wreck, and had receiv'd several shot between wind and water, one of which was afterwards discover'd to have penetrated into her magazine. The Fowey was so much damag'd in her masts and rigging, that she was obliged to undergo a thorough repair at Jamaica. When the Ventura struck, neither ship had a boat that would swim, or tackles left to hoist one out with. By nailing a tarpaulin over the shotholes of a small boat, Captain Mead contriv'd to get a Midshipman and six men on board the prize, and to receive the Captain of the ship, the Captain of the soldiers, and six or seven more prisoners on board the Fowey. The Midshipman employ'd good usage, and some finesse, to induce the Spaniards to co-operate with him in bringing the Ventura into Port-Royal harbour. The Ventura lost about 40 or 50 men in this action. The Fowey had 10 killed and 24 wounded; two of the latter, died soon afterwards of their wounds. The Lieutenant, two Mates, and 24 private sailors, were in the harbour. The Master got drunk, and disappointed the Captain of his assistance, and the gunner was wounded in the first part of the engagement. Under all these disadvantages, the capture of so strong a frigate, may be justly reckon'd among the gallant actions of the war. Mr. Mead, when he was an inferiour Officer, serv'd under Mr. Mostyn, and was the inventor of a machine for cleaning a ship's bottom at sea, known to the sailors by the name of Mead's Hog. While he commanded the Crown store ship, he gave repeated proofs of his diligence and conduct. He is the Author of a little pamphlet, intituled "*An essay on currents at sea:*" for which he receiv'd the thanks of the Lords of the Admiralty.

March 17. The squadron which sailed from Brest on the 24th of January, under the orders of the Count de Blenac, arriv'd at Cape François in Hispaniola. It was compos'd of one ship of 80 guns three of 74, three of 64, three of 32, and one of 16; and had on board, the regiments of Foix Quercy, and Boullonois, amounting to 2000 men, commanded by the Viscount de Belsunce, the Chevalier de St. Croix, and the Count de la Tour Auvergne. The Dragon of 64 guns, belonging to this squadron, was lost in attempting to enter the harbour, but the men, artillery, and stores, were saved.

April 3 and 4. The Hussar frigate attack'd four ships, lying under a fort in Tiberone Bay; one of them of 16 guns was burnt, another of 14 sunk the third of 16, and the 4th of twelve, laden with flour and indigo, were cut out, and carried into Jamaica. The Hussar had one man kill'd and 1 wounded, The French, 17 kill'd and 35 wounded The crews of the Enemy's ships, got on shore in their boats, during the engagement.

April 6. General Luckner at the head of 160 horse, came up with the Marquis de Lortang who was retreating to Gottingen with 1800 horse and 2000 foot, and immediately fell upon the rear of this corps, kill'd 30, took 80 prisoners and brought of 100 horses. About the same time a French Officer and 50 Hussars, were taken by Major Wintzingerode, in the Country of Eichsfeld

April 19. The Castle of Arensberg, defended M. Muret, surrender'd at discretion to the Hereditary Prince of Brunswick. 231 men, exclusive

9 Officers, were made prisoners, and 26 pieces of cannon taken.

May — The Huffar frigate Captain Carket being on a cruize off Hispaniola, struck upon the shore, and was lost: three men were drowned; the Captain and the rest of the crew were taken prisoners.

May 5. A treaty of peace was sign'd at Petersbourg, by the Baron de Goltze in the name of the King of Prussia, and by the Count de Woronzof Great-Chancellor, in the name of the Emperor of Russia.

May 7. The Achilles, Captain Teague, with a cargo valued at 60 or 70,000 pounds, was burnt, by accident, off Carthagena.

May 9. By accounts receiv'd from Duffeldorp of this date, it appear'd that the Hereditary Prince of Brunfwick had difpers'd the corps of M. Conflans which was at Elberfeld, and had taken hoftages to fecure the payment of thofe contributions, which he had demanded of the Duchy of Berg.

May 9. A powder magazine having blown up at Miranda de Douro, a city of Portugal in the province of Tralos Montes, whilft the Marquis de Sarria, commander of the Spanifh forces, was preparing to befiege it; the Portugueze Governor determin'd to capitulate. Upwards of 800 men, were either deftroy'd by the explofion, or obliged to furrender prifoners of war.

May 12, 13, 14. Prince Henry of Pruffia furpriz'd the left wing of the Auftrians near Dobeln in Saxony,

Saxony, and took General Zetwitz, 43 officers, and 1536 men prisoners, together with three pieces of cannon. He afterwards made himself master of Freyberg, where he found a considerable magazine. The Austrian General Maquire retir'd from Freyberg to Dippoldswalda. The account, receiv'd in England, of some subsequent successes, was never confirm'd.

May 21. The Active frigate Captain Sawyer, and the Favourite sloop Captain Pownal, took off Cape St. Vincent, and carried into Gibraltar, the Hermione, a Spanish register ship of 26 or 28 guns, bound from Lima to Cadiz. On board this ship there were 2,600,000 hard dollars, registred for the Court of Madrid. Her whole cargo was of an immense value.

May 21. General de Luzinsky possess'd himself of Chemnitz, after having defeated the Prussian Major General de Bandemer, and taken one Lieutenant Colonel, 14 Officers, and about five or six hundred private men prisoners. The Austrians obtain'd other considerable advantages, on that day and the 24th, near Wilsdruf.

May 22. A treaty of peace was sign'd at Hamburgh, between the Kings of Sweden and Prussia, by their respective Plenipotentiaries.

May 23. Portugal declared war against Spain and France ; and soon afterwards Spain declared war against Portugal.

May 25. La Lagera, one of the King of Spain's galleys was driven on shore by the Warspight, afterwards

terwards brought off by the ſhip's boats, and carried into Gibraltar.

May 26. Lieutenant Colonel de Belgrady with 300 men, under the orders of Colonel Torreck, fell upon three Pruſſian ſquadrons and 200 foot, by ſurprize, near Freyberg; kill'd many, made near 80 priſoners, diſpers'd the reſt, and took all their Baggage.

May 29. M. de Magyary attack'd a Pruſſian poſt at Schluben, cut in pieces 21 men, made 69 priſoners, officers included, moſt of them belonging to the regiment of Dingelſtedt, and took 145 horſes.

May 31. Major General M. de Kleefeld, under the orders of General de Luzinſki, attack'd Colonel Dingelſtedt, near Gerinſwalde, and oblig'd him to retreat to the poſt of Waldheim, with the loſs of 189 men made priſoners, including five officers. The Auſtrians had only 6 kill'd, and 40 wounded.

June 2. The Pruſſian advanc'd poſts in Saxony, were attack'd by Marſhal Serbelloni and General Reid. According to letters from Prince Henry's army, the Pruſſians repulſed the enemy, with the ſmall loſs of 200 men; but the Auſtrian account ſeem'd to be the moſt authentic, which ſaid, that the loſs of the Pruſſians conſiſted in 3 Majors, 26 officers, and upwards of 450 private men made priſoners, near 500 deſerters, and two pieces of cannon taken.

June —— The garriſon of Teſchen in upper Sileſia, conſiſting of 200 men, ſurrender'd to the Pruſſian General Werner.

June 10 and 11. Colonel de Torreck made 60 Prussian Hussars prisoners, near Mitweyda.

June 20. The Brilliant privateer, Captain Crichton, together with the York privateer of Bristol, a sloop of 10 three pounders, silenc'd a fort upon Cape Finisterre, mounting two 18 pounders and eight 9 pounders, struck the Spanish, and hoisted English colours, sunk two vessels in the harbour, and brought away four others laden with wine for the Spanish fleet at Ferrol. The privateers had 2 men kill'd and 12 wounded.

June 20. France declar'd War against Portugal.

June 24. Prince Ferdinand surprised and defeated the French army commanded by the Marshals D'Etreés and Soubise, in their camp at Graebenstein. General Luckner with six battalions of grenadiers, four squadrons of dragoons, and his own regiment of Hussars, marched from Hollenstadt near the Leine to Mariendorf, formed between the last place and Udenhausen, and attacked the Marquis de Castries in the rear, who was posted at Carlsdorf to cover the right wing of the French: at the same time General Sporcken, with twelve Hanoverian battalions and a body of cavalry, charged this corps of the enemy in flank; having marched from Sielem, over the Dymel, and formed between Hombrexen and Udenhausen. The Marquis de Castries retired with small loss; and the two Hanoverian Generals continued their march, in order to take the camp at Graebenstein both in flank and rear: Lord Granby with the reserve under his command, crossed the Dymel at Warbourg, and passing by Zieremberg and Ziebershausen, possessed

seſſed himſelf of an eminence oppoſite to Furſten-wald, and was prepared to fall upon the enemy's left wing: Prince Ferdinand paſſed the Dymel, marched through the Langenberg, and came upon the centre of the French which occupied an advantageous eminence. In this critical ſituation, the enemy ſtruck their tents and retreated. M. de Stainville preſerved their whole army by throwing himſelf into the woods of Wilhelmſtahl, and ſacrificing the flower of his infantry to cover the retreat. The grenadiers of France, the royal grenaniers, and the regiment of Aquitane, ſuffered ſeverely in this action. M. Reideſel intirely routed the regiment of Fitz-James, horſe. The Britiſh troops conſiſted of the grenadier guards, the firſt, ſecond, and third battalions of guards, Welſh's and Maxwell's grenadiers, Hodgſon's and Barrington's regiments, Keith's and Campbell's Highlanders, Fraſer's Chaſſeurs, the blues, and Elliot's horſe. The firſt battalion of grenadiers belonging to Colonel Beckwith's brigade diſtinguiſh'd itſelf extremely. Lord Granby behaved with his uſual intrepidity, and had a great ſhare in the victory. The loſs of the Allies amounted to 108 killed, 271 wounded, and 318 miſſing; in all, 697; of whom 437 were Britiſh. Two pieces of cannon and three ammunition waggons were taken by the Enemy. Some ſtandards and colours fell into the hands of the Allies. Lieutenant Colonel Townſhend of the firſt regiment of Foot Guards, was the only Officer of diſtinction who fell in this engagement. The French retreated under the cannon of Caſſel; and a great part of their army afterwards paſſed haſtily over the Fulda. They owned the loſs of near 900 men killed and wounded; and it appeared, by an account in the London Gazette, that the number of their priſoners amounted to 2732,

among

among whom there were 5 Colonels of the grenadiers of France, the Viscount de Broglie, and 156 other Officers. The Chevalier de Narbonne Lieutenant Colonel in the Royal grenadiers, was killed. The Duc de Picquigny and the Marquisses of Peyne and la Roche Lambert were wounded. The Chevalier de Muy and many general officers lost their baggage. The corps de reserve under Prince Xavier of Saxony, which was encamped near Dransfeld in the territory of Hanover, retired over the Werra and joined the French main army, with the loss of its hospital, baggage, medicines, and the escorte that conducted them. After the action, Prince Ferdinand occupied Fritzlar, Feltzberg, Lohr, and Gudensberg.

June 25. The Hereditary Prince of Brunswick at the head of 400 horse, attacked the French troop of Conflans at Recklinghausen, but was repulsed with the loss of 20 men killed and 200 taken prisoners.

June — Major General Grant, Commandant of Neisse in Silesia, defeated an Austrian corps near Otmachau; and made General Draskowitz and several officers, together with 400 men, prisoners of war.

June 27. The Robuste of 74 guns, L'Eveille of 64, La Garonne of 44, and the Licorne of 30, together with a bomb ketch, landed a body of troops under the Count de Hansonville in the bay of Bulls in Newfoundland; and after possessing themselves of the small settlement in that bay, they march'd directly for St. John's Fort, which surrendered on the 27th; the garrison and inhabitants capitulating to be prisoners during the war, unless sooner exchanged,

changed, and to be secure in their persons and properties. Every thing in the Northern Harbors of service to the fishery was destroyed. These ships commanded by M. de Ternay, fell in, on the eleventh of May, with the East India, West India, and North American fleets, under convoy of the Superbe of 74 guns, the Gosport of 44, and the Danae of 38; but the French, notwithstanding the superiority of their force, declined an engagement; in order to reserve their full strength for the expedition against Newfoundland.

July 1. The brigades of infantry and cavalry under M. de Rochambeau near Hombourg, were attacked and defeated by the brigade of the British grenadiers, Elliot's horse, the Blues, and four Hanoverian squadrons, all commanded by Lord Granby. Elliot's regiment made the first charge, and was in great danger; till Colonel Harvey at the head of the Blues passed the village of Hombourg on full gallop, overthrew every thing in his way, and came seasonably to its rescue. These two gallant regiments maintained an unequal combat till the arrival of the infantry, when the Enemy retreated in the utmost hurry. The loss of the Allies in killed, wounded and taken, fell short of 100 men; that of the French was considerable; the number of prisoners alone amounting to upwards of 250. Lord Frederic Cavendish's corps came up during the retreat; and the Hussars of Baver and Reidesel push'd on to Rothenbourg, where they destroyed a considerable magazine. The Colonels Harvey and Erskine, and the Majors Forbes and Ainsley, distinguish'd themselves greatly in this engagement.

July 2. Lieutenant Colonel Riedefel burnt 150,000 rations of hay, 40,000 rations of oats, and carried off 70 fat oxen belonging to the French.

July 3. The army under the Prince of Conde, made Major Scheiter, two officers, and upwards of 120 men, prifoners of war; and afterwards took the little village of Rhene where they found fome fmall magazines.

July —. Captain Bonell of the Harriot packet-boat was attacked in his paffage from New York to Falmouth, by a French privateer of a much fuperior force in guns and men, which he repulfed two different times, and at laft got clear off. The poft-office acknowledged the Captain's bravery by promoting him to the command of a Lifbon packet, and by making him a prefent of 100 guineas which he generoufly diftributed among the crew.

July 6. General Neuwiedt, or the Count de Wied, made three unfuccefsful attacks upon the Auftrian General Brentano, who guarded the defiles of Adelfbach with 8000 men. The cannonade continued from three in the morning till after eight. His Pruffian Majefty was prefent, and much expofed during the whole attack: he loft upwards of 1000 men in killed, wounded, and prifoners. The Baron de Tillier, Mr. de Riefe, and Mr. de Fabris, diftinguifhed themfelves on the part of the Auftrians.

July 6 and 7. According to accounts from the French army, M. de Viomenil under the orders of the Prince of Condé ruined, without the lofs of a man,

man, many magazines of the allied army upon the lower Embs and the Haze, to the amount of 76 loaded waggons, 62,800 facks of grain, 46,880 facks of oats, and 400,000 rations of hay. The total lofs was computed at four millions of livres. A very fmall party of the French deftroy'd, foon afterwards, one of the largeft magazines on the Embs, confifting of near two millions of rations of forage.

July 7. The Count de Wied penetrated to Weiffe in Bohemia, and made 300 Auftrians prifoners.

July 7. The corps under General de Brentano on their march to cover Braunau, engaged a fuperiour number of Pruffians near Ditterfbach; killed many men, and took feveral prifoners, with little lofs on their fide.

July — The Count de Vaux attacked and defeated a large party of M. de Luckner's corps near Uflar; made one Lieutenant Colonel, one Captain, and 81 private men prifoners, and took many horfes.

July — The French Partizan Monet with his whole corps was taken by General de Luckner, at Schaffhoff, at the diftance of 200 paces from Caffel.

July 9. The Emprefs of Ruffia was declared reigning Sovereign and Autocratrix of that extenfive Empire, in the room of her hufband Peter the third.

July

July 10. The Marquis de Chamborant destroyed part of the British bakery and provision waggons near Warbourg; rendered 20 horses unfit for service, took 210, and made the English Commissary, together with 83 other persons, prisoner of war.

July 10 and 11. The Prussian irregulars set fire to, and pillaged, the towns of Jaromirz and Konigsgratz in Bohemia. A large magazine, and some small ones, were burnt or destroyed at the latter place.

July 11. The Castle of Waldeck, eleven leagues from Cassel, surrendered to General Conway, and the garrison of 160 men capitulated on the terms of not serving against Great-Britain or her Allies for one year.

July 12 and 13. Five hundred marines of Commodore Young's squadron made a descent upon the banks of the river Orne in lower Normandy, with a design to destroy 13 vessels guarded by two batteries at the mouth of that river: they succeeded in nailing up the cannon of the batteries, but were obliged to reimbark without making any attempt upon the vessels.

July 16 and 17. M. de Valliere took 400 horses from the Allied army, and entirely defeated one of their detachments near Ulfen.

July 18. The Prussian General Kleist attacked General Plunket near Einsiedel, took 500 prisoners, and obliged him to retire to Aussig.

July

July 21. Five Transports, being Part of the second division from New York for the Havannah, having on board 350 regulars of Anstruther's regiment and 150 provincials, were taken near the passage between Maya Guanna and the North Caicos, by two French ships of the line, three frigates and fix sail of brigantines and sloops.

June 21. The King of Prussia attacked and made himself master of the fortified heights and Villages where the right of Marshal Daun's army was posted under M. de Brentano. The Austrians lost a battery of 14 cannons at Ditmansdorf, and near 1000 men were made prisoners in the several attacks, 1000 deserters returned to the Prussian Colours. The King of Prussia's loss was comparatively inconsiderable. The Austrians estimated their own at near 1400 men and 13 pieces of cannon of different bores. Schweidnitz was left to be defended by its proper force. The Russians were not in this action, but remained quiet in their camp.

July 21. General Seidlitz came up with the army of the Empire near Averbach, obliged one part to retire to Plaven and the other to Eybenstock, made upwards of 300 men prisoners, and took a quantity of baggage..

July 23. A body of Hanoverian and Hessian Troops under the command of the Generals Zastrow and Gilsen, defeated part of the right wing of the French army intrenched at Lutterberg and commanded by the Count de Lusace. The Allies marched through the Fulda up to their wasts, clambered up the mountain, took four palisaded redoubts, and drove the Saxons from all their intrenchments.

trenchments. In the mean time Major General Walthaufen gained the rear of their right flank, and took or deftroyed a whole regiment of Saxon horfe. The Enemy had many men killed in this gallant attack, and 1100 were made prifoners; among the latter was the Prince of Ifenbourg. 13 pieces of cannon and two ftandards were taken. Prince Frederic of Brunfwic entered and demolifhed the ftrong lines on the heights of Kratzberg, which were abandoned by the French upon the defeat of the Count de Luface. The enemy in their account of this affair deminifhed their own number and lofs, and almoft claimed the victory. They declared pofitively that they had taken, on their part, near 300 prifoners. The intrepidity and fpirit of the Allies cannot be difputed on this occafion; but their fuccefs was not attended, at that time, with any very advantageous confequences.

July 23. The Prince of Bevern and General Werner abandoned Troppau and Gratz.

July 23. The Pallas Captain Clements, attacked two Spanifh Chebecks at the entrance of the Bay of Cadiz, one of which was of 34 guns and the other of 24, and obliged them both to fhelter themfelves under the cannon of their own forts with confiderable lofs.

July 23. The auxiliary corps of Ruffians commanded by General de Czernichef, having feparated itfelf from the Pruffian army, repaffed the Oder at Auras on their return to the Viftula.

July 24. The Chefterfield of 44 guns and four tranfports ran on Cayo Confite, the entrance of the Bahama ftreights on the Cuba fide, an hour before
day-

day-light, and were stranded; all the seamen and troops got on shore, and were afterwards transported safe to the Havannah.

July 25. Prince Ferdinand marched up to the main Body of the French army with an intention to attack them; but finding their position too strong, he drew off his Troops after a cannonade of two hours. The French repassed the Fulda in the night according to Prince Ferdinand's expectations, and Lord Granby took possession of the heights of Melsungen, a post which the enemy had declared to be impregnable.

July 25. General Stainville with four regiments of Dragoons fell into an ambuscade at Morschen. These regiments were routed and dispersed with great loss by General Freytag, whose troops made a considerable booty on the occasion.

July 25. General Luckner made himself master of Fulda, took 200 prisoners, and carried off a booty consisting of 300 oxen, a considerable quantity of wine, and a contribution of 70,000 florins.

July 28. The Count de Stainville defeated 400 light troops of the Allies near Vacha.

July —— Messrs. de Rochechouart and de Lostanges dispersed a detachment of the Allies near Uslar, and made near 200 prisoners: they afterwards divided their forces, and took or destroyed, at Carlshaven and Beverungen, one magazine and 29 large boats laden with provisions. About the same time Mr. de Verteuil ruined another magazine at Brackel, and took 120 horses together with

with 60 soldiers and some officers. The Baron du Blaisel marched from Giessen to Amoeneburg, and surprised 400 of the Allies, whom he made prisoners of war.

August 2. The French made an unsuccessful attack, at Neu-merssen, upon the troops commanded by General Freytag.

August 2. The Prussians to the number of 12000 under the command of the Generals Seidlitz and Kleist, attacked the Prince of Lowestein at the head of 8000 Austrians near the village of Gradrop at a small distance from Toplitz in Bohemia. After a warm dispute, the former were obliged to retire with the loss of 500 killed, between 3 and 400 made prisoners, and 400 deserters. General Kleist renewed the attack the next day but with the same bad success; upon which he evacuated Bohemia. The Prussians gave a different account of this affair, asserting that they engaged the enemy with an inferiour force, that they had taken 400 men prisoners, and that their whole loss in killed, wounded, and missing, amounted only to 200 men. The Austrian relation appeared to be the most credible.

August 2, 3, 4. The Prussians plundered the town of Dux in Bohemia; the damages they occasioned to the inhabitants amounted to 80,000 florins with little advantage to themselves.

August 4. The Tyger frigate Captain Fabre, from St. Domingo for Bourdeaux, of 26 nine pounders and near 240 men, valued at between two and three millions of livres, was taken by the King George privateer Captain Read of 26 nine
pounders

pounders and 130 men, after an engagement of two hours and an half. The Tyger had about 80 men killed and wounded; the King George only three killed and thirty two wounded. This important Service was not the first which the gallant Captain Read had rendered to his Country.

August 7. Eight hundred Men under the Count de Stainville threw red hot balls into the castle of Friedwalde, made the garrison of 50 men prisoners of war, plundered the village, and stripped the inhabitants of all their substance. This castle is three leagues distant from Hirschfeld.

August —. The St. Peter, a packet of 14 guns and 60 men, bound from St. Sebastians to the Caricoas, was taken by the Dreadnought privateer of Bristol.

August 7. Prince Frederic of Brunswick possessed himself of Muhlhausen, Eschwege, and Wanfried, behind the French army.

August 7 and 8. M. de Conflans attacked the town and redoubt of Pattenberg, took possession of that post, and made 72 men prisoners of war.

August 8. Eight battalions of regulars and 1000 croats sallied out upon the Prussians before Schweidnitz, routed the battalion of Falkenhayn, made the Colonel and some officers prisoners, and killed and wounded 100 men.

August 9. Lieutenant General D'Affry made himself master of the castle of Ulrichstein, and the garrison of 110 men surrendered at discretion.

Q 3 *August*

August 10. M. de Conflans carried Frankenberg by assault, made 143 men prisoners, three officers included, and took four pieces of cannon.

August — M. de Rome, under the orders of the Marquis de Lostanges, took at Stadt-Worbes five officers, 133 grenadiers, 26 horses, the military chest of the Turkish regiment, and many carriages loaded with bread for the Allies.

August 13. The Havannah, with all its dependencies, and the ships of war and merchandize in the harbour, surrendered by capitulation to Sir George Pocock and the Earl of Albemarle. Sir George passed through the old streights of Bahama with his whole squadron, consisting of 19 ships of the line, several frigates, and a large number of transports, between the 27th of May and the evening of the 5th of June. On the 2d of June the Alarm, Captain Almes, engaged and took the Thetis of 22 guns 180 men, and the Phœnix storeship of 18 guns 75 men, together with a brigantine and a schooner, all bound to Segoa in the Streights, to load with timber for the use of the fleet at the Havannah. The Thetis had 10 men killed and 14 wounded; the Alarm 7 men killed and 10 wounded. The army under Lord Albemarle landed on the 7th of June without opposition between two forts on the rivers Bocanao and Coximar, about six miles to the eastward of Moro Castle. Captain Hervey in the Dragon silenced Coximar Castle and enabled the army to pass that river unmolested. On the 8th a small corps under Colonel Carleton repulsed and dispersed the Spanish regiments of Edinburgh dragoons, two companies of grenadiers and many officers, together with a body

body of militia on horſeback, the whole amounting to near 6000 men advantageouſly poſted upon a riſing ground between the Britiſh army and the village of Guanamacoa. On the 11th the fort of Chorera (on the weſt ſide) was abandoned by the Spaniards after having been battered by the Belliſle Captain Knight; and Colonel Carleton attacked a redoubt upon the Cavannos (an Hill above Moro Caſtle) which he carried with little reſiſtance and loſs: A poſt was eſtabliſhed here under the name of the Spaniſh Redoubt. By the 12th the Spaniards had ſunk three ſhips of the line in the entrance of the harbour's mouth, by which it was effectually blocked up and ſecured. On the 15th a detachment of 1200 men under Colonel Howe and 800 marines under the Majors Campbel and Collins were landed and encamped at Chorera about ſeven miles to the weſtward of the Havannah, where they engaged the attention of the enemy and proved of conſiderable ſervice. After the previous and neceſſary preparations were compleated, which employed the time of the army from the 12th of June to the firſt of July, the artillery began to play upon Moro Caſtle. The enemy landed on the 29th of June two detachments from the Havannah of 500 men each, conſiſting of grenadiers and choſen troops together with armed Negroes and Mulattoes, to interrupt the beſiegers in their operations. One of theſe detachments marched upon the right under the Moro; the other upon the left near the Lime-kiln, where the Beſiegers had raiſed one or two batteries to remove the ſhipping to a greater diſtance which had annoyed them conſiderably: the picquets and advanced poſts repulſed theſe detachments, wounded many, and killed or took priſoners 200 men, with the loſs only of 10 men killed and wounded on their ſide. On the firſt of of July the Cambridge of 80 guns, Dragon of 74, and Marlborough of 66, all under the command of Captain Hervey, attacked the north-east part of Moro Castle for the space of near six hours, when they were called off. The two former ships received great damage from the height of the fort, whilst the fort itself suffered very little from their fire. This attack divided the attention of the garrison, and enabled the army to obtain a superiority of guns on the land side. Captain Goostry of the Cambridge was killed in the beginning of the engagement; and his place was supplied by Captain Lindsay of the Trent, who acquitted himself with honour during the remainder of the action. The conduct of Captain Campbell of the Stirling Castle was censured by Captain Hervey, and ordered to be examined into by a court martial. 42 seamen were killed and 140 wounded in this desperate service. Captain Mackenzie of the Defiance brought the Venganza frigate of 26 guns and the Marte of 18 out of the harbour of Port Mariel, after some firing. All but 20 men had left them. The harbour of Port Mariel is about seven leagues to the leeward of Chorera, and was afterwards taken possession of by Sir George Pocock as a place of security for the shipping against the dangers of the season, in which he was at that time advanced. A schooner loaded with coffee, and bound from Hispaniola to New Orleans, fell into the hands of the cruizers belonging to the fleet. On the 2d of July the grand battery caught fire, and the labour of 5 or 600 men for seventeen days was destroyed. Had not this accident intervened, the castle would probably have been reduced in a short time. On the 11th the merlons of the grand battery again caught fire, and the whole was irreparably consumed. Amidst these difficulties, and the uninterrupted

-rupted communication which the castle maintained with the town of the Havannah and the ships, together with the nature of the soil which was all rocky, and the consequent necessity of carrying on all the approaches above ground, the siege proved a work of time. From the 17th to the 22d the besiegers proceeded against the Moro by sap and mines. About four in the Morning of the 22d, fifteen hundred men made a sally from the Havannah, divided into three parties; two of these parties were repulsed and driven back into the town; the third retreated without venturing upon an engagement. Lieutenant Colonel Stuart of the 90th regiment at the head of 30 men only, sustained the attack of one of these parties for an hour, when he was supported by about 100 sappers and the 3d battalion of royal Americans. The loss of the Spaniards was computed at near 400 men in killed, drowned and taken: That of the British troops amounted to about 50 killed and wounded; Brigadier Carleton was among the latter. On the 26th a two decked Spanish merchant ship was sunk by an Howitzer; and on the 28th a large merchant ship was destroyed by lightening in the harbour. The works were continued from the 23d to the 30th, and the usual advances were made, step by step; on the 30th two mines were sprung; one in the counterscarp; the other in the right bastion; the latter had the most considerable effect, and made a practicable breach. Orders were immediately given for the assault. Twenty two officers, 15 serjeants, and 281 rank and file commanded by the gallant Lieutenant Colonel Stuart of the 90th regiment, together with 150 sappers under a Captain's command; all sustained by 17 officers, 14 serjeants, and 150 rank and file, making in the whole 499 men; mounted with the greatest

reso-

resolution, formed expeditiously on the top of the breach, drove the enemy from every part of the ramparts, and planted his Majesty's standard upon the bastion. Thus fell Moro Castle after a siege of 29 days. Of the Spaniards, Don Louis de Velasco, Captain of the Reyna, Colonel and Commander in chief of the castle, was mortally wounded in defending the colours sword in hand; a brave officer, deservedly regretted both by friends and enemies; the Marquis Gonzales Captain of the Aquilon, Colonel and second in command in the castle, was killed; their loss in the assault amounted to 343 killed or drowned, 37 wounded, and 326 made prisoners; in all, 706. The loss of the British troops was trifling, consisting in 14 killed and 28 wounded. On the 10th of August in the morning, the batteries being prepared to play from the Cavannos on the east side, and ground being ready to be opened on the west side, Lord Albemarle summoned the Governor of the Havannah to capitulate, who returned a civil but resolute answer; the next day, the artillery men and sailors silenced, in about six hours, all the guns in the Punta Fort and the north bastion of the town. The Governor hung out a white flag and beat a parley. The capitulation was signed on the 13th, by which the town of Havannah with all its dependencies surrendered to his Majesty's arms; *all* ships in the harbour, *all* money and effects *whatever* belonging to the King of Spain; all the artillery, arms, ammunition, and naval stores without reserve, and all the Catholick King's slaves, were to be delivered up to Sir George Pocock and Lord Albemarle; the regular troops, sailors and marines, all making part of the garrison, were to be transported to the nearest port of old Spain at the expence of his Britannic Majesty; and the militia were

were to deliver up their arms to the Commiffary appointed to receive them. The Tigre, Reyna, Soverano, Infante, and Aquilon of 70 guns, the America, Conqueftado, San Genaro and Santo Antonio of 60 guns, fell into the hands of the conquerors; the Neptuno of 70, the Afia of 64, and the Europa of 60, were funk in the entrance of the harbour; there were two more fhips of war on the ftocks, and feveral merchant fhips. The regulars who capitulated, were compofed of the fecond regiment of Spain, the fecond regiment of Arragon, the Havannah regiment, artillery companies, Edingburgh and Havannah dragoons, amounting to 936, exclufive of the prifoners on board the men of war, and the fick and wounded on fhore. In the courfe of the fiege, the lofs of the Britifh troops confifted in eleven officers, 15 fergeants, 4 drummers, and 260 rank and file killed; 19 officers, 49 fergeants, 6 drummers, and 576 rank and file wounded; 39 officers, 14 fergeants, eleven drummers, and 632 rank and file dead of difeafes and the climate; and one fergeant, 4 drummers, with 125 rank and file miffing; 4 officers, 1 drummer, and 51 rank and file died of their wounds. The whole amounted to 1822. The officers of note were, the Lieutenant Colonels Thomas, Gordon, and Leith; the Majors M' Neil, Mirrie, and Ferron; the Captains Suttie, Tyrwhitt, Schaak, M' Donald, Menzies, Crofton, Windus, and Goreham *dead*; Captain Strachey *killed*; Brigadier Carleton and the Captains Balfour, Morris, Spendlove and Gordon, *wounded*. 351 pieces of brafs and iron ordnance were found in the Moro Caftle, Punta, and the town of Havannah. Major General Keppel commanded the attack of the Moro Caftle. Sir George Pocock, Commodore Keppel, Lieutenant-General Elliot, in particular; and, in general, every officer, soldier, and sailor, carried on the service with the greatest spirit and zeal. The seamen chearfully assisted in landing cannon and ordnance stores, manning batteries, making fascines, and supplying the army with water. The unanimity which subsisted between the army and fleet cannot be better described than in Sir George Pocock's own Words. "Indeed," says he, "it is doing injustice to both, to mention them as two corps; since each has endeavoured, with the most constant and chearful emulation, to render it but one; uniting in the same principles of honour and glory for their King and Country's service." This capture of 12 great ships of the line, (including the three which were sunk) besides two men of war on the stocks, three frigates, and an armed storeship, was a more severe blow to Spain than that which she felt from England in 1718, when Sir George Byng and Captain Walton took or burnt off Cape Passaro and on the coast of Sicily, one ship of 74 guns, one of 70, four of 60, two of 54, one of 44, three of 40, one of 36, one of 30, and one of 24; in all, 15. And if the situation of the Havannah, and the treasure found in it, are considered; perhaps it may be safely affirmed, that the Spaniards have not suffered such a sensible and humiliating loss since the defeat of their celebrated Armada. — An account of the killed and wounded seamen had not been collected, when the express left the Havannah. — The narrow pass between the town and castle having been closely watched, a letter was intercepted from the Governor of the former to the Governor of the latter, desiring him to maintain himself in the possession of the castle, and expressing his own inability to make any defence. After the castle was gallantly taken by assault, Lord Albemarle

bemarle acquainted the Governor of the town that he had been well informed of the weak state of the place, and that it would save much bloodshed to surrender; this was refused. Lord Albemarle afterwards sent his own letter to him, which immediately brought on the capitulation.

August 16. The corps of the Duke of Bevern posted upon the heights of Peile beyond Reichenbach, was attacked about 5 o' clock in the afternoon by 33 battalions, eleven regiments of cavalry, and three of Hussars, commanded by the Generals Beck, Brentano, Lascy, and Odonel, under the orders of Marshal Daun; the view of the Austrians was to relieve Schweidnitz. The Duke of Bevern maintained his ground with resolution, till the King of Prussia came in Person to his assistance, with 30 battalions and 8 squadrons. His Majesty charged and defeated the five regiments of cavalry under General Odonel, after a warm and obstinate dispute. Night coming on, the Austrians abandoned their design. According to the Prussian account, the total loss of the Austrians exceeded 2000 men. Five standards fell into the hands of the conquerors. The Austrians asserted that, on their part, they had taken 500 prisoners, and two pieces of cannon, and reduced their own loss to 17 officers wounded or prisoners, 131 private men killed, 354 wounded, and 336 missing, in all 1838. They owned that the Prussians had made themselves masters of three standards. It was said that General Lauhdon commanded the vanquished troops.

August 16. The garrison of Gottingen destroyed the fortifications of that place, and retired to Witzenhausen; having first set fire to the powder magazine,

gazine, by the explosion of which 50 Saxons were killed. The enemy left in Gottingen three brass guns and a great quantity of ammunition of all kinds.

August 17. The French abandoned Munden in the night.

August ⸺ M. Conflans was dislodged from Padberg or Pattenberg by Colonel Riedesel, with the loss of a Captain, seventy private men, and many horses.

August 22. The hereditary Prince of Brunswick charged the vanguard of the Prince of Conde under the orders of M. de Levis. The French lost about 150 men on this occasion.

August 25. The Marquis d'Auvet bombarded Ham, ruined several houses, and retreated upon the approach of 4000 men from the allied army.

August 25. The Prince of Conde gained an inconsiderable advantage over the hereditary Prince of Brunswick, and obliged him to retreat after a smart cannonade, with the loss of three field pieces.

August 25. The principal operations of the Spaniards from their first invasion of Portugal to this date, may be related in few words. They made themselves masters of Miranda, Braganza, Torre di Moncorvo, and Chaves. They demolished the fortifications of the two former cities, and left a strong garrison in the latter. They divided their forces, which were in the Province of Tras-os-Montes, into three parts; the principal body was

en-

encamped near Miranda; the second, consisting of 5000 men, at Torre di Moncorvo; the third of the same number near Chaves. Another corps of 8000 men entered the Portugeze frontier near Almeyda; this corps suffered by desertion, and its detached parties were often repulsed by the militia of the country. The summer months in that warm climate are unfavourable to military expeditions; and the Spaniards could do little more than chastise the peasants of several villages, whose natural aversion overcame the oath of obedience which they had taken, and who did every thing in their power to cut off the convoys of provisions designed for their camp: *These*, and the Portugueze companies called auxiliaries, were easily defeated and dispersed. At last the Spaniards formed the siege of Almeyda, a frontier town in the province of Trasos-montes, 16 miles distant from the Spanish city of Cividad Rodrigo. On the 25th of August the fortress was surrendered, after a siege of nine days, and before a practicable breach had been made, by the Governor Alexandro de Pallares Coello de Brito, for which he was afterwards put under confinement at Coimbra. 1500 regulars and 2000 peasants were permitted to retire with the honours of war, on the condition of not serving against the King of Spain or his Allies for six months. 83 pieces of brass cannon, eleven of iron; 9 brass mortars for bombs; 31 brass mortars and one of iron for grenades; 700 quintals of powder and other implements of war, together with a quantity of ammunition and provisions, were found in the place.

August 26. The Hunter sloop cruising off the Texel, fell in with four Dutch ships under convoy of a man of war, and desired leave to search them;
but

but was refused: the Hunter, on proper signals being made, was joined between the 23d and the 26th by the Trial sloop, the Diana, and the Chester, and two cutters. Captain Adams of the Diana, acting as Commodore, politely demanded the usual permission to search the merchantmen; but the Commander of the Dutch man of war persisted in his refusal; upon this Captain Adams prepared himself for force, and ordered the boats of the ships, with an English jack hoisted in each of them, to search the convoy, threatening the Dutch Captain with a broadside if he insulted the English flag. The Dutchman immediately fired two shot at the Hunter's boat, which were answered by a single shot from Captain Adams, and returned by the Dutchman's whole broadside. Thus the engagement commenced between them, which lasted about 15 minutes; the man of war and convoy struck, and were brought into the Downs. Not one man was killed or wounded on board the Diana; two men were killed on board the Dutchman; and the Captain, with two others wounded. The frigate was called the Dankbaarheld of 26 guns, commanded by Solomon Dedel the younger; she did not strike, according to the Dutch account, till she had received the fire of the Chester.

August 27. Brigadier General Burgoine, ordered part of his regiment of light dragoons to push into the Spanish town of Valença d' Alcantara sword in hand. The guards in the square were all killed or made prisoners before they could use their arms; after the body of the English regiment was come up and formed in the square, some desperate parties attempted an attack; but all of them were destroyed or taken. The General gave no quarter to those who fired single shots from the windows
of

of the houses; at last he forced some Priests through the town, to declare to the people that he was determined to set fire to it at the four corners, unless all the doors and windows were instantly thrown open. This menace had the desired effect. Major General Don Michael d' Irumberri and Balança, with his Aid de Camp; one Colonel and his Adjutant; two Captains, 17 Subalterns, and 59 private men were made prisoners; the rest of the regiment of Seville were destroyed. Three colours were taken. The dragoons were sent into the country to bring in all who had escaped. A detached servant, and six men only, fell in with a Spanish subaltern and 25 dragoons, who were unbroken and prepared to receive them; of these, they killed six, made the rest prisoners, and took every horse. The loss of the English in the attack of Valença was inconsiderable; one Lieutenant, one Serjeant, and three private men were killed; two Serjeants, one Drummer, and 18 private men were wounded. Ten horses were killed, and two wounded. Brigadier Burgoyne and Colonel Somerville gallantly conducted the troops in person; the British grenadiers under the command of Lord Pulteney dislodged the enemy's infantry from the houses; and Captain Singleton distinguished himself in this affair. The Spanish officers themselves publickly commended the generosity of General Burgoyne in handsome terms.

August 30. The hereditary Prince of Brunswick and General Luckner with 19 battalions and 40 squadrons, engaged the different corps under the Prince of Conde, Count Stainville, and the Chevalier de Levis, near Neuheim and Friedberg. The French were at first driven from the steep mountain of Johannes-berg into the plain below, by the vigorous charge of the allies; but the grand army of France under the Marshals D'Etrees and Soubise having sent them a considerable reinforcement, the attack was renewed with vivacity and success. The Allies, repulsed in their turn, were obliged to repass the Wetter. The hereditary Prince was wounded in the hip, whilst he was endeavouring to rally his disordered troops. Prince Ferdinand, better informed of the situation of the French army than the hereditary Prince appears to have been, marched with a considerable part of his forces from his camp at Nidda to the support of the Allies; he came in time to prevent the Enemy from pushing their advantage. Major General Elliot's dragoons and the chasseurs under Lord Frederick Cavendish were the only Brittish troops concerned in this action. Colonel Clinton was wounded; yet he continued with the gallant hereditary Prince two hours afterwards; and did not discover his misfortune, till the Prince desired him to carry an account of the battle to Prince Ferdinand, which obliged him to acknowledge that he was rendered incapable of executing his commands. On the part of the enemy, M. de la Guiche Lieutenant General and Commander of the brigade of Boisgelin, was taken prisoner. The French troops in general exerted themselves on this occasion with intrepidity and spirit. The regiment of Boisgelin had a particular share in the sufferings and glory of the day. The loss of the enemy, according to their own estimate, did not exceed 500 men in killed and wounded; whilst they calculated that of the allies at about 600 killed and 1500 prisoners (including 400 wounded) besides two standards and fifteen pieces of cannon taken. A letter from Prince Ferdinand's head quarters confessed only the loss of 1398 men killed, wounded, and prisoners,

soners, together with ten small pieces of cannon. The French, accustomed to defeat, demonstrated their sense of this Victory by publick rejoycings. M. de Boisgelin, Colonel of the regiment of his own name, who carried the news to Versailles, was promoted to the rank of Brigadier General.

September 1. The Duke de Nivernois was appointed Minister Plenipotentiary to Great Britain.

September 2. Captain Lebras in the Lion, took the Zephyr frigate of 26 guns, which had on board 200 troops, brass mortars and cannon, ammunition and stores, and was bound from Brest for St. John's in Newfoundland.

September 2. The St. Joseph, a Spanish ship of above 1200 tons, capable of carrying 60 guns and mounting 32, bound from the Caraccas to Port Passage with a cargo of hides and cocoa, was attacked in Aviles Bay by the Æolus Captain Hotham. The enemy took to their boats, and abandoned the ship, after a very faint resistance. The ship being now in the possession of the English, the Spaniards quitted a battery of three guns erected upon an eminence, and Lieutenant Campbell with a party of marines went on shore in the evening and spiked the guns. This valuable prize unfortunately bulged in the night, and was burnt by the orders of Captain Hotham.

September 4. The Duke of Bedford was appointed Minister Plenipotentiary to France.

September 9 and 10. A detachment of the French army harassed the Allies in their retreat, drove

two

two battalions out of Laubach, and took some pontoons and baggage.

September 11. The Austrian Colonel de Lanius attacked, with an inferior force, the Prussian General le Grand, Commandant of Neisse, near Sandhubel; and obliged him to retreat with precipitation to Neisse after the loss of 121 killed, 103 made prisoners, and two pieces of cannon taken. Only 7 Austrians were killed and 40 wounded.

September 13. The Prussians under General Schmettau took Zittau, after having permitted the garrison to retire to Gabel: they abandoned it the next day, carried away hostages with them from that town and the neighbouring places, and returned to Gorlitz, of which they had taken possession just before.

September — General Freytag defeated, between Alsfelt and Newstadt, a body of the French under M. de St. Victor, which had attempted to intercept the bread-waggon train.

September 16. Prince Ferdinand marched to Wetter through the same routes which the Prince of Condé had opened for the French army; and on the 16th he drove the enemy's garrison out of that place, and obliged the Prince of Condé to repass the Lahne. On the same day the French abandon'd Schweinsburg.

September 18. The Humber of 40 guns ran on the south of Happysborough sands, and was entirely lost.

Sep-

September 18. Lieutenant Colonel Amherst, under the orders of Sir Jeffery Amherst, sailed with the transports from New York and got into the harbour of Halifax on the 26th of August, after the Fleet under Lord Colville had left it. Not having a sufficient number of transports with him, he took up shipping to the amount of 400 tons, reached Louisburg on the 5th of September, and sailed out of that harbour on the 7th with his whole embarkation. On the eleventh he joined Lord Colville a few leagues to the southward of St. John's; on the 13th he landed his troops at Torbay about three leagues to the northward of St. John's, drove the enemy from an hill on the opposite side of Kitty Vitty river, and took Post. On the 15th the enemy were dislodged with great resolution by Captain M'Donell, from a steep and difficult hill in the front of Colonel Amherst's advanced posts; Lieutenant Schuyler was killed, and the Captain himself wounded in this gallant affair: in the night the French fleet under M. de Ternay, equal in number to the British squadron, and superior in guns and men, made their escape by a shameful flight, after having been blocked up by Lord Colville in the harbour of St. John's for three Weeks; they afterwards got safe to Corunna. On the 16th Colonel Amherst acquainted the Count d' Hauffonville by letter, that in case he should execute his intended design of blowing up the fort when he quitted it, every man of the garrison should *then* be put to the sword. On the night of the 17th a mortar battery was opened against the fort; and the next day it capitulated, before any other batteries had begun to play. M. de Ternay, flying in the utmost confusion, left his anchors and the grenadiers of the army behind him. The garrison amounted to 689 men,

men, staff and other officers included: they capitulated on the terms of surrendering prisoners of war, and of being transported to the coast of Brittany at the expence of his Britannick Majesty. The total number of prisoners made on this occasion did not fall much short of 800; a very fine body of men, and almost as numerous as the regulars of the British army. On the part of the conquerors, one Lieutenant and eleven rank and file were killed; 3 Captains, 2 serjeants, 1 drummer, and 32 rank and file were wounded; in all, 50. Lieutenant Colonel Tullikin and Captain M'Donell were honourably mentioned by Mr. Amherst.

September 20. The French attacked, and made themselves masters of a redoubt and a mill situated upon the left bank of the river Ohm, at the foot of the mountain of Amoeneburg.

September 21. The French, favoured by a fog, opened a branch of a trench before Amoeneburg on the 20th, and established their batteries against that castle, which was occupied by a battalion of the British legion and a detachment of 200 men from the reserve of the allied army. The stone bridge over the Ohm at the Brucker-Muhl, was guarded by 200 men of Hardenberg's regiment; the greatest part of which were posted in a small work on the right of the bridge. The enemy were also in possession of a little work beyond the bridge. About these two posts there commenced a warm and bloody action on the 21st, which continued from six in the morning till dark night. A fire of cannon and small arms was kept up on both sides for fourteen hours with the utmost severity and the most determin'd resolution. There was no attempt on either part to pass the bridge. Fresh troops were

were reciprocally sent to support the posts which each maintained on the opposite banks of the river, as fast as the several reliefs had expended their ammunition. The mill occupied by the enemy, afforded rather more shelter to them, than the redoubt did to the allies. History hardly furnishes an instance of such an obstinate dispute. The execution of near 50 pieces of cannon was confined to the space of near 400 paces. The fire of the artillery and musquetry was not intermitted one single moment. On the part of the allies, 17 complete battalions were employed, at different times, in this destructive service. Lieutenant Colonel Manlove, Major M'Lean, the Captains Twisleton and Reynell, and Ensign Clive brother to Lord Clive, were killed; Lieutenant Colonel Hale, the Captains Peter Campbell and Wyvil, together with seven inferiour officers were wounded. The total loss (including that of the Hanoverian corps) amounted to 161 killed, 460 wounded, and 17 missing; in all, 638. A subsequent general account increased it to near 800. 19 horses were killed, and 4 pieces of cannon were rendered unserviceable. The French acknowledged the loss of 300 killed and near 800 wounded; among the latter were the Marquis de Castries and the Chevalier de Sarsfield. Letters from Frankfort to the Hague, received in England, made the wounded on the part of the French amount to near 2000 men.

September 22. A practicable breach having been made, the Castle of Amoeneburg surrendered to the French; and the garrison were made prisoners of war, to the number of eleven officers and 553 private men.

September 27. A small corps of the enemy under M. de Poyanne was attacked, defeated, and pursued to Alsfeldt, by Major General Freytag. The total loss of the French upon this occasion amounted to near 400 men.

September 27, 28, and 29. The Austrians and Imperialists under the orders of General Haddick, obliged the Prussians under Prince Henry to abandon their advantageous situation at Wilsdruf, Pretschendorf, Fravenstein, and Burckenheim. The attack and defence were vigorous, and the loss on each side considerable. In the night between the 29th and 30th, Prince Henry made the whole Prussian army repass the Mulda, which they did with success, and ranged themselves the next morning in order of battle on the other side of that river. The Prince afterwards retired to Freyberg, and General Hulsen towards Katzenhausen.

September 30. Major General Freytag dislodged the French from Bergemunden.

October — The Scorpion sloop was lost on the Liverpool station.

October 5 and 6. The Marquis de Sarria having solicited and obtained his dismission from the command of the Spanish army in Portugal, with the Order of the Golden Fleece in recompence of his past services, the Count d'Aranda succeeded to the post of General in chief of his Catholic Majesty's Forces. On the 28th of September the Portugueze abandoned Celorico; the Spaniards afterwards took possession of Penamacor, Salvaterra, and Segura; in the second of these places there was a
gar-

garrison of upwards of 400 men, which capitulated on the condition of not serving against the Catholic King or his allies for the term of six months. Early in October the Spaniards made themselves masters of the Defilé of St. Simon, and and of Villa Velha a Moorish castle near the Tagus: The latter was supported for some time by Brigadier Burgoyne across the river. Three hundred men and upwards, of whom the garrison was composed, surrendered prisoners of war. The Portuguese infantry under the Count de St. Iago being obliged to file off by the road of Sobreira Formosa, Lord Loudoun with four British regiments, six companies of Portuguese grenadiers, some light dragoons and Portugueze cavalry, brought up the rear-guard and kept the Spaniards in awe: The Portugueze grenadiers merited upon this occasion the approbation of Lord Loudoun, who spake of them in very handsome terms. Between the 5th and 6th of October, Colonel Lee with 100 grenadiers, 200 royal volunteers, 50 British dragoons and 50 of St. Payo's horse, all under the orders of Brigadier General Burgoyne, marched up to, attacked, and forced, a small Spanish encampment near Villa Velha, burnt some magazines, spiked up six pieces of cannon, brought off about 60 artillery mules, a few prisoners, and a quantity of valuable baggage. Lieutenant Maitland of Burgoyne's dragoons distinguished himself in this affair, and repulsed the enemy's cavalry. The loss of the British troops consisted in one corporal killed, 8 private men wounded, and one missing. By the Spanish account, one Colonel and one Ensign were wounded on their part, two Lieutenants killed, one Captain and one Sub-Lieutenant taken prisoners. The loss of their private men is uncertain. The dexterity of General Burgoyne, and the resolution of the

British

British troops commanded by Colonel Lee, deserved great commendation.

October 9. Schweidnitz capitulated to the King of Pruffia, when the trenches had been opened before it for two months and two days. Lieutenant General Guafco and his brave garrifon were obliged to furrender prifoners of war, after having made feveral fruitlefs efforts to obtain more favourable terms. On the 8th of October a grenade from the befiegers fell upon a magazine of powder, did great damage to the fort N°. 2, and blew up 205 men officers included. A mine took full effect in the night between the 8th and 9th, carried away part of the rampart, made a confiderable breach in the covered way, and filled up the ditch with the rubbifh. The garrifon marched out of the fortrefs with all military honours, layed down their arms and were made prifoners of war, and were promifed the preference in cafe of an exchange: In the courfe of the fiege they had 32 officers and 1249 foldiers killed ; 53 officers and 2223 foldiers wounded ; and the number of the prifoners of every denomination, including the fick and wounded, amounted to 238 officers and 8784 private men; in all, 10303. The artillery and military ftores found in the place were confiderable. The lofs of the Pruffians confifted in 25 officers and 1084 fubalterns and private men killed or dead of their wounds, and in 61 officers and 1845 fubalterns or private men wounded : in all, 86 officers and 2929 foldiers. M. de Griboval acted as engineer to the garrifon; and M. Le Fevre to the befiegers. Thus Schweidnitz changed its mafter for the fourth time in the progrefs of the war. The Emprefs Queen took it on the 12th of November 1757. after 16 days of open trenches; the King of Pruffia recovered

vered it on the 17th of April 1758, upon the 17th day after the opening of the trenches; General Laudohn made himself master of it by assault between the 30th of September and the 1st of October 1761, and the King of Prussia is now once more in possession of it, after a long, memorable, and destructive siege.

October 14 and 15. General Haddick and the Prince of Stolberg, attacked General Belling on the 14th in the Rathswald or the Wood of Raths, and dislodged him from that post; but the latter receiving a considerable reinforcement from Prince Henry, repulsed the enemy in his turn: On the 15th the Prussian General was charged again by the Austrians and Imperialists, before he had sufficient time to resume his posts. The dispute was sharp and continued, but in the end the Prussians were driven from the wood with loss. The regiments of Kleist and Salmouth suffered severely in the engagement. Freyberg was abandoned in consequence of this success. Prince Henry retired in two columns towards Nossen and Roswein. The Imperialists behaved with spirit. Near 2000 Prussians were made prisoners; eight or nine pieces of cannon, eight colours and two standards were taken. The Hungarian regiment of Giulay performed wonders in this engagement. The conduct and military arrangements of General Haddick and the Prince of Stolberg were spoken of by the Austrians in high terms of praise.

October —— The Austrian General de Zollern surprised, at Kirchayn in lower Lusatia, part of a regiment of cavalry under the orders of General Dingelstedt, made 300 prisoners, and took some horses belonging to the baggage.

October 20. La Folle, a French frigate of 24 guns and 250 men, was taken by the Phoenix Captain Bethell, after a chase of six hours.

October 29. Prince Henry of Prussia attacked, near Freyberg, and defeated the combined army of Austrians and Imperialists, which was commanded by the Prince de Stolberg in the absence of General Haddick. According to the Prussian account, the action began at day-break and lasted till two in the afternoon, when the enemy was entirely routed, obliged to abandon the field of battle and the town of Freyberg to the Prussians, and to retire to Dippoldswalde. On the part of the vanquished, according to the same account, Lieutenant General Baron de Rodt, one Colonel, one Major, 24 Captains, 41 Lieutenants, eleven Ensigns, 159 under officers, and 4174 private men were made prisoners; 27 pieces of cannon were taken, together with nine standards and colours. As the action continued many hours, it is reasonable to presume that the loss on both sides, in killed and wounded, could not be inconsiderable.

October 30 and 31. The French Partizan Cambefort took and plundered the City of Osnabrug, which had no garrison to defend it.

November 1. Cassel surrendered to Prince Frederic of Brunswick, after the trenches had been opened before it from the night of the 16th of October. The garrison obtained all the honours of war, and were escorted to the French army under the command of the Marshals D'Etreés and Soubise.

November 3. The preliminaries of peace were signed at Fontainebleau by the Count de Choiseul, Secretary of State for foreign affairs, on the part of France; by the Duke of Bedford Minister Plenipotentiary on the part of Great-Britain; and by the Marquis de Grimaldi Ambassador Extraordinary and Plenipotentiary from the Court of Madrid, on the part of Spain. The most Christian King rewarded the services of the Count de Choiseul in this negotiation, by creating him a Duke and Peer of France with the title of Duc de Praslin.

A list

A lift of many confiderable privateers and armed merchantmen, taken by his Majesty's ships of war from the 31st of December 1761 to the signing of the preliminaries of peace.

January.	guns.	men.	captors.
Duc d'Ayen of Dunkirk	16	120	taken by the Tweed C. Pafton.
A fmall French privateer			Tartuffe cutter.
The Bearnoife of Bayonne	14 carriage 12 fwivels	82	Richmond Capt. Elphinftone.
February.			
The Efperance of Bayonne	6 carriage	60	Æolus Captain Hotham.
The Creole of Bayonne.	8	84	Venus Captain Harrifon.
The Perla Catalana de Barcelona from Spain to St. Domingo, reported to have had 100,000 dollars on board			carried into Gibraltar by a man of war.
Le Guerrier of Bourdeaux of 500 tons	24		Arethufa Captain Vane.

	guns.	men.	captors.
Aimable Marie from Bourdeaux to St. Domingo, of 250 tons with wine and provisions.			Fame and Lyon.
The Foudroyant, a letter of marque of 450 tons from Bourdeaux to St. Domingo, with wine, provisions, and dry goods.			

March.

	guns.	men.	captors.
L' Esperance	4 carriage 6 swivels	45	Essex Captain Schomberg.
Le Bien Aimé	4 carriage	52	ditto.
L' Escureuil frigate	10	80	Fame and Lyon.
Le Villeveau from the isles of Bourbon for L' Orient, with 4000 bales of coffee.			ditto.
Le Soujon	1	45	Renown Captain Maitland,
Count d' Heronville	16	129	ditto.

	guns.	men.	captors.
The Cerbere of St. Maloe	12 carriage 16 swivels	105	Tartar Captain Knight.
The Augustin of ditto	10 carriage	80	ditto.
The Romain of Dunkirk	20	130	Essex.
Snow privateer of Bayonne	12	120	Bellona Captain Dennis.
Amabile Josepha Spanish privateer of St. Sebastians	14	183	Venus Captain Harrison.
Amabile Maria of Bourdeaux bound to St. Domingo			ditto.
The Sequier of Dunkirk	12 swivels 10 carriage	99	Adventure Captain Middleton.
L'Audacieux of Brest	10 carriage 6 swivels	104	Coventry Captain Carpenter.
Eagle of Brest	2 carriage 10 swivels	50	Diligence and Albany sloops.
La Mannen of St. Maloe	6 carriage 6 swivels	50	Looe Captain Penny.
L'Esperance of St. Maloe	6 carriage 6 swivels	66	Brilliant Captain Loggie.

	guns.	men.	captors.
Auguftine of Dunkirk	12 carriage	80	Effex.
Le Gloire of Bourdeaux with wine, flour, brandy, and bale goods	16 carriage fix pounders 10 fwivels	94	Milford C. Mann — The Captain and firft Lieutenant were killed in the Engagement.
The Domerville	8 carriage 8 fwivels	64	Renown Captain Maitland.
The Guerrier of Bayonne	10 carriage	120	Coventry Capt. Carpenter.
A French privateer	22	240	Actif.
A French privateer	18		carried into Leghorne by the Gibraltar frigate.
A valuable French Merchantman from St. John de Acre			carried into Leghorne by the Quebec.
The Bien Acquis of 250 tons from Bourdeaux to the Miffiffippi	10	160 amongft whom there were feveral principal officers	carried into Barbadoes by the Edgar.

April.

A privateer of St. Maloe	6 carriage 4 fwivels	34	Diligence Capt. Ofborne.

	guns.	men.	captors.
The Curieux of St. Maloe	6 carriage	33	Æolus and Brilliant.
The Malouin of ditto	10	80	Ditto.
The Mignion of Bayonne	8	63	Ditto.
The Grand Admiral of Bayonne	10	85	Liverpool Captain Knight.
Neuftra Senhora de la Piedad alias Golondrina	8	65	Aldborough Captain Graham.
The Duc de Fronfac armed ſhip of 420 tons (afterwards fold for 2810 pounds) with 89 regulars for Louiſiana			Mermaid.
Another ſhip of 250 tons bound for Louiſiana			Ditto.
A Spaniſh packet boat of St. Sebaſtian's with iron and flour for the Havannah	14	59	Royal William.
Le Baillen of Rochelle	14	160	Royal William.
La Minx of Rochelle	10	68	Ditto.
The Fortune from Smyrna to Marſeilles			carried into Leghorne by the Gibraltar.

	guns.	men.	captors.
L'Etoile de la Mer, a Spanish Register ship from Campeachy, worth 200,000 piastres. A piastre amounts to 3ˢ and 7ᵈ sterling			A frigate.

May.

	guns.	men.	captors.
The Jupiter of Bayonne	22 nine and six pounders. 10 swivels.	185	Looe Captain Penny.
Two large French sloops and a snow valued at upwards of 10,000 pounds			Alarm Captain Almes.
A Spanish ship of 500 tons, having a part of her loading on board estimated at upwards of 30,000l, taken near Port Omoha at the entrance of the Golfodolce in the Bay of Honduras	32 carriage		Port-Royal sloop Lieutenant Duff, together with the Westmorland privateer of 16 guns, C. Balfour Commander.

	guns.	men.	captors.
A French ship valued at upwards of 10,000 pounds			carried into Guadalupe by the Foudroyant.
The Micollet of Bayonne	14	136	Venus Captain Harrison.
A French privateer	12		
Ditto	14		Echo.
Ditto	12		
Two large prames destroyed off Dunkirk			Lowestoffe Captain Stirling.
A privateer brig of Cape François			Levant.
Nostra Senhora de Begonia of Bilboa.	16 six pounders 20 swivels	195	Venus.

June.

	guns.	men.	captors.
The Revenge of Marseilles	10	62	Pallas Captain Clements.
Le Volage of Dunkirk	2 carriage some swivels	65	Alarm cutter Lieut. Anningson.
The Mars of Marseilles	10 carriage 6 swivels	50	Dolphin Captain Keeler.

	guns.	men.	captors.
The Maria and Joſeph Spaniſh privateer.	4 carriage	30	Looe Captain Penny.
July.			
Le Serviceable of Morlaix	8	90	Mermaid Captain Watſon.
The Skuer lugſail privateer	2 carriage 6 ſwivels	46	Liverpool Captain Knight.
A rich Spaniſh ſnow			ſent into Oporto by Sir Edward Hawke's fleet.
The Duc de Broglio, with ſix ranſomers on board	14 carriage	80	Diſpatch ſloop Captain Bertie.
A Domingo merchant-man and four Spaniſh ſnows laden with wine and proviſions			Shannon frigate.
Le Jacques French privateer	2 carriage 8 ſwivels	41	Liverpool.
The Savage cutter privateer of Dunkirk	4 ſwivels	15	taken and ſunk by the Hazard ſloop Captain St. John.

August.	guns.	men.	captors.
La Dunkerquaife of Dunkirk, with ranfomers on board for 800 guineas	4 carriage 4 fwivels	30	Diana Captain Adams.
A fmall French privateer			deftroy'd by the Grace cutter.
A French lugfail privateer			Lyon cutter Lieutenant Reeves.
A merchantman from St. Domingo, richly laden.			Lynn.
A fmall privateer and two fchooners			carried into Jamaica by the Fowey Captain Mead.
September.			
The Carnabel privateer of St. Sebaftians	8 carriage	80	Venus and Lark.
La Galga of St. Sebaftian's	6	56	Juno Captain Falconer.
Duc de Penthievre, of Bayonne	14	106	Venus and Lark.
The Count de Flandre of Dunkirk	10	70	Diana.
The Galgo Spanifh privateer, pierced for 18 guns.	14	136	Venus and Lark.

	guns.	men.	captors.
The Cantabria Spanish privateer	14	115	Looe Captain Penny.
A large French frigate with military stores for Newfoundland			Dragon Captain Hervey.

October.

	guns.	men.	captors.
La Parfaite Spanish privateer	12	103	Arethusa Captain Vane.
Le Charlequint	8	30	Grace and Endeavour cutters.
The Levrette of Nantz	6	55	Cornwall Captain Mann.
The Crozon	6	36	Venus Captain Harrison.
The Amitié	18	77	Arethusa.
Le Victoire of Bayonne	12	77	Niger.

November.

Le Hercule	2 carriage 6 swivels	19	Martin sloop Captain Caldwall.

The CONCLUSION

HAVING brought down their Annals to the figning of the Preliminaries of Peace between Great-Britain, France and Spain; I thall now conclude with fome particular Obfervations. But, in the firft Place, I hope the candid Reader will pardon me, when I inform him, that I have not defcended into a minute Relation of every Circumftance which may have diftinguifhed the feveral Engagements by Land and Sea. A very entertaining French Biographer has declared, that "We ought to be diffident of "thofe Perfons who enter into a full Detail "of modern Hiftory, and penetrate into the "Secrets of the Cabinet, who pretend to give "Us an exact Account of every Battle, when "even the Generals themfelves would find "much Difficulty in doing it." The only Thing which I dare affert, is, that I have taken fome Delight in tracing the Succeffes of my Country, without forming the fmalleft Pretenfions to the Opportunities and Dignity of an Hiftorian.

—*Sumite fuper Palfa a Rerum.*

Thofe who defire a more diffufed Account, may be led, by the Dates, to the Store-Houfe of the public Papers, from which this Epitome has been generally extracted. It will be enough for the Author, that leaft he may be thought not to have abufed his own idle Identary.

The CONCLUSION.

Having brought down thefe Annals to the figning of the Preliminaries of Peace between *Great-Britain, France,* and *Spain*; I fhall now conclude with fome particular Obfervations. But, in the firft Place, I hope the candid Reader will pardon me, when I inform him, that I have not defcended into a minute Relation of every Circumftance which may have diftinguifhed the feveral Engagements by Land and Sea. A very entertaining French Biographer has declared, that "We ought to be diffident of "thofe Perfons who enter into a full Detail "of modern Hiftory, and penetrate into the "Secrets of the Cabinet; who pretend to give "Us an exact Account of every Battle, when "even the Generals themfelves would find "much Difficulty in doing it." The only Thing which I dare affert, is, that I have taken fome Delight in tracing the Succeffes of my Country, without forming the fmalleft Pretenfions to the Copioufnefs and dignity of an Hiftorian.

— *Summa fequor Faftigia Rerum.*

Thofe who defire a more diffufed Account, may be led, by the Dates, to the Store-Houfe of the public Papers, from which this Epitome has been generally extracted. It will be enough for the Annalift, if at leaft he may be thought not to have abufed his own idle fedentary

dentary Hours, whilst he was employing them in this Recapitulation of the many gallant Services performed by his Fellow Citizens in an active Military Life.

The Peace is yet in its Infancy; and before we venture to determine peremptorily upon its Stability and Continuance, it may be proper to wait till the mutual Animofities of the contending Parties have cooled by infenfible Degrees. The Sea continues in Agitation after the Storm is over; and the Waves do not immediately fubfide into a perfect Calm: Or, to exprefs myfelf in the Lines of *Statius*,

*Ut fi quando ruit, debellatafque reliquit
Eurus Aquas,* PAX IPSA TUMET, *Pontumque jacentem
Exanimis jam volvit Hiems.*

One Thing however may be afferted with Confidence; which is, that the Poverty and Diftrefs of the principal Powers of *Europe* will be ftronger Guarantees of Peace than the Faith of a modern Treaty.

Upwards of two hundred pitched Battles have been fought in *Europe* within the fpace of fourfcore Years: Few have been more bloody and lefs decifive than thofe of the War which I have been commemorating. The Fruits of the Victory near *Prague* were loft in the Defeat at *Kolin*. The celebrated Actions of *Rofbach* and *Liffa*, together with the Reduction of *Breflau* and *Schweidnitz*, coft the Enemies of the King of *Pruffia* 50,000 effective Men;

Men; Yet that very Monarch received two severe Checks from the *Auſtrians* in the Courſe of the following Year. The other Battles were attended with a Diverſity of Succeſs, and only enabled the exaſperated Adverſaries to ravage and depopulate the moſt fruitful Provinces. The *Ruſſians* were conquered at *Zorndorf*; at *Zulicau* and *Cunnerſdorf*, they triumphed in their Turn: Thouſands fell upon thouſands in thoſe long and deſperate Engagements. The *Swedes* and *Pruſſians* in *Pomerania*, were more innocent Antagoniſts; confining their Views principally to the taking and retaking of *Anclam* and *Demmin*, two weak and defenceleſs Places. The moſt diſtinguiſhed Actions of the War between the *French* and the Allies were included in a ſmall Tract of Country: The ſeveral Armies marched again and again over the ſame ſpot of Ground: In the mean time the Troops ſuffered from Fatigue and Want, and the plundered Inhabitants died of Famine. Through the Extent of the largeſt Part of *Germany*, it ſeemed a Matter of Emulation *who* ſhould occaſion the greateſt Diſtreſs. The Operations of a Campaign were ſeldom determined by the Severity of the Seaſon. Conſiderable Marches were made, and Battles given, in the Winter Months. In 1759, four thouſand Men in the *Auſtrian* and Imperial Armies periſhed through the Cold; and, without Doubt, the *Pruſſians* ſuffered in the ſame Proportion. According to an Account in the public Papers,

the

the *Austrian* Party in *Holland* confessed that they had lost 56,000 Men in that Year. The *Brussells* Gazette, which was favourable enough to the *French*, acknowledged that, in 1761, *France* expended between seven and eight Millions Sterling upon the *German* War. From this summary Relation, it appears with sufficient Evidence, that the principal Powers concerned in the War had Reason to wish for the return of Peace, in respect to their own particular Sufferings, as well as to the general Misery of Mankind.

The partial *Spaniard* entered late into the Dispute; but in the short Course of an unequal Contest, he became in a very literal Sense of the Words,

Dedecorum pretiosus Emptor.

The Reasons which the Court of *Madrid* published to the World, to justify their Invasion of *Portugal*, are hardly to be paralleled but by those which *Peter* the Great alledged against *Charles* the twelfth; viz. that he, the *Czar*, had not received sufficient Honours when he passed *incognito* through *Riga*, and that Provisions had been sold too dear to his Ambassadors. Under the Pretext of these curious Grievances, *Peter* ravaged *Ingria* with 100,000 Men. *Voltaire* observes, that the young King of *Sweden* did not dream of a different Morality for Princes and private Persons. In Truth, the Laws of Morality are equally obligatory upon Both; and Kings *may* be as virtuous as the meanest of their Subjects:

jects: In Fact, to the Shame of Christian and Catholic Monarchs, *la Queſtion de Morale ſe-mêle peu de la Conduite des Souverains*—Family Connections, and the various Diſtreſſes of *Portugal*, ought to have prevented the Deſolation of that Kingdom; But Ambition avails itſelf of thoſe Calamities which Nature reverences. A fatal Earthquake; a daring and wicked Attempt upon the Life of the Sovereign; the very dreadful Puniſhment afterwards inflicted upon the noble Families which were concerned in that Attempt; the Expulſion and total Ruin of the Jeſuits; *all theſe working together*, had weakened to a great Degree that reciprocal Affection and Confidence, which conſtitute the true Happineſs both of Prince and People. In this Ferment of Men's Minds, the Conſequences of an Irruption on the Part of *Spain* were dubious. Such an Irruption, unprovoked and cruel as it was, might have given Spirit and Power to Diſaffection; or it might have called back the Attention of the Court and Nation to their mutual Intereſt, and have at leaſt united a wretched Country before it was ſubdued. Upon the whole, it ſeems to have done neither: The King maintained his Prerogative, and the Subject abandoned himſelf to his Cowardice. The *Portugueze*, (ſome of the Peaſants and Regulars excepted) anſwered the Character which Lord *Peterborough* gave of them in one of his Letters from *Valencia*; "You may have received (ſays he) by *Italy*,
"be-

"before these come to Hand, some Letters
"which I writ in the Uncertainty of what the
"*Portugueses* might do. By all Accounts, the
"least Opposition would have made them
"turn back. It was hard enough to make
"them *walk* to *Madrid*, 'tho' meeting no Re-
"sistance." — In the Introduction to the second Part of these Annals, I expatiated with Pleasure upon the bright Pages of their History; I wish they had afforded me fresh Matter of Praise. The following Extract out of a little printed Description of *Portugal*, which I read when I was in that Country, ought to make a modern *Portugueze* blush, upon the Comparison of his Ancestors Virtue with his own Degeneracy. *Resolveo-se el Rey D. João a buscar o Exercito* Castelhano, *seguindo o parecer do Condestavel; Marchou com poucos e valerosos Soldados, e se toparão os dous Exercitos na conhecida Campanha de* Algibarrota. *Virão os Castelhanos o Exercito* Portuguez *com Desprezo, e teve entaõ Disculpa, a sua Vaidade, fundada no seu Podér. Era taõ desigual o Numero da nossa Gente, que se pode duvidar, se foy mayor Acçaõ resolver a Batalha, ou vencer. A* 14 *de Agosto do Anno de* 1385, *Dia sempre fausta na nossa Memoria, ganhamos aquella celebre Victoria, que confessaõ fielmente as Historias de Castella, escrevem com Espanto as estrangeiras, e referem as nossas com Modestia.* "The King Don *John*,
"following the Advice of the Constable, determined

"termined to go in Search of the Army of
"*Caſtile*; he marched with a ſmall Body of
" valiant Soldiers; the two Armies placed
" themſelves in the well-known Plain of *Al-*
"*gibarrota*. The *Caſtilians* looked upon the
" Forces of *Portugal* with Contempt; and, at
" that Time, their Pride, founded on their
" Power, received a juſt Puniſhment. The
" Number of our Troops was ſo unequal, that
" it may be a Matter of Doubt, whether it was
" a greater Action to reſolve upon the Battle,
" or to conquer. On the 14th of *Auguſt* in
" the Year 1385, a Day always to be ſtampt
" as a fortunate one upon our Memory, we
" gained that famous Victory, which is con-
" feſſed faithfully in the Hiſtories of *Caſtile*,
" recorded with Aſtoniſhment in thoſe of fo-
" reign Nations, and related with Modeſty in
" our own." — Whenever the *Portugueze*
ſhall again riſe into the ſame Activity and Vigour by which they were diſtinguiſhed during
this ſhining Period, or during that ſucceſsful
War (termed by them *the War of the Accla-
mation*) which they commenced againſt *Spain*
in 1640; it will *then* be prudent in us to ſup-
port their eſſential Intereſts with our Treaſure
and our Blood: And they ought to conſider
with themſelves, that neither the *Spaniards*
may be always deſtitute of Proviſions, nor the
Rains always fall in a critical Seaſon: But
whilſt their military Genius continues in its
preſent feeble and languiſhing State, I cannot
but be concerned when I reflect, that their

only

only Neighbour may once more become their worſt Enemy, and that *we* are obliged to be their Friends.

Providence was ſo wonderfully favourable to *us*, in the whole Courſe of the War, that we felt but a ſmall Part of thoſe Calamities which diſtreſſed the Continent. Our Succeſſes were often improved and heightened by the little Loſs with which they were obtained. Admiral *Boſcawen* purchaſed his naval Conqueſt at the Expence only of 56 Men killed and 196 wounded. Freſh Gales, heavy Squalls, and an horrid Coaſt, did not prevent Sir *Edward Hawke* from making a ſhort Winter's Day for ever glorious in the Annals of his Country. On the 20th of *November* and the following Days, the number of the *French* killed, wounded, and drowned, amounted to between three and four thouſand; that of the *Engliſh* fell ſhort of 350. The Danger of the Iſlands and Shoals which the *Britiſh* Fleet eſcaped, is always to be remembered with Gratitude; for had not the Admiral brought to when he did, the whole Squadron by general Confeſſion had been loſt in leſs than half an Hour. Our very *Defeats* seemed only to enhance the Pleaſure of our *Victories*. The Advantage which attended the *French* at *Corbach* was more than balanced by the Surprize at *Erxdorf*. The Fortreſſes of *Munſter* and *Minden*, with their large Garriſons, ſurrendered to the Enemy; and our Fears were alarmed for *Hanover*. The Battle of *Minden* drove

drove the *French* from the Banks of the *Weser*, almost to the *Maine*. We had hardly Time to read the Account of our Misfortune at the Falls of *Montmorenci* before we received the News of a Victory on the Heights of *Abraham*, and of the Surrender of *Quebec*. A Letter from General *Murray* informed us of the Loss of a Battle near the same Heights; We were immediately in Pain for our new Conquest: A second Letter from the same General, assured us that the Siege of *Quebec* was raised with the utmost Precipitation. Our Repulse before *Belleisle*, and our successful Landing upon that Island, made only the Difference of fourteen Days: To these I may add the important Reduction of the *Havannah*, after the inevitable Delays of an obstinate and lingering Siege, by which our Hopes and Fears had been alternately agitated for many Weeks. In this, and every similar Instance, *Ipsa Solicitudo commendat Eventum, et quasi lenocinatur Voluptati.*

The domestic Concerns of *Russia* will probably engage the Attention of that Government, and leave it neither Liberty nor Inclination to take a large Share in the Affairs of *Europe*. The People may be kept in their Obedience by the Clergy; and the Clergy may be treated with Respect: *Peter* the third experienced the fatal Effects of a different Conduct; and the Empress *Catherine* will study to avoid the Errors and Misfortunes of her Husband: The interiour Quiet of this Country

T   may

may be secured by equal Laws, and a sensible Administration; Yet, granting all these Things are done, many Regulations must be still wanting, to civilize the *Russians* themselves, and to refine them into a polished and cultivated People. That vast Empire is in Length from *West* to *East*, upwards of 6000 Miles; and in Breadth from North to South, about 2400: But it is very thinly inhabited in Proportion to its Extent: Nothing will more distinguish the Capacity of the Sovereign, or give a greater Lustre to her Reign, than a regular and determin'd System of Policy; by which Commerce may flourish, Manufactures increase, Arts receive fresh Life and Vigour, and the Number of the People augment equally with the Riches of the State. A Plan of this kind is vastly to be preferred to the Acquisition of foreign Conquests; as it is infinitely more glorious for Princes to encourage the Wealth and Populousness of their own Country, than to bring Destruction and Slavery upon any other People.

The reigning Empress has faithfully executed the Treaty, which the late Emperor concluded with the King of *Prussia*, in its material Articles; and has evacuated *Prussia* and *Pomerania*. The keeping of the *Russians* at their present Distance from *Germany* will *now* deserve the Consideration of *Europe*: It has already been too long the Custom to invite them *into it*, upon any important Difference between rival Powers. The Allies who attacked *Charles*
the

the 12th of *Sweden* in the Decline of his Fortune, watched their Confederate *Peter* the Great with a rational Jealousy, and would not suffer him to get the least Footing in the Empire. They did not know how soon such a formidable Prince might aim at the first Dignity in *Germany*, to the Oppression of every Sovereignty but his own: The unfortunate *Charles* the Sixth, the last Heir Male of the House of *Austria*, was the Person who introduced the *Russians* into the Empire, by calling them to his Assistance in the War of 1733. A large Body of them actually marched to the *Rhine* at his Request; and the Czarina *Anne* promised another of the same Force, in Case of Necessity. Towards the close of the War of 1741, *Russia* made a respectable Figure; and, according to some Politicians, contributed not a little to the Peace of *Aix la Chapelle*. Thirty seven thousand Negotiators of this Nation came into *Germany*; The first Column of them reached *Furth*; The second, *Ebelfeld*, in the Bishoprick of *Bamberg*; The third advanced beyond *Hoff* in *Moravia*. A Junction was originally intended between these Troops and the Allies in the Low Countries; but *France* arrested them in their Progress, by a Convention, which she made at *Aix* with *Great-Britain* and the States General, on the 2d of *August* 1748. She stipulated on her side to send a proportionate Number of her Forces, which were then in the Low Countries, into the interiour Parts of her Dominions, upon the im-

mediate

mediate Signature of this Convention; and to disband the same Troops, or an equal Number, within one Month after she had received authentic Intelligence of the Departure of these *Russian* Auxiliaries from *Germany*, towards their own Country. In the War of 1756, the *Russians* added Discipline to Valour; and brought the first Prince in *Germauy* to the very Verge of Ruin. Let therefore the Ministers of every southern Potentate think with Seriousness, before they spread fresh Temptations in the way of these Northern Heroes, which may prevail upon them in the End to exchange a cold uncomfortable Climate for an advantageous Settlement in a mild and temperate Country.

It does not appear that the *Swedes* had any private or personal Quarrel with the Brother of their Queen: Their only real one was with the Treaty which they concluded at *Stockholm* on the 21st of *January* 1720 N. S. By this Treaty, a Part of *Swedish Pomerania* was ceded to the House of *Brandenburg*. To give a clearer Idea of the Motives which prevailed upon *Sweden* to enter into the War, it may not be improper to mention the *Swedish* and *Prussian* Pretensions to that Province. Upon the Death of *Boleslaus*, Duke of *Pomerania*, whose Family had enjoyed this Dutchy 700 Years, the legal Right of Succession to all *Pomerania* devolved upon the House of *Brandenburg*: But *Gustavus Adolphus* had already taken Possession of it, and the Power of the *Swedes* was
in-

vincible. The Elector, who was the Anceſtor of the preſent King of *Pruſſia*, aſſerted his Claim in a curious and ſingular Manner: He ſent a Trumpet to the States of the Dutchy, and ordered them to fall upon the Troops of *Sweden*: He was afterwards obliged to ſubmit to Neceſſity, and to cede the beſt and moſt fruitful Part of *Pomerania* to his Competitor, by the Treaty of *Weſtphalia*. Upon the Defeat of *Charles* the twelfth at *Pultowa*, it was natural to expect that the Affairs of *Sweden* would be brought into a miſerable ſituation. In Fact, they were ſo: *Ruſſians*, *Danes*, *Pruſſians*, and *Saxons*, united to cruſh a falling Power. *Frederic William* King of *Pruſſia* paid 400,000 Crowns to *Denmark* and *Ruſſia* for *Stetin*, which he agreed to hold in Sequeſtration: The Regency of *Sweden* conſented to this Bargain; but *Charles*, untractable in every Fortune, refuſed to ratify it. The King of *Pruſſia* afterwards offered to deliver up *Stetin*, on the Re-payment of the 400,000 Crowns, and on a Promiſe from the King of *Sweden*, that he would not invade either *Saxony* or *Poland* through *Pomerania*: But this Offer never took Effect. *Charles* the twelfth being killed in 1718 at the Siege of *Frederickſtadt* in *Norway*, the *Swedes* made great Sacrifices for the Sake of Peace: By the third and nineteenth Articles of the Treaty of *Stockholm*, they granted the City of *Stetin*, the Diſtrict between the *Oder* and the *Pehne*, the Iſles of *Wollin* and *Uſedom* (which command the Navigation of the *Oder*) together with the

Cities

Cities of *Damm* and *Golnaw* situated beyond the *Oder*, to the King of *Prussia* in Perpetuity; to be possessed by that Monarch, exactly as they had been by *Sweden*, according to the tenth Article of the Treaty of *Westphalia*. The King of *Prussia*, on his Part, engaged to pay two Millions of Rixdollars to the Queen of *Sweden*. Things remained upon the Footing of this Treaty till 1757, when the Danger which surrounded and threatened the present King of *Prussia* on every Side, seemed to point out to *Sweden* the critical Opportunity of recovering the Places which she had relinquished: She therefore entered into a secret Convention with the Court of *Vienna*, stipulated to make a Diversion in Favour of the Enemies of *Prussia*, and was promised, in Return, the Possession of a Part of *Pomerania*. This Fact was insisted upon in the Memorial of the Court of *Berlin*. The King knew (says that Memorial) that it was the Acquisition of this Province, ceded by the most solemn Treaties, and sold for considerable Sums to the late King of *Prussia*, which was the Object of the Ambition of *Sweden*, and the Reason of her Enterprize, whilst the Peace of *Westphalia* was to be the Pretext. — After a Contest equally tedious and insignificant, *Sweden* was disposed to leave off just where she had begun: This first, and baffled Attempt, will in all Probability deter her from entertaining any Thoughts of a second, for many Years to come.

The present Century has been fatal to *Saxony*: Her Distresses indeed are extreme, and more properly a Subject for Pity, than for Dissertation. Under King *Augustus the Father*, the Electorate became a Prey to *Charles* the twelfth, who made it his military Chest, and subsisted his Army out of its Revenues. The Repartee of King *Augustus* deserves to be repeated here: When *Paikel* the *Livonian*, who had served as an Officer in the *Saxon* Troops, was condemned by the Senate of *Stockholm* to lose his Head for High Treason, he endeavoured to obtain his Pardon by pretending to communicate the Secret of the Philosopher's Stone. *Charles* rejected the Applications which were made in his Favour: Upon which *Augustus* observed, ", that it was no Wonder the King " of *Sweden* shewed such Indifference about " the Philosopher's Stone, since he had found " it in *Saxony*." Under King *Augustus the Son*, this Electorate has twice felt the Superiority of *Prussia*; and there is hardly a single Calamity of War, to which it is a Stranger: It has afforded a convincing Proof to the World, that in the Disputes between the Houses of *Austria* and *Brandenburg*,

——— *imparibus se immiscuit Armis.*

For three Years, the King of *Prussia* maintained himself in the Possession of *Dresden*: During that Time, this rich and harrassed Country was obliged to answer every Demand which the Necessities of a Conqueror prescrib'd.

Saxony

Saxony is now divided between its Friends and Enemies; *Dresden* is yet in the Hands of the *Austrians*, and *Leipsick* in those of *Prussia*. General *Haddick* and the Prince of *Stolberg* had obtain'd some important Advantages over Prince *Henry* in the middle of last *October*; They flattered themselves that those Advantages would have been permanent, for the Season of the Year had already proved sharp and rigorous; a Quantity of Snow had fallen the very Day after their Success, which was driven by a Wind so cold, as to pervade the warmest Cloathing: But all their promising Expectations were of a short Duration. Prince *Henry*, at the Head of an inferiour Force, supported by the Abilities and Intrepidity of the Generals *Kleist*, *Seidlitz*, *Stutterheim* the Elder, and *Belling*, gave a compleat Defeat to the *Austrians* and *Imperialists* under the Prince of *Stolberg*, restored the Honour of the *Prussian* Arms, and established himself firmly in his Part of the Electorate. The Loss of the Enemy at a moderate Computation amounted to 7000 Men; whilst that of the Conqueror hardly exceeded 1400. When Peace is once more concluded in *Germany*, we may flatter ourselves that King *Augustus*, reclaimed by Experience, will take a Lesson from his Misfortunes, and prevent a Repetition of these Evils by a total Change of his political System: Nothing less than a settled and perfect Tranquility, can ever repair the Desolation, which his hereditary Dominions have suffered, or enable him to recover his

his Confederation and Influence amongst the Princes of the Empire.

Voltaire has ftated the Nature of thofe Claims, which the King of *Pruffia* firft made upon *Silefia*, with an elegant Brevity. " Il y prétend
" doit quatre Duchés, dont fa Maifon avoit
" été, autrefois en Poffeffion, par des Achats
" & par des Actes de Confraternité. Ses Ayeux
" avoient renoncé a toutes leurs Pretenfions
" par des Tranfactions réiterées parce qu' ils
" étoient foibles; Il fe trouva puiffant, & il les
" reclama." *Silefia* is, at prefent, in no Danger of changing its Mafter: *Auftria* left to herfelf alone will manage with Difficulty an unequal War. It is to be wifhed, rather than expected, that the Emprefs Queen of *Hungary*, and the King of *Pruffia*, would at laft drop the Memory of their old Provocations, and permit the true Intereft of their refpective Countries to prevail over the mutual Injuries which they have done and fuffered. A firm and cordial Friendfhip between two fuch powerful Sovereigns would foon heal the Wounds of *Germany*: Political Diftractions, intermixed with religious Differences, have long weakened the Empire; and the Weaknefs of the Empire has been the Strength of *France*.—The following extraordinary Anecdote is too remarkable to be omitted in this Place, efpecially as it refts upon fufficient Authority; but whether it moft diftinguifhes the *Spirit* or the *Art* of the Emprefs Queen, I will not take upon me to determine.

mine. In the Year 1758, while the King of *Prussia* was besieging *Olmutz*; the *French* Ambassador, alarmed at the probable Consequences of that King's Success, was desirous of persuading the Empress Queen to think of some Terms of Accommodation. He ventured to ask her, if, in Case of bad Fortune, she would wait for her victorious Enemy at *Vienna*, and stand a Siege in her Capital? No, Sir, said that Princess; when he advances to *Vienna*, I will retreat to *Presburg*: And what, Madam, replied the Ambassador, if *Vienna* should not be able to arrest the Conqueror in his Progress? You will hardly throw yourself into the Arms of the *Turk*. That I will never do, answer'd the Empress; I will collect my faithful *Hungarians*, and perhaps I may give Battle to the King before *Presburg*: Should I be defeated, I will write a Letter to him, in which I will let him know that our Differences are *inexpiable*; That therefore I will meet him, at a Place to be named, in my Post-Chaise, with a Brace of Pistols; That we will draw up near to each other, and *He* shall then perceive, that I have a Courage above my Fortune, and a Resolution superiour to my Sex.

The general Happiness of Mankind would tempt me to desire (if such a Desire corresponded with the established Constitution of Things) that something similar to the *last Determination* of our House of Commons, in the Case of a controverted Election, might effectually take Place

in

in the public Concerns of *Europe*; And that all future Treaties of Peace might carry with them a certain and perpetual Obligation upon the contracting Parties. Extensive Power has indeed been too frequently founded upon Usurpation and Violence; But if the pillaged States were never to be satisfied, till they had obtained the Restitution of their dismembred Provinces, there could not be any such Thing as Peace in the World: War transfers the Property of the vanquished: And it is better to acquiesce at once, even under an Act of prosperous Injustice, than to be involved in a cruel and endless Struggle upon a Dispute of Right.

It has been asserted upon fair Grounds of Probability, that *France* was drawn with Reluctance into her close Connections with *Spain*; That she did not care to increase the Load of her own Difficulties, by taking those of another upon herself; That she would have finally desisted from her Pretensions to a Satisfaction for the Captures made upon her before the Declaration of War, and that she would not have played her last deep Game of the Family Compact, if she had not previously lost the hope of obtaining a Peace upon those Concessions, to which she had determined her Submission. *Spain*, on the contrary, encouraged a Continuation of the War; flattering herself with the Expectation of Seeing us at last bend under our enormous and growing Debt, and of seizing upon that favourable Opportunity to plunge us into Destruction.

Destruction. With a View to this Policy, the Marquis *de Grimaldi* privately threw every Obstacle in the Way of Mr. *Stanley*, which could serve to interrupt the Course of the Negotiation. If these material Facts should ever be clearly ascertained, it will be no easy Matter to comprehend *how* or *wherefore* Peace came to drop through our Hands in 1761. Nor let it be imagined that *Great-Britain* and *France* were moving on *pari passu*, to Ruin: *We* had Glory and Credit to lose; *France* had lost both long before: The Constitution of our happy Government secures the Fortune of the Subject. *Britons* are free in the noblest Sense of the Word.

———— *Soli magnis agitant sub Legibus Ævum.*

Amongst us, Individuals are rich in the midst of national Poverty: In *France*, the public Wants *will* be supplied, whatever may be the Fate of private Property.

I desire to be ranked in the Number of those who respect a late Administration. I confess with Pleasure, that we were awakened from a Lethargy of Despair; that a new Life animated our Measures, to the Amazement of ourselves, and the Confusion of our Enemies; that the Gentleman who took the Lead at this critical Season, formed and executed his Designs with the same Spirit; that he was neither startled at Difficulties, nor intimidated by Expence; that during the entire Continuance of his activity, Success attended, like an obedient Handmaid, upon his vigorous Councils. To him therefore

therefore I may addrefs myfelf with Propriety, in the Words of a Panegyrift, " *Initium La-* " *boris mirer, an Finem? Multum eſt quod per-* " *feverafti ; Plus tamen, quod non timuiſti ne* " *perfeverare non poſſes.*" This able Minifter withdrew himfelf aftewards from the Conduct of public Affairs: And I cannot help thinking that he defcended *one Moment* from his Greatnefs, when he voluntarily charged himfelf with a fuppofed Fault, and indirectly cenfured thofe, who might be obliged to venture upon the Repetition of it; For he willingly owned, that he had departed from his private Judgment at the Time of his confenting to reftore to the *French* the Liberty of fifhing upon the Banks of *Newfoundland:* He owned too that he had yielded in this important Article, to prove his Readinefs and Practicability in the Courfe of the Negotiation; Yet he declared that the Expences of another Year would be amply fatisfied, by obtaining an exclufive Right to the whole Fifhery on thofe Banks. What he *did*, gave the *French* an Advantage, which I am perfuaded, they would have never parted with; What he *faid*, could not fail of being a Stumbling Block in the Way of any other Minifter.

The glorious Events which marked the Progrefs of our late War ftill left behind them a Weight and Oppreffion of Debt, which grew heavier Year after Year, beyond the Experience and Belief of the paſt, and perhaps beyond the poffible Ability of fucceeding Times. Government

ment no longer impofes Taxes upon the Luxuries or Comforts of Life; It has now reached the Neceffities of it. Real and fenfible Wants will raife the Price of Labour; The Price of Labour will advance that of the Manufacture; And the advanced Price of the Manufacture, will enable the Rivals of our Trade to underfell us in a foreign Market. The Failure of our Negotiation in 1761. coft us many Millions; The Failure of it in 1762. would have coft us as many more; And the nearer we approached our Deftruction, the Submiffion of our Enemies would, I am afraid, have been at the greater Diftance. Policy, Reafon, Duty to the prefent and to every future Generation, all called upon us to ftop here. A Peace well adjufted, and well adminiftred, might relieve us from fome of thofe Burthens, which a Continuation of the War would have certainly increafed: And that Peace, confidered in a civil or religious View, would probably be the moft durable, which left enough for ourfelves, and yet gave fomething to our Enemies. There is a Defpotifm by Sea as well as by Land; And if we had affected to be upon the Ocean, what we have often accufed *France* of labouring to be upon the Continent; Our averfion would not have been to the Power, but only to the Hand which held it. Like a victorious Wreftler at the old Olympic Games, we are defervedly proud of thofe mighty Efforts, which we have made; Like him too, we fhould remember, that we are weakened and debilitated

even

even by the very Exertion of our Strength: Time and undisturbed Rest are necessary to refresh and recruit our exhausted Spirits. Let us therefore reflect with a grateful Satisfaction, that the Conquests which we have retain'd, will, under the Protection of Providence, place our Colonies beyond the Reach of future Insult, and will extend our Navigation and Commerce; Whilst those which we have restored, will serve as a convincing Proof to the World, that we have been fighting for Security, not Ambition. Permit me therefore to apply to my Country, the expressive Words which *Pliny* applied to *Trajan*. " *Ut ipsa nolis pugnare,* " *Moderatio; Fortitudo tua præstat, ut neque* " *Hostes tui velint.*"

The Study of the *Roman* History generally makes a Part of our early Education; And the dangerous Merits of those Republicans are so deeply impressed upon our tender Minds, that we are apt to consider every Thing which relates to them under an habitual Prejudice. Yet *Rome*, in Fact, was the Tyrant, and the Oppressor of Mankind: Her Ambition and her Valour were equally unbounded; One Conquest was the Prelude to another; And her own particular Glory became the Cause of universal Misery. We seemed, not long ago, to be acting upon the same Principles, and to influenced by the same domineering Spirit; But we did not recollect, that in the brightest Times of the Commonwealth, *Poverty* was compatible with *Greatness*. Consuls and Dictators despised Wealth as heartily as they despised an Enemy.

*Privatus illis Census erat brevis
Commune magnum.*

The Case of this Country is unfortunately the Reverse; And I hope we shall never imitate *Roman* Pride, without the smallest Pretension to *Roman* Virtue. If we are ready enough to admire the military Perfections of *Rome*; we are not less so to boast of her Laws and of her Liberty: But by one of the Laws of the *Twelve Tables*, a capital Punishment was enacted against the Publishers of defamatory Compositions: It is contained in few Words; *Si quis Carmen occentassit, quod alteri Flagitium faxit, Capital esto. Cicero* declares his full Approbation of this Law, *Præclarè*; *Judicis enim ac Magistratuum Disceptationibus legitimis, propositam Vitam, non Poetarum Ingeniis, habere debemus; nec Probrum audire, nisi eâ Lege, ut respondere liceat, et Judicio defendere.* Our own Laws are particularly tender of every Man's Reputation: The Reason is sensible and evident; The Character of a Man is his Property; and it is the noblest that he can possibly acquire; A Jury of *Englishmen* will in most Cases consider any great Injury done to the Fame in the same Manner as if it had been done to the Fortune of another. If a fair and honest Name is dear to the meanest Individual, I presume it is equallly so to those who fill an high Station, and

and are charged with the Affairs of Government. Succefsful Obloquy, in the latter Inftance, is of a worfe Complexion; becaufe it fpreads a fatal Poifon far and wide, and makes even the Virtues of our fuperiours dangerous to themfelves, and ufelefs to their Country. I wifh the Gentlemen who indulge and cherifh a Fault of this Malignity, would confider both its Guilt and its Aggravations.

It is one of the cleareft and moft indifputable Principles of Liberty, that the *Governed* have a Right to interpofe their Opinion upon every Subject of national Importance; Yet the more important the Subject is, the greater ought to be the Decency and Candour with which it is debated. A fober Appeal to the Reafon of the People will always be attended to with Pleafure, and often with Conviction: But an inflammatory Addrefs to their Weakneffes, or their Prejudices, is nothing better than a *Libel* upon Freedom itfelf. It turns into Poifon the very Food which was intended for our Nourifhment, and fhakes our whole political Syftem under the Pretence of preferving it: And I could almoft venture to afk my Countrymen in their cooler and more difpaffionate Moments, if the popular Sufpicion and Jealoufy which brake out with fo much Fury on the firft Report of the negotiating of the Preliminaries, did not offer Violence to the acknowledged Prerogative of the Crown, affront the Virtues of the Prince who wears it, and prostitute, to the Purposes of Faction, the boasted Liberty of the Press? What the constitutional Liberty of the Press *is*, it may be difficult to say with Precision: Perhaps, like the Privilege of the Peerage, it is more secure by not being strictly and minutely defined: And every one who wishes well to this Liberty, (as I very cordially do) should wish also that the Blasphemy and Licentiousness of the present Age, the wanton Abuse of Religion and Government, may not render it necessary for the Legislature to *determine* its Boundaries by a clear and positive Law.

——— *in Vitium Libertas excidat, et Vim Dignam Lege regi.*

But I think it is easy to say what *is not* the constitutional Liberty of the Press. It is *not* then the Overflowing of personal Calumny and Invective; It is *not* the Sowing of Sedition in the Hearts of the People, and the seducing of their Affections from their native Sovereign; It is *not* the torturing of Texts of Scripture to the most profane Senses, in equal Defiance of the Laws of God and Man. Whoever commits these enormous Offences against his Country, and yet pretends to shelter himself under the Privilege of the Press, appears to me to be acting the Part of another *Clodius*, who first destroyed the House of *Cicero*, and afterwards had the Assurance to consecrate the whole

whole Area upon which it stood to the Goddess *Liberty*.

The Mask of public Zeal covers the Deformity of private Resentment. "*Potentia apud Unum;* "*Odium, apud Omnes,*" is an Axiom practically recommended by modern Politicians: *Tacitus* applies it to a low and worthless Character; They are for giving to it a free and unlimited Application. He who enjoys the *Power*, ought indeed to guard against the *Hatred*, with every Degree of Circumspection and Address. If the Hatred must necessarily pursue him, still Common Sense will persuade him to tread carefully a slippery Path; and to make the Effects of such an Hatred justly chargeable upon the Conduct of his Adversaries, not his own. He will never disgust Equals by Haughtiness, or Inferiours by Contempt; For that would be to brave an impetuous Torrent, which nothing can oppose. A Strength able to defeat Resistance, is only to be mastered by Dexterity.

I do not know, even by Sight, the noble Lord who has long been honoured with the Confidence of his Prince; I am willing to believe that he has not yet deserved to forfeit this Confidence, by vitiating the Mind of his Master with false Knowledge, or licentious Opinions: It has been asserted, that he was better qualified to act the Part of a Schoolmaster, than of a Minister: Let him therefore be intitled to the *Credit* of having encouraged

U 2 those

those happy Principles which he found in his royal Scholar, and which have already rendered him the Delight of his Subjects: And when this Credit shall ripen more and more by the improving Testimony of his Majesty's Virtues, perhaps it may at last be rewarded with the Approbation of a grateful People.

   Abilities and Integrity are the great Qualifications which the Spirit of our Constitution requires in those who are nominated to the first Offices of Government: If there is no Deficiency here, it will be a Matter of extreme Indifference to me, *Who* are Ministers; Only Duty and Inclination oblige me to *respect* the Choice of my Sovereign: But if once the Nation is worked up into a Dispute, not about Things, but about Persons; If Pretensions to Trust and Influence shall be regarded as a Right of Prescription under one Man, and shall yet be deemed haughty and tyrannical under another; I cannot then but lament the Infatuation of my Countrymen, who have countenanced such a Variety of incendiary Papers, to prove this particular Person a Favourite, and to promote the Views of an insolent Aristocracy. The Law is a Stranger both to the one and the other; But there is this essential Difference between them; An Aristocracy is always formidable; A Favourite is seldom so, when the Affections and Interests of the Prince are known to be inseparably united with the Public Good. And let us not be deceived by an idle Notion,

                                     that

that the Erection of an Aristocratical Power in this Kingdom will stifle the Rage of Party-Divisions amongst us. The Confederacy of great Men is dissolved, as soon as the Rival Authority which connected it is subdued. An honest *Irishman* once ventured to shut some Game Cocks up together, *because they were matched on the same Side*; But upon his returning to feed them, he discovered with Astonishment, that for Want of an Enemy, they had begun the Battle amongst themselves, and were actually picking out each other's Eyes.

The same Persons who have clamoured loudest against the Preliminaries of Peace, might perhaps have exalted their Voices against the Continuance of the War; such Gentlemen even Impossibilities would not satisfy. A fair and temperate Judgment of the Merit or Demerit of any Peace is not to be formed upon the single Consideration of the Articles themselves, but upon an exact Knowledge of the Comparative Situation and Ability of the contending Parties at that particular Point of Time in which the Peace is made. — A War upon the Continent, incapable of being maintained or relinquished; An unfortunate Ally, whom it was equally dangerous to abandon or to defend; A gallant Nation, consuming itself between *Hanover* and *Portugal*, and almost overpowered by a full Tide of Success; These Circumstances, combined together, obliged us to consult our immediate and future Safety.

The Reader may perceive the gradual Increase of our annual Expence, if he will cast his Eye upon the following Account. Having been misled myself by erroneous Calculations of the Supplies granted by Parliament during the War, and having printed these Calculations at the End of the respective Years; it is particularly incumbent upon me to correct my own Mistakes: I have therefore faithfully extracted this Account from the several appropriating Acts, and from those alone.

Years.	Supplies.
1755	4,520,327. 12 8
1756	7,915,430. 4 6¼
1757	8,330,906. 6 5½
1758	10,475, 7. 0 1
1759	12,705,339. 3 8⅔
1760	14,636,930. 15 9½
1761	17,301,119. 19 9¾
1762	16,794,153. 18 11½
Total	92,679,215. 02 2/7

The Supplies granted by Parliament for the Service of the Year 1754 (which was the last Year of Peace) amounted to two Millions two hundred sixty five thousand and sixteen Pounds ten Shillings and two-pence: If the Reader multiplies this Sum by eight (the

Years

Years of the War) it will come to ——— — 18,120,132. 1 4

And the multiplied Sum being deducted from the great Total above, the Remainder will be —— 74,559,083. 0 8 2/7

This Remainder is, to a Trifle, the extraordinary Expence which the Government has incurred in the Profecution of the late War. Twelve Millions, more at leaft (I am afraid) are ftill wanting, and muft be raifed, to enable the Publick to re-enter upon its own ftanding Revenue, and to difcharge Anticipations, Exchequer-Bills, the Navy-Debt, the bringing home of our Armies and Fleets from the different Parts of the World, and the fubfequent difbanding of them. Thefe Twelve Millions being added to the Account, the War will, upon the whole, have coft this Nation the amazing Sum of —— 86,559,083. 0 8 2/7

In

It is impossible to suppose that the ordinary Charge of Government in Time of Peace, can be circumscribed within the Limits of that Sum which was raised in the Year 1754. Our additional Possessions demand an additional Expence. But we may hope, that the regular Commerce flowing in upon us from our Conquests and the Cessions made to us, will in a few Years answer this Expence, by a proportionate Increase of the sinking Fund. *Portugal* may also favour our Trade, either by taking off the Duty which she imposed upon it soon after the Earthquake, or by abolishing the late Monopoly of Brandy: We have not ungenerously worked upon the *Fears* of a *distressed* Kingdom; and we may reasonably expect a Recompence, from the *Gratitude* of one which we have *relieved*.

In this State of Things, the Preliminaries of Peace have been signed and ratified: By the several Articles of the Preliminaries, the most Christian King guaranties to *Great-Britain* in the most ample Form, the following Tracts of Country in *America*; *Nova-Scotia*, or *Acadia*, with all its Dependencies; *Canada*, with all its Depedencies; The Island of *Cape-Breton*, with all the other Islands in the Gulph and River of *St. Lawrence*; The River and Port of *Mobile*, and every Thing that the said King does or ought to possess on the left or East Side of the River *Mississippi*; (the Town and Island of of *New-Orleans* only excepted;) fixing irrevocably the Boundaries of the *French* and *British* Dominions upon the Continent of *North-America*, by a Line drawn along the middle of the River *Miſſiſippi* from its Source down to the River *Iberville*, and by another Line drawn along the middle of the latter River, and of the Lakes *Maurepas* and *Pontchartrain* to the Sea or Gulph of *Mexico*; declaring the Navigation of the *Miſſiſippi* to be exempted from every Duty, and entirely free and open to the Subjects of both Nations in its whole Breadth and Length, from its Source to the said Sea or Gulph of *Mexico*, and that Part expreſly which is between the Iſland of *New Orleans* and the right or weſt Bank of the *Miſſiſippi*, together with the Paſſage both in and out of the Mouth of that River. — The moſt Chriſtian King guaranties in like Manner, to *Great Britain*, the Iſlands of *Grenada, Grenadillas, St. Vincent, Dominica,* and *Tabago*. — In *Africa, Senegal* is guarantied to Us. In *Aſia,* the moſt Chriſtian King renounces the Acquiſitions which he has made on the Coaſt of *Coromandel,* ſince the Commencement of Hoſtilities between the two Companies in 1749; and engages not to erect any Fortifications, or to keep any Troops in *Bengal*. By this Engagement, the Territory and Trade of the *Engliſh* Eaſt-India Company are ſecured; both which have been enlarged ſince the Year 1749, by the Power of their own Arms, and the Neceſſities of the Subas of *Bengal*.

In

In *Europe*, the moſt Chriſtian King promiſes to reſtore *Minorca* to *Great-Britain*; and all the Conqueſts which he has made upon the Dominions of *Hanover*, *Heſſe*, *Brunſwick*, and *Lippe-Buckebourg*, to their reſpective Sovereigns; and to replace faithfully all the Artillery, that ſhall have been removed from the ſeveral Fortreſſes: He engages alſo to evacuate *Oſtend* and *Nieuport*; together with *Cleves*, *Weſel*, *Gueldres*, and, in general, all the Countries belonging to the King of *Pruſſia*. This Stipulation in Favour of his *Pruſſian* Majeſty, and the Sum of 2,680,000*l*. Sterling which that Prince has received from our Generoſity, by the ſeveral Conventions of the Eleventh of *April* and the ſeventh of *December* 1758, the ninth of *November* 1759, and the Twelfth of *December* 1760, will be ſufficient Proofs to *Europe*, that *Great-Britain* has not been a barren and an unprofitable Ally.—The Town and Port of *Dunkirk* are to be put into the State fixed by the laſt Treaty of *Aix la Chapelle*, and by former Treaties: The *Cunette* is to remain in its preſent Condition, if the *British* Engineers ſhall declare that it is only of Uſe for the wholſomneſs of the Air and the Health of the Inhabitants.

In Regard to *Great-Britain* and *Spain*, the Catholic King deſiſts from his Pretenſion to the Right of Fiſhing about the Iſland of *Newfoundland*; ſubmits the Validity of the Prizes made upon his Subjects in Time of Peace, to the

the Determination of the Courts of Juſtice of *Great-Britain*; and aſſures to the *Britiſh* Subjects trading for Logwood in the Bay of *Honduras*, or elſewhere, the free Exerciſe of that Branch of Commerce, with the Liberty of building Houſes and Magazines; on this ſole Condition, that the Fortifications erected in the Bay, and in the other Parts of the *Spaniſh* Territory, ſhould be demoliſhed within four Months after the Ratification of the definitive Treaty.—The Catholic King guaranties likewiſe to *Great-Britain* all *Florida*, or the Poſſeſſions of *Spain* upon the Continent of *North-America* to the Eaſt or to the South-Eaſt of the River *Miſſiſſippi*: By this Ceſſion, the vaſt Territory of *Great-Britain* upon that Continent is entirely and perfectly connected: *Fort-Auguſtine*, which in former Wars committed frequent Depredations upon the Trade of *Charles-Town* in *South-Carolina*, will be put into our Hands; and a ſenſible Service will be rendered to the Commerce of that very flouriſhing and important Colony.

The King of *Portugal* is expreſly included in theſe Preliminaries, as the Ally of *Great-Britain*: Every Thing taken from him in *Europe* or *America* is to be reſtored; and the Peace and Friendſhip which before ſubſiſted between *France*, *Spain*, and *Portugal*, are to be re-eſtabliſhed.

The Prisoners made on each Side during the War are to be released: And the Sovereign of the Country in which they shall have been detained, is to receive Satisfaction for the Subsistance and Maintenance which he has afforded to them.

Great-Britain and France mutually engage themselves to cause all their Troops in Germany to retire as soon as possible into the Territories of their respective Sovereigns, and not to furnish any Succour of any Kind to their Allies in the Empire; with this Exception, that the most Christian King shall be at Liberty to acquit all the Arrears of his former Subsidies.

By the latter Part of the Sixth Article of the Treaty of *Utrecht*, the *French* King consented and engaged, that he would not for the Interests of his Subjects hereafter endeavour to obtain, or accept of, any other Usage of Navigation and Trade to *Spain* and the *Spanish West-Indies*, than what was practised in the Reign of the late King *Charles* the Second of *Spain*, or than what should be likewise fully given and granted, at the same time, to other Nations and People concerned in Trade. The Treaty of *Utrecht* is a Treaty which existed before the late War; And the present Preliminaries renew and confirm all the Treaties, of what Nature soever, which existed before the War; as well between *Great-Britain* and *France*,

France, as between *Great-Britain* and *Spain,* as also between either of them and *Portugal, notwithstanding whatever may have been stipulated to the contrary by any of the high contracting Parties;* And all the said Parties declare, that they will not suffer any Privilege, Favour, or Indulgence to *subsist,* contrary to the Treaties above confirmed. Thus the Danger, with which the Family Compact menaced our commercial Interests, is, I hope, effectually removed.

To recompence the Restitutions and Cessions made on the Part of *France, Great-Britain* consents that the Subjects of the most Christian King shall have the Liberty of fishing and drying their Fish on a Part of the Coasts of *Newfoundland,* agreeably to the 13th Article of the Treaty of *Utrecht,* and also of fishing in the Gulph of *St. Laurence*; with this Reserve, that the *French* shall, in the Exercise of these Fisheries, keep at the Distance of three Leagues from all the Coasts of the Continent, or of the Islands in the Gulph of *St. Laurence,* and at the Distance of 15 Leagues from the Coasts of the Island of *Cape Breton.* The Islands of *St. Pierre,* and *Miquelon* (the former three Miles broad, and the latter six) are to be ceded to *France* for the Uses of her Fishery, the most Christian King obliging himself upon his *royal Word* to erect no Fortifications, and to maintain only a small Guard of 50 Men for the Police, — *Guadeloupe, Mariegalante*

riegalante, *Defirada*, *Martinico*, and S^te. *Lucie* or *Santa-Lucia*, are given back to *France*. Thefe are the Terms granted to that Crown in *America*. — In *Africa*, *France* recovers the Poffeffion of *Goreé*. — In *Afia*, *Pondicherry ruinés de fond en comble*, is reftored to her; together with the feveral Comptoirs which belonged to her *Eaft-India* Company in *Bengal*, and on the Coafts of *Malabar* and *Coromandel*. This Reftitution fuperfedes that Part of the Treaty concluded between the Nabob and the *Englifh* Company in 1757, in which the *French* were for ever prohibited from fettling in the three Provinces of *Bengal*, *Bahar*, and *Orixa*. In *Europe*, the Ifland of *Belleifle* is given back to *France*.

The King of *Great-Britain* reftores to *Spain* all that he has conquered in the Ifland of *Cuba*.

The Time reciprocally permitted to the Inhabitants of the ceded Countries for their Emigration, is fixed to Eighteen Months from the Ratification of the definitive Treaty.

Between the Rupture of the Negotiation in 1761, and the Signature of the prefent Preliminaries, *Great-Britain* had acquired *Martinico*, *Santa Lucia*, *St. Vincent*, *Grenada*, the *Grenadillas*, and the *Havannah*. I do not recollect that we took any formal Poffeffion in *Tobago*.

Portugal

Portugal relieved, *Florida* ceded, and our Disputes adjusted with *Spain*, are a reasonable and solid Equivalent for the *Havannah*.

In Return for *Martinico*, we have obtained the *French* Possessions on the left or East Bank of the *Missisippi*, and the Cession of *Grenada* with the *Grenadillas*.

The following appear to me to be the most material Variations between the Articles which miscarried in 1761, and these which have been now brought to Maturity.

In 1761, the Lakes *Huron*, *Michigan*, and *Superiour*, were to be comprehended within the Limits of *Canada*; and these Limits were to be further described and distinguished by a Line traced from the Lake *Rouge*, and taking in, by a winding Course, the River *Ouabache*, to its Junction with the *Ohio*; and from that Junction, the said Line was to continue along the *Ohio* to its Point of Confluence with the *Missisippi*: But the two Crowns were not perfectly agreed in Regard to the *Indian* Nations situated between the *British* Settlements and the *Missisippi*. — All Differences about the Boundaries and the *Indian* Nations are *now* happily terminated; The most extensive and the clearest Limits are given to our Possessions on the Continent of *North-America*, beyond the Reach of future Sophistry and Debate.

In

In 1761, it was ſtipulated that the Subjects of *France* ſhould exerciſe their Cod-Fiſhery on a Part of the Coaſts of *Newfoundland* and in the River *St. Laurence,* according to the Tenor of the 13th Article of the Treaty of *Utrecht,* abſtaining from *every other Part* of the Coaſts belonging to *Great-Britain,* whether of the Continent, or of the Iſlands. The Iſland of *St. Pierre,* without Fortifications, was to have been ceded to them for the ſole Purpoſes of their *own* Fiſhery, ſubjected to the Reſidence and Inſpection of an *Engliſh* Commiſſary. — The Iſland of *Miquelon* is *now* added to that of *St. Pierre*: The moſt Chriſtian King's royal Word is preferred to the keeping of an *Engliſh* Commiſſary upon the Spot; but the *French* are not permitted to fiſh within a *certain ſpecified Diſtance* of our Coaſts.

In 1761, the *French* demanded *Akra* and *Anamaboo* in Exchange for *Gorée* and *Senegal*; or *Senegal* in Exchange for *Gorée.*— *Now* they have obtained *Gorée.*

In 1761, we conſented to treat of an equal Partition of the four neutral Iſlands; but *France* inſiſted that *Santa Lucia* ſhould be declared a Part of her Diviſion. — *Santa Lucia* is *now* reſtored to *France,* and the other three remain with *Great-Britain.*

In 1761, the *French* conftantly and peremptorily refufed to evacuate and reftore the Territory of the King of *Pruffia*. Now they have confented to evacuate it.

In 1761, the Difputes between the two Companies in the *Eaft-Indies* were to be fettled by Commiffaries, and to be concluded at the fame time with the Negotiation between the two Crowns. *Now* thefe Difputes are effectually determined.

In 1761, the *French* propofed and we rejected a mutual and abfolute Renunciation of the *German* War. *Now* this Meafure will be carried into Execution.

In 1761, the *French* demanded Satisfaction for the Captures made upon their Trade before the Declaration of War. — *Now* this Demand is paffed over in profound Silence.

In 1761, the Prifoners were to be reciprocally fet at Liberty without Ranfom. *Now* Satisfaction is to be made for their Maintenance and Support.

In 1761, *France* declared that fhe would preferve the Cunette of *Dunkirk* for the Salubrity of the Air and the Health of the Inhabitants. — This Cunette is *now* fubjected to

X the

the Inspection and Judgment of the *British* Engineers.

In 1761, the Term of Emigration for the Inhabitants of the ceded Countries was confined to one Year.—It is *now* enlarged to Eighteen Months.

Nothing can be *restored*, which has not been *first lost*. If therefore we consider our Glory and Acquisitions as dearly bought with the Millions which they have cost us; What must the *French* think or say, who have purchased Disgrace and Losses at such an enormous Expence?

But it is now Time to dismiss the Reader; and I hope he will pardon me, if I dismiss him with a short Reflection. It was a daring and infamous Saying of a Marshal of *France*, " *Le bon Dieu é toujours du Coté des gross* " *Battalions.*" I persuade myself that the unexampled Success of the late War; the " *con-* " *tecti cædibus Campi, et infecta Victoriis Ma-* " *ria*" have left a serious Impression upon our Minds, and instructed us to glory in acknowledging that " *through God we have done these* " *great Acts,* and that it was He who trod " down our Enemies." Yet something more is wanting to perfect our Gratitude; which is, to express it in our whole Conduct: Peace and War, Life and Death, are in his Hands. Nations are rewarded and punished in this World.

Public

Public Reformation belongs to our Governors; Private, to every Individual in the Kingdom: And let it be always remembred, that among the various Blessings which are promised to the virtuous Person, *this* also is particularly mentioned, that, " *He shall see* Jerusalem *in Prosperity all his Life long.*" Thus will the best Man, be, in Fact, the best Citizen; and the sincerest Observer of divine and human Laws, will approve himself the truest Friend to the Peace and Happiness of his Country.

By a list of the Hungarians & Croates that have been kill'd during the late War it appears that thirty two thousand Women of those Nations are become Widows since 1756, without counting the unmarried Men that have been kill'd.

Lond[on] *Gazette, April 20th 1763*

APPENDIX.

ADVERTISEMENT.

The Reader is desired to observe, that any supposed Ambiguity in the wording of the Preliminary Articles, may, and doubtless will, be explained and removed by the Definitive Treaty: For his Majesty has been graciously pleas'd to declare, that, in what remains to be done, the Publick may depend upon the utmost Care and Attention on his Part to settle every Thing which concerns the Interests of his Kingdoms upon a solid and durable Foundation. The Affair of the Antigallican's Prize (to which some of the News-Papers have referred) could not have been introduced into the Preliminaries with any Propriety, because the Fifteenth Article submits the Validity of all Prizes made upon *Spain* in Time of Peace, to the Determination of our own Courts.

The Compiler is so diffident of himself, and so fearful of imposing upon the Reader, that he must entreat him not to take *any* of his Remarks upon Trust, but to depend upon his own Judgment and a more accurate Information.

APPENDIX.

THESE Annals terminating with the Signature of the Preliminaries, the Compiler of them is excused from taking Notice of any Facts under a more recent Date. But it will not be imputed to him as a Fault, if he observes that the Ratifications of the Preliminaries were exchanged at *Versailles*, with the Duke of *Bedford*, by the Ministers Plenipotentiary of *France* and *Spain*, on the 22d of *November*; and that a Cessation of Arms was published in *Great-Britain*, by Proclamation, on the 26th of the same Month.

The following Accounts are prior to, or of the same Date, with the third of *November*.

October 26. The Sheerness of 24 guns, Captain Clarke, put into Villa Franca in the Mediterranean, after having been pursued by a French ship of 64 guns, and two frigates. These three men of war came to an anchor in the same harbour, soon after the arrival of the Sheerness. The Minerve, one of the frigates of 24 guns, struck upon a rock, and was lost in less than two hours. A very high sea prevented all assistance from the shore, but did not intimidate Captain Clarke; who sent his people to the relief of their enemy. The British sailors exerted themselves so effectually, that the whole French crew, about 25 only excepted, (who were carried away by the violence of the surf) were preserved. The French Commodore waited afterwards upon Captain Clarke, to thank him for his seasonable assistance, fiftance, and to exprefs the great fenfe which he entertained of fuch benevolence and generofity.

November 2. The Marquis de Marigny, bound from Bourdeaux to Cape-François pierced for 24 guns, and mounting 20 nine pounders with 148 men, was taken by the Terpfichore Captain Ruthven, after a fmart Engagement.

November 3. General Kleift penetrated into Bohemia, by Enfiedel.

November 3. The Auftrians began to abandon their Camp at Fravenftein in Saxony.

N. B. It is highly probable, that the city of Manila, the capital of the ifland of Luconia, and the chief of the Philippines, will be in our poffeffion before the expiration of the term limited for a ceffation of hoftilities in that part of the world. Perhaps the Portugueze forts and settlements on the Rio de Janeiro in Brafil, may also be in the hands of the French and Spaniards. If either of thefe events fhould be found to have happened before the third of *November* 1762, the reader will be fo good as to fupply the place of this unavoidable deficiency.

The following fhips are reported to have been taken, loft, deftroyed, or retaken, which, are not to be found in this collection.

FRENCH.

Ships.	Guns.	
Northumberland	of 70	loft.
Leopard	of 60	loft.

FRENCH.

APPENDIX.

FRENCH.

Ships.	Guns.	
Alegon	of 50	destroyed.
Aigle	of 50	lost.
Chariot Royal	of 36	taken.
Comette	of 32	taken.
Sauvage	of 30	lost.
Emeraude	of 28	taken.
Oiseau	of 26	taken and carried into Gibraltar, by the Blonde, Capt. Tonyn.
Bienfaisant	of 22	destroyed.
Marquis Marloye	of 18	destroyed.

ENGLISH.

Ships.	Guns.	
Mars (formerly French)	of 64	lost.
Harwich	of 50	lost.
Winchelsea	of 24	retaken.
Gramont (formerly French)	of 20	taken.
A sloop of war from the Havannah		taken.
Ferret	of 16	lost.
Pheasant (formerly French)	of 16	lost.
Peregrine	of 16	lost.
Diligence	of 14	lost.
Duke (in the service of the East-India Company)		lost.

A Bomb Vessel and two armed Ships detained or taken.

A GENERAL INDEX of the BATTLES;
NAVAL ENGAGEMENTS; SHIPS OF WAR and
the most confiderable MERCHANTMEN, Taken,
Loft or Deftroyed, SKIRMISHES of Importance,
and FORTRESSES Befieged, Taken, Relieved
or Evacuated.

BATTLES.

EUROPE.

Lowofitz, page 10
Prague (near) 17
Kolin, 18
Hastenbeck, 24 and 25
Grofs-Jagerndorf or Norkitten, 25
Roſsbach, 29
Breſlau (near) 30
Leuthen or Liſſa, 31
Crevelt, 55
Sandershaufen or Sagershaufen, 57
Zorndorf, 62
Lutterberg or Lutzenberg, 65
Bergen, 85
Hoch-Kirken, 65 and 66
Kay near Zulichau, 91
Minden, 94 and 95
Cunnersdorff, 97 and 98
Maxen, 108
Landshut, 128 and 129
Warbourg, 132 and 133
Pfaffendorff, between the King of Pruſſia and General Laudohn, 134 and 135
Campen, 141
Torgau or Siptitz, 142, 144 and 145
Langenſaltza, 189

AMERICA.

Fort Duqueſne, (near) 2
Lake George, 4
Ticonderoga, 67
Montmorenci, (near Quebec) 93 and 94
Heights of Abraham, (near Quebec) 101, 103, 125 and 126

ASIA.

Between Colonel Clive and the Nabob, 15
Plaſſey, 19
Between the Marquis de Conflans and Colonel Coote at Wandewaſh, 69
Between Colonel Coote and the Mogul Prince, in Chincura.

Ebuſbury, page 189
Kloſter Beeckern, 197 and 198
Wilhelmſthal, 234 and 235
Luterberg, Reichenbach, 253
Nauenburg, 257, and 258
Brücker Mühl, 262 and 263
Willſtatt, &c. 264
Rheinwald, or the wood of Rahn, 267
Freyberg, near, 268, 296.

A GENERAL INDEX of the BATTLES; NAVAL ENGAGEMENTS; SHIPS OF WAR and the moſt confiderable MERCHANTMEN, Taken, Loſt or Deſtroyed; SKIRMISHES of Importance; and FORTRESSES Beſieged, Taken, Relieved, or Evacuated.

BATTLES.

EUROPE.

Lowoſchitz, page 10
Prague, (near) 17
Kollin, 18
Haſtenbeck, 23 and 24
Groſs Iægerſdorf or Norkitten, 25
Rosbach, 29
Breſlau, (near) 30
Leuthen or Liſſa, 31
Crevelt, 55
Sanderhauſen or Sangerhauſen, 57
Zorndorf, 62
Luttenberg or Lanwerenhagen, 65
Hoch-Kirchen, 65 and 66
Bergen, 85
Kay near Zulicau, 91
Minden, 94 and 95
Cunnerſdorf, 97 and 98
Maxen, 108
Landſhut, 128 and 129
Warbourg, 132 and 133
Pfaffendorf, between the King of Pruſſia and General Laudohn, 134 and 135
Campen, 141
Torgau or Siplitz, 143, 144, and 145
Langenſaltzen, 188

Grunberg, page 189
Kirch Denckern, 197 and 198
Wilhelmſtahl, 234 and 235
Peile beyond Reichenback, 253
Neuheim, 257 and 258
Brucker-Muhl, 262 and 263
Wilſdruf, &c. 264
Rathſwald, or the wood of Raths, 267
Freyberg, (near) 268, 296

AMERICA.

Fort Duqueſne, (near) 2
Lake George, 4
Ticonderoga, 57
Montmorenci, (near Quebec) 93 and 94
Heights of Abraham, (near Quebec) 102, 103, 125 and 126

ASIA.

Between Colonel Clive and the Nabob, 15
Plaiſſey, 19
Between the Marquis de Conflans and Colonel in Golconda, 69

Chincura,

INDEX.

Chinçura, (near) page 110 and 111

Wondivash, 119 and 120
Patna, 185

NAVAL ENGAGEMENTS.

EUROPE.

Off Rochfort, between the Colchester and the Lyme on one side, and the Aquilon and Fidelle on the other, 6 and 7
In the Mediterranean, between Admiral Byng and the Marquis de la Galissoniere, 7.
Between the Terrible and Vengeance Privateers, 14
Between the King George privateer and the Hirondelle, 14
Between the Britannia and Granville Privateers, 21
Off the High-land of St. Albans, between the Southampton and five French vessels, 23
Off Ostend, between the Seahorse frigate, Raven and Bonetta sloops, and two French frigates, 24
30 leagues from Scilly, between the Prince Edward, and a large French frigate, 25
Off Cape de Gatt, between part of Admiral Osborne's Squadron and part of the French Squadron under M. de la Clue, 47
In the Mediterranean, between the Glasgow and Oiseau frigates, 88
Off Cape Lagos, between Admiral Boscawen and M. de la Clue, 98, 99 and 188
Between Sir Edward Hawke, and Marshal Conflans, page 108 and 109, page 288
Between Captain Elliot and M. Thurot, 123
Between the Biddeford and Flamborough on the one side, and the Opale and Malicieuse on the other, 125
Between the Danae and a French frigate, 223
Between the Harriot packet boat and a French Privateer, 238
Between the Pallas and two Spanish Chebecks, at the entrance of the bay of Cadiz, 242

AMERICA.

Off Cape Race, between part of Admiral Boscawen's squadron, and part of the French squadron under M. du Bois de la Mothe, 1 and 2
Off Louisburg, between Captain Holmes and M. Beaussier, 9
Off Cape François, between three British men of war under Captain Forrest, and four French men of war together with three frigates under M. de Kersin, 28 and 29
Near Guadalupe and Montserat, between the Buckingham on the one side and the Florissant, &c. on the other, 67

ASIA.

INDEX.

ASIA.

Off Alamparvey, between Admiral Pocock and M. d'Aché, page 51

Off Carical, between Admiral Pocock, and M. d'Aché, page 59 and 60

Between Admiral Pocock and M. d'Aché, 101.

Between the English and Dutch in the river Bengal, 110

SHIPS of WAR, and the most considerable MERCHANTMEN, Taken, Lost, or Destroyed.

ENGLISH.

Doddington Indiaman, page 3.
Warwick, 6, 186
Greenwich, 14, 46
Merlin sloop, 18, 25
Tilbury, 28
Invincible, 46
Prince George, 50
Bridgewater, 50
Triton, 50
Bolton Tender, 53
Stork sloop, 63
Winchelsea, 65
York Indiaman, 67
Litchfield, 68
Grantham Indiaman, 77
Falcon Bomb, 82
Resolution, 109
Essex, 109
Mermaid, 111
Hunter Cutter, 114
Esther Cutter, 112
Marquis of Granby Bomb Ketch 119
Ramillies, 122
Hawke Cutter, 122
Thames Merchantman, 123
Tartar's prize, 124
Penguin, 124
Denham Indiaman, 124

Prince of Wales Merchantman, page 126
Lowestoffe, 127
Eurus, 136
Dublin Tender, 136
Virgin sloop, 139
Lyme, 140
Conqueror, 142
Duke of Aquitain, 185
Sunderland, 185
Newcastle, 185
Queenborough, 185
Protector, 186
Cumberland, 186
Griffin Indiaman, 186
Ajax Indiaman, 187
Speedwell Cutter, 192
Fatalasam Indiaman, 203
Griffin, 207
Biddeford, 211
Raisonable, 222
Hussar, 231
Achilles Merchantman, 231
Chesterfield, 242
Humber, 260
Scorpion sloop, 264
Hawke sloop retaken, 213

FRENCH.

INDEX.

Munden upon the Orcke, 138
Witzenhauzen, 183
Saalfeld, 190
Queifs near Greiffenberg, 193
The Solling, 201
Convent near Goftin, page 204
Colberg, (near) 204
Treptow, 207
Sanglow near Golnow, 207
Dobeln, (near) 231 and 232
Chemnitz, (near) 232

Hombourg, (near) 237
Adelsbach, (near) 238
Ditmansdorf (Heights of) 241
Lutterberg, 241 and 242
Gradrop near Toplitz, 244

AMERICA.

Loyal Hannon, page 65
Niagara, 92

FORTRESSES Befieged, Taken, Relieved, or Evacuated.

EUROPE.

Fort St. Philip in Minorca, page 9
Bielfeld, 18, 97
EMBDEN, 22, 48, 204
Memel, 22
CASSEL, 22, 49, 68, 89, 99, 133, 189, 268
Gottingen, 22, 59, 89, 133, 136, 253, and 254
Oftend and Newport, 22
Gabel, 23
Zittau, 23, 260
Hamelen, 24
HANOVER, 24, 47
Minden, 24, 48, 90, 96
Brunfwick, 25
Wolfenbuttle, 25, 205, 206
Verden, 25
Gueldres, 25
Bremen, 26, 46
Bautzen, 26
Gorlitz, 27, 260
Aix, (Fort of) 27, 200
BERLIN, 28, 140
Lignitz, 28, 32, 202
SCHWEIDNITZ, 30, 50, 205, 245, 266 and 267
BRESLAU, 30, 31, 32 and 133
Harburg, 32

Demmin, 32, 77, 107, 135, 199
Anclam, 32, 78, 108, 120, 135
Iagerndorf, 32, 86
Troppau, 32, 46, 86, 242
Tefchen, 32, 233
Rottenburg, 46
Koningsberg, 45
Zell, 47
Pennamunde, (Fort) 48, 59, 84
Munden, 48, 68, 89, 92, 133, 254
MUNSTER, 49, 91, 100, 108
Paderborn, 49, 89, 97, 134, 196
Lipftadt, 49, 96
Vechte, (Caftle of) 49
Kaiferworth, 54
Cleves, 54, 140
Nuys, 56
Olmutz, 56
Duffeldorf, 56, 61
Ufedom, (Ifle of) 59, 102
Nordheim, 59, 134, 188
Ruremonde, 60
Cherburg, 61
Wachtendonck (poft of) 60
Cuftrin, 62
Sonneftein, 63
Landfparg, 64
Fehrbellin, 64

COLBERG,

INDEX.

COLBERG, 66, 138, 204, 206, 209 and 210
Coflin, 203
Neiffe, 67
Cofel, 68
Torgau, 68, 99, 100, 139
LEIPSICK, 68, 96, 102, 140, 142
Freyberg, 68, 193, 232, 267, 268
DRESDEN, 68, 100, 132
St. Goar and Rhindfels, 69
Damgarten, 77, 89, 200
Francfort, 77
Erfurth, 81
Pofen, 81
Hirfchfeld, 81, 82, 189
Vacha, 81, 243
Fulda, 82, 189
Schwerin, 82
Grieffenberg, 82, 90
Saalfeldt, 82
Hoff, 83
Meinungen, 83
Ulricftein, 84, 245
Bamberg, 88
Cronach, 89
Erbefeld, 89
Ziegenhayn, 89, 99, 134
Fritzlar, 89, 188, 236
Eimbeck, 89, 208
Ritberg, (Caftle of) 89
Havre de Grace, 89, and 90
Ofnabruck, 92, 205, 268
Detmold, 97
Halle, 97, 136, 205
Naumbourg, 97, 222
Zeitz, 97, 124
Halberftadt, 97
Wittenberg, 99, 139, 140, 142
Templin, 102
Paffewalk, 107, 139
Dillenbourg, 119, 131
Carrickfergus, 122
Noffen, 126
Landfhut, 128, 145
Glatz, 128, 132

MARPURG, 100, 102, 129, 138, 188
Ifle Dumet, 136
Zierenberg, 136
New Stetin, 185
Burwalde, 185
Stadtbergen, 187, 209
Afchaffenburg, 189
Gudersberg, 188, 236
Duderftadt, 189
BELLEISLE, 191 and 192, 194, 195, 206
Warbourg, 196
Horn, 201
Waldeck, 202, 240
Dorften, 203, 204
Treptow, 204, 207
Scharsfels, 205
Golnow, 206
Stepnitz, 207
Munde, (Fort) 209
Munden, (Fort) 209
Arensberg, 230
Miranda de Douro, 231
Chemnitz, 232
Cape Finifterre, (Fort on) 234
Amoencburg, 244, 263
Friedwalde, 245
Pattenberg or Padberg, 245, 254
Frankenberg, 246
Braganza, 254
Torre di Moncorvo, 254
Chaves, 254
ALMEYDA, 255
Valença d'Alcantara, 256 and 257
Laubach, 260
Wetter, 260
Bergemunden, 264
Celorico, 264
Penamacor, 264
Salvaterra, 264
Segura, 264
Villa Velha, 265

AMERICA.

INDEX.

AMERICA.

Monongahela, (Fort) Introduct. page 13
Log's Town (Fort) Introd. 13
Fort-Neceffity, Introduct. 13
Beaufejour, (Fort) 2
Gafperau, (Fort) 2
St. John, (Fort) 2
Bull, (Fort) 6
OSWEGO, (Fort) 9
Fort William Henry, 15 and 16, 24
Grand Ance Bay, (Fort of) 45
LOUISBURG, 57 and 58
Fort Frontenac, 63
Fort du Quefne, 64, 68
MARTINICO, 77, 222, 223, 224, 225, 226, 227
GUADALOUPE, 78, 86 and 87
Marigalante, 87
Ticonderoga, 92
Niagara, 92
Crown Point, 96
Venango, 97
Prefque Ifle, 97
La Buef, 97
QUEBEC, 104, 126, and 127
Eftatoe, 127
Sugar Town, 127
Etchoey, 129 and 130
Fort Loudon, 133 and 134
MONTREAL, 137
Dominica, 194
Cherokee-Nation, 196, 210
Santa Lucia or S^{te}. Lucie, 227
Grenada and Grenadillas, 227
St. Vincent, 227
NEWFOUNDLAND, 236, and 237, 261 and 262
HAVANNAH, 241, 243, 246, 247, 248, 249, 250, 251, 252, 253

ASIA.

Severndroog, (Fort) page 1
Goa, (Fort) 1
Bancote 1
Geriah, (Fort) 5
Coffimbuzar, (Factory) 7
Calcutta or Fort William, 8, 13
Busbudigia, (Fort) 12
Hughley, 13
Chandenagore, 16
Cutwa, (Fort) 18
Vizagapatam, 20
Cuddalore or Gondelour, 53
Fort St David. 54
Davecotah, 54
Tanjore, 61
MADRASS, 78 and 79
Narfipore, 80
Concale, 80
Surat, 81
Maffulipatam, 82, 84
Conjeveram, 85
Trivatoor, 105
Wandewafh-Pettah, 105, 111
Seringham, 106
Gombroon, 106
SUMATRA, (Coaft of) 107, 124
Carangoly, 112
Chittiput, 120
Timmery, 121
Arcot, 121
Carical, 125
PONDICHERRY, 185
Mahe, 187

AFRICA.

Fort Lewis on the River Senegal, page 53
GOREE, 53, 69

THE END.

www.ingramcontent.com/pod-product-compliance
Lightning Source LLC
Chambersburg PA
CBHW030302240426
43673CB00040B/1031